Econometric Modeling of Japan and Asia-Pacific Economies

ECONOMETRICS IN THE INFORMATION AGE: THEORY AND PRACTICE OF MEASUREMENT

Series Editors: Lawrence R Klein *(Univ. of Pennsylvania)*
Kanta Marwah *(Carleton Univ.)*

Published

Vol. 1 Selected Papers of Lawrence R Klein: Theoretical Reflections and Econometric Applications
edited by Kanta Marwah

Vol. 2 Interregional Input-output Analysis of the Chinese Economy
edited by Shinichi Ichimura & Hui-Jiong Wang

Vol. 3 Econometric Modeling of China
edited by Lawrence R Klein & Shinichi Ichimura

Vol. 4 Macroeconometric Modeling of Japan
edited by Shinichi Ichimura & Lawrence R Klein

Vol. 5 Econometric Modeling of Japan and Asia-Pacific Economies
edited by Soshichi Kinoshita

Econometrics in the Information Age: Theory and Practice of Measurement – Vol. 5

Series Editors: Lawrence Klein & Kanta Marwah

ECONOMETRIC MODELING OF JAPAN AND ASIA-PACIFIC ECONOMIES

Editor

Soshichi Kinoshita

Nagoya University, Japan

World Scientific

NEW JERSEY • LONDON • SINGAPORE • BEIJING • SHANGHAI • HONG KONG • TAIPEI • CHENNAI

Published by

World Scientific Publishing Co. Pte. Ltd.
5 Toh Tuck Link, Singapore 596224
USA office: 27 Warren Street, Suite 401-402, Hackensack, NJ 07601
UK office: 57 Shelton Street, Covent Garden, London WC2H 9HE

British Library Cataloguing-in-Publication Data
A catalogue record for this book is available from the British Library.

Econometrics in the Information Age: Theory and Practice of Measurement — Vol. 5
ECONOMETRIC MODELING OF JAPAN AND ASIA-PACIFIC ECONOMIES

ISBN-13 978-981-4368-62-9
ISBN-10 981-4368-62-8

In-house Editor: Samantha Yong

Typeset by Stallion Press
Email: enquiries@stallionpress.com

Printed in Singapore.

Preface

During the recent three decades, the Japanese economy has experienced a period of rapid growth and two stagnant decades with serious financial distress. In the course of this process, Japan undoubtedly succeeded in establishing herself as a strong base for manufacturing industries in the world economy. But the drastic changes in the energy and other resources markets in the world and her trading and financial relationships with the US and Asia-Pacific economies have brought about several new issues; such as energy and resource price hikes, trade and investment conflicts, ever-stronger Japanese Yen exchange rate, FDI outflow and CO_2 emission problems, among others. These issues are global in nature, and must be analyzed by an international framework and solved by policies which are implemented through international cooperation.

The main purpose of this book is to offer some basic econometric models to be used for analyzing such issues. We developed several models to quantitatively analyze the interdependencies among Japanese, the US and East Asian economies and applied those models to observe the dynamic impacts of alternative policies to tackle the issues mentioned above. The introduction chapter gives a short survey of the similar econometric models constructed in Japan.

Chapter 1 examines the changing pattern of international speciaization and interdependence among Japan, Asia-Pacific, the US and EC economies since the 1970s. After examining the changes in their comparative advantages in terms of RCA (revealed comparative advantage) indices, it constructs a small link model to analyze the interdependence among Japan, ASEAN, Asian NIEs, the US and EC economies.

Chapter 2 presents a world model of industry and trade, and quantitatively studies the impacts of changes in international economic policies, particularly export promotion of developing countries and protectionism in the US and EC countries upon sectoral productions, foreign trades, employment in Japan and her close trade partners.

In the recent ten years or so, many developed economies have been suffering from new types of issues both internally and externally. One centers arounds lower growth, higher inflation and unfavorable imbalance of payment in these countries. The other important issue is related to the industrial restructuring required by higher oil price,trade frictions among developed economies and rapid industrialization of newly and semi-newly industrializing countries. Simple-minded macroeconomic policies do not seem to solve them. Thus, they have been greatly concerned with the way with which they should enhance and maintain the structural adaptability of domestic economy to the new international circumstances.

Chapter 3 applies the world model of industry and trade explained in Chapter 2. It is applied to evaluate the probable global impact of robotization on the macro and sectoral economies. Robotization in Japan and Korea are found to have a positive impact on domestic economic growth, whereas robotization in the United States apparently has a negative impact on economic growth. Externally impacts of robotization in Japan are negative for the United States, but positive for the Korean economy.

Chapter 4 recompiles the Asian international input-output table for 1995 to analyze the interdependence between Japanese firms, their subsidiaries in the US and Asia on the one hand and the foreign companies on the other. The production of Japanese subsidiaries in the US is hardly affected by the situation in Japan as a whole, but depends heavily on the US market. Japanese subsidiaries in Asia have a relatively large interdependence with Japan, especially in the machinery sectors. Overseas production affects the home country in two different ways: the induced production effect and the substitution effect. If the degree of substitution were the same as the ratio of Japanese exports for each sector, production in Japan as a whole would increase when its overseas production grew. However, hollowing-out may occur in the transport equipment sector.

Chapter 5 evaluates the effects of the recent unprecedented stimulus packages that China and the United States carried out since 2008, as well as the effects of fiscal expansion in China, Japan, the US and Korea. The econometric model employed here was originally developed to analyze the changing properties of the trade relations between Asian countries and the US. It is a small Asian Link Model involving China, Japan, the US and Korea with the bilateral trade linkage models. This model is an expansion of the conventional econometric model in several directions. One objective is to further investigate the changing bilateral trade patterns of more flexible form among those four countries using a translog specification. The second objective is to use forward-looking variables to evaluate the anticipated expectations in a new economic policy.

Chapter 6 presents a multi-sectoral econometric model of China and discusses the economic impacts of the improvement of energy efficiency and a shift of energy demand with the model. It analyzes the scenarios for the pipeline project of the Chinese government and the natural-gas thermal power plant project. According to this simulation, China will continue to grow at a relatively high rate, though the rate will decline gradually to less than 5% per year. The amount of real GDP in 2020 will become 2.78 times the amount in 2000. The overall energy demand in 2020 will increase to 1.95 times the amount in 2000. Also, CO_2 emissions will grow in volume 1.91 times from 2000 to 2020. Investment in the projects expands total demand in the economy, which requires more energy and increases CO_2 emissions. However, the shift in demand from coal to natural gas adopted by the projects has the effect of reducing CO_2 emissions. Although these two effects offset each other, the CO_2 reduction is large enough for the simulation periods throughout. The CO_2 reduction cost for the economy as a whole is estimated at US$30.39 per ton of CO_2 for the pipeline project, and at US$21.48 per ton of CO_2 for the power plant.

Lastly, I wish to express my hearty gratitude to Professors Shinichi Ichimura and Lawrence R. Klein for providing me with the opportunity to publish this book and their invaluable advices. I also thank the

Economic Research Institute of former EPA for giving me a chance to organize the three-year project of constructing a multi-sector world model in cooperation with its excellent researchers. This book is the final fruit of the modeling studies that I have done with my research group since then.

In addition, I owe a great deal of our econometric studies to many professors: Chikashi Moriguchi, Mitsuo Saito, F. Gerard Adams, Shuntaro Shishido, Hideki Imaoka, Hisashi Yokoyama and Hiroshi Osada, among others. As for research grants, I have received a research grant from ICSEAD in Kitakyushu for two years 2001–2002, and a Grand-in Aid for Scientific Research from JSPS (formerly Ministry of Education, Culture, Sports, Science and Technology) for 1999 to 2000 and 2003 to 2005. For all these, I wish to express our hearty gratitude.

May 21, 2011
Soshichi Kinoshita

Contents

Introduction: A Short Survey of Linked Econometric Models in Japan

Econometric modeling effort started in Japan in the late 1950s. Since then, various types of macro and multi-sector econometric models have been constructed in some successive stages as a common tool for forecast and policy simulation. Comprehensive and excellent surveys of econometric modeling in Japan have been offered among others by Kazuo Sato (1981, 1991) and Shinichi Ichimura (2010). They covered almost all of the econometric models of the Japanese economy as a whole produced at universities, government organizations and private research institutions up to the present. In particular this introduction will focus on the internationally linked models and survey only those which incorporate the interdependencies among Japan, the US and other countries.

1. Internationally Linked Econometric Models in the Late 1970s

As the previous surveys stated, the 1970s marked a turning point of econometric modeling in Japan for several reasons. The two oil crises and shifting from the fixed to the floating exchange rate system completely changed the international economic conditions surrounding Japan and the rest of developed and developing economies. As the result, international trade conflicts between Japan and the US and/or EC have aggravated in the global scale. These circumstances increased the needs for economic forecast and policy analysis. At the same time, computer facilities substantially had improved by then, and more adequate data became available even in developing countries.

These changes urged the model-builders to re-examine the structure of econometric models. As the result, in the late 1970s a number of new econometric models were constructed with new SNA data, incorporating global and lnter industrial interdependencies among Japan and other countries or regions.

Representative models were the following six.

1. Asian Link (1985): The Center for Southeast Asian Studies, Kyoto University; Asian Link Model.
2. ELSA (1984): Institute of Developing Economies; ELSA Model.
3. EPA (1982): EPA; World Econometric Model.
4. EPA-Kinoshita (1982, 1983, 1989): EPA-Kinoshita; World Trade and Industry Model.
5. T-FAIS (1981): University of Tsukuba; Tsukuba-FAIS Model.
6. FUGI (1983): Soka University; FUGI-GREM Model.

These models were all based on the idea of Project Link, which started its activities in 1968 under the leadership of L. R. Klein and other leading econometricians then. Their common features were that real national and sectoral outputs in each national model were basically determined by the demand side with the capacity constraints, and that those national and regional models were linked together using a trade linkage model or the world trade matrix. There were some characteristics, however, among them to be explained here.[1]

The first two Asian Link and ELSA models differed from the other ones in the objectives and scope. Both aimed at analyzing mainly the economic relationships in the East Asian region[2] *Asian Link model of Kyoto-CSEAS* covered Japan, the US and nine East Asian countries (Korea, China, Taiwan, Hong Kong, Indonesia, Malaysia, Philippines, Singapore and Thailand) and linked them and the rest of the world through the trade models based on constant shares approach with

---

[1] A. Amano (1985) [1] provides a detailed comparison of the performance of the models.

[2] A pioneering work of developing a system of linking national econometric models of East and Southeast Asian countries was initiated by the project organized by Shinichi Ichimura at Kyoto University. See S. Ichimura and M. Ezaki (1985) [7].

adjusting factors.[3] *ELSA of IDE* also included the same countries as Asian Link except for China and analyzed the interrelationships among those economies. China was not included mainly due to unavailability of SNA-based data. This model linked the simple monetarist-variant models of Japan and the US with eight Asian countries' models using a trade linkage model á la Samuelson-Kurihara (1980).

EPA model was a world-wide macro-econometric model connecting nine major countries (Japan, the US, UK, France, Germany, Italy, Canada, Australia and Korea). It was estimated with quarterly data primarily for the short-term forecast in the context of changing world circumstances and secondly for an evaluation of economic policies under the new regime of floating exchange rate. Each country had its own model, whereas the rest of the world was divided into six regions. These countries and regions were connected by a trade linkage model based on Samuelson-Kurihara (1980) method. Exchange rates were endogenously determined in the balance of payment block.

EPA-Kinoshita model was developed by Soshichi Kinoshita of Nagoya University and his team as a multi-country, multi-sector annual model of international trade and industry. It evolved from an original three country models of Japan, the US and Korea to four regions (EC12, Asian NIEs and ASEAN, other developed) and the rest of the world. Those national models (with 21 sectors) and the four regional models are linked through a trade linkage model based on Moriguchi (1973) method. The impacts of the shifting comparative advantages and protectionistic policies for specific sectors in the trading-partners were evaluated by the use of this model.

T-FAIS model was developed by Shuntaro Shishido (Tsukuba University and FAIS) as a worldwide annual econometric model. It is designed for medium- to long-term projection and policy simulation. The model covered 19 countries and four regions including OPEC, other developed, developing and centrally planned economies. Trade was divided into two groups: primary and manufacturing, and

[3]A national model of China was included in Asian Link model but not fully in the simulation of linked system due to the differences in national income accounts.

manufacturing trades were further disaggregated into 11 sectors in the sub model.

FUGI model was developed by Akira Onishi of Soka University and his associates and the biggest world model. It covers 54 countries and 8 regions with equations about 12,000. It was used for medium- to long-term projections and primarily concerned with North-South problems. As for the trade linkage among countries and regions, bilateral export and import equations were estimated for each pair of countries. Its huge size, however, did not permit the journal articles to provide more than parts of the estimates nor the explanations of the structural equations of the model.

2. Development of Linked Models in the 1990s and Later

In the 1990s, when the cold war was over and Chinese development became unignorable, these modeling efforts were either completed as the projects or revised to take into account the politico-economic changes in the world.[4] The dramatic success of Chinese high growth was obvious throughout the 1980s and later, but the drastic changes in the other East Asian economies since the mid-1980s were also very noticeable; for instance, the rapid Yen appreciation and the associated changes in foreign direct investment flows. Japan's greater involvement in the East and Southeast Asian economies has become bigger and stronger than before. Another change is the increasing role of expectation in the decision of households and private businesses due to the uncertain and risky environments. All these changes in the circumstances seem to have necessitated the reconstruction of linked econometric models in the more globalized world economy. Here are outlined 9 newly constructed or expanded linkage-type models, which focus on the impacts of domestic policies and international policy coordination among Japan, the US, EC and East Asian economies. Except for FUGI global and Sakurai models, other seven models focus their analyses on the relationships among Japan, the US and the East

[4]EPA world econometric model were successively revised to the fifth version, and then the project was completed in 1995.

Asian economies. The rest of the world is treated as exogenous in the Link simulation.

1. FUGI (2011) (Soka University, M200 Model)
2. Sakurai (2002) (Socio-Economic Research Center, CRIEPI)
3. ERINA (1999, 2007) (ERINA, DEMIOS-NAMIOS Model)
4. ESRI-Ban (2002) (ESRI, Cabinet Office)
5. Ozaki (1999, 2010) (Kyoto Gakuen University, Asian Link Model)
6. Kinoshita (1992, 1994, 1996) (Nagoya University, Kinoshita Model)
7. ICSEAD (1994, 1999) (ICSEAD-Konan University, ICSEAD World Link Model)
8. Uemura (2001) (APEC Study Centre IDE)
9. Kamada-Takigawa (2005) (Monetary Statistics Department of BOJ, Quarterly Model)

FUGI model is an extended version of former FUGI macro-econometric model described above, and now classifies the world into 200 countries/regions where each model is treated as globally interdependent. Countries in the East Asian region are individually modeled. Each model has nine subsystems. Including subsystems, the number of structural equations is over 170,000. The main purpose of this model is to provide a simulation framework to internationally coordination the development strategies for the sustainable global economy.

Sakurai model was developed by Norihisa Sakurai at the Socio-Economic Research Center of CRIEPI and covered G-7 countries (the US, Japan, Germany, France, UK, Italy and Canada) and ten Asian countries (Asia NIEs, ASEAN and India). It is a demand-determined model with a particular focus on the impact of global linkage and transmission of influences of demand and supply shocks among G-7, East Asian countries and rest of the world. Its trade linkage model depends basically on Samuelson-Kurihara (1980) method.

ERINA model was constructed by a research group of S. Shishido. It consists of two models: DEMIOS for Japan and NAMIOS for Northeast Asia that are linked together for the policy-oriented analysis of the economic interrelations among Japan, six Northeast Asian countries (China, Hong Kong, South Korea, North Korea, Mongolia, and Russia) and two sub-regions (Northeast China and Russian Far East). NAMIOS consists of the five-sector annual macro econometric model for individual countries and two sub-regions, and a trade linkage model. This model is linked with DEMIOS to analyze the mutual interdependence between Japan and Northeast Asia in the medium-term simulation. The relevant variables thus obtained from these simulations are fed into 34-sector IO sub-model in DEMIOS to consistently obtain 34 sector outputs. In the long-term simulation, however, NAMIOS treats Japan and the US as exogenous,

ESRI-Ban model was constructed by Kanemi Ban (Osaka University) and his associates and was a new type of Asian LINK model, following the Mark III version of MULTIMOD developed by the IMF. It covers Japan, the US, EU and eight Asian economies (Korea, Thailand, Malaysia, Indonesia, Philippines, Singapore and China including Hong Kong) and connects each model together, assuming the nominally fixed trade share matrix in the base year. It pays a special attention to the roles of asset prices as the driving forces in the bubble and burst of the Asian and Japanese economies in the 1990s. For this purpose, the model introduced forward-looking expectations in the specification of household and business behaviors. As the balanced budget rules were adopted in the fiscal simulation with the model, taxes rates are endogenously determined for securing government solvency.[5]

Ozaki model was constructed by Taiyo Ozaki (Kyoto Gakuen University) as a compact world quarterly model with forward-looking expectations), consisting of eight countries (Japan, the US, Korea, Taiwan, Australia, Germany, France and the UK). Each national model is made of ten equations with the common structure and GDP identities and introduces forward-looking expectations in determining personal consumption, business investment and foreign exchange rate. Ten countries were connected through export volumes and competitive prices, both of which were determined by trade partner's

[5]Balance budget rules are usually adopted into the forward-looking models such as NiGEM of NIESR and MULTIMOD of the IMF. See Laxton *et al.* (1998) and NIESR home page (www;niesr.ac.uk).

trade-weighted exports and GDP deflators. The rest of the world was excluded, and the linkage of world economy was confined within the ten countries. At present Ozaki model is integrated with the Asian annual Link model of Japan, the US, China and Korea to analyze the cross impacts of alternative policies of each country within the increased interdependences among these four countries.

Kinoshita model was developed by S. Kinoshitafor APEC study on the economic interdependence of trade among the Asia Pacific economies. The model covers 13 countries and regions; namely, the developed, Japan, the US, Canada and EC12, and newly developed or developing, Korea, Taiwan, Hong Kong, Singapore, Indonesia, Malaysia, Philippines and Thailand. They are linked together through a trade model, which first estimates the total imports of country j based on her domestic demand/output and relative price (defined import price/domestic price), and then the allocation of j' imports to country i (i's exports from j's country) is determined by the total imports and price competiveness of country i in the world market. In most of the bilateral export equations, the short and long-run elasticity with respect to relative prices is significantly estimated.

ICSEAD world link model was constructed by Yoshihisa Inada and associates at the ICSEAD. Initially it was built as a tool for analyzing economic policy issues in both Japan and the US, and then expanded to include China, Taiwan, Korea and two regions (EU12 and ASEAN5). Bilateral trade equations are estimated one by one to connect five countries and two regions. The model was applied to evaluate the effects of regional integration in the APEC region.

Uemura model was constructed by Jinichi Uemura (IDE) for APEC Study project at IDE to evaluate the macroeconomic impacts of trade liberalization under FTA configuration in the APEC region. The model covers six countries (Japan, China, South Korea, Hong Kong, Taiwan and Russia), four regions (ASEAN, NAFTA, Oceania and Latin America) and the rest of the world. Bilateral trade equations are estimated as a trade linkage model. Parameters are estimated on the basis of the observations from 1989 to 1998.

Kamada-Takigawa model was constructed at the Bank of Japan as a simple quarterly Asian Economy model to discuss policy issues on policy coordination among the East Asian economies. The model covers Japan, the US, nine East Asian economies including China and the rest of the world. Behavioral equations of the model are specified in term of the 1st difference of log variables and parameters are estimated using the quarterly data. The main equations to be estimated in each model are total import, domestic demand, Philips curve and policy rules equations. GDP and exports are approximated by definitional identities under the assumption of bilateral fixed import shares. One of the unique characteristics is that current imports are determined by future exports, reflecting the rapid changes in the international production network, which have been developing across the Asia-Pacific area.

The above link-type models focusing on East Asian countries and Japan have some similarities and differences. The former are the size of the model, countries and/or economies covered and demand-determined structures. The latter are the role of expectation (adaptive or rational), unit of observation (annual or quarterly) and the specification of trade linkage model (bilateral equations, Samuelson-Kurihara and so on).

As regards the future development for the Japan and Asian link-type model, quarterly modeling is quite useful to analyze the short-term repercussion of economic shocks among the interdependent countries, and for its purpose a simple trade linkage model based on fixed share matrix may be workable.

In this introduction, we have referred little to the GTAP-based CGE (computable general equilibrium) Model, which are widely used for industry and trade policy analyses covering multi-sector multi-country issues. The main reasons are, first, the rigor of assumptions underlying the household' and businesses' decision making that people are fully rational and forward-looking, basing their current decisions on a full lifetime plan.[6] Second, the research results appear to relay on particular assumption heavily. It is reported that relaxing some of the model assumptions can result in different results.[7] Third, the

[6]see CBO (2009) for the comparison of macroeconomic forecasting models with CGE (computable general equilibrium) models.

[7]see Hakim Ben Hammounda and Patrick N. Osakwe (2008).

projections of the CGE model cannot be comparable to historical data and those by traditional link-type econometric models.

References

Amano, Akihiro (1985). "International Linked Macro-econometric Models of Japan: A Survey," *Working Paper 8504*, School of Business Administration, Kobe University (in Japanese).

Ban, Kanemi *et al.*, (2002). "An East Asian Macro-econometric Link Model-Structure and Simulation Properties," *The KEIZAI BUNSEKI (The Economic Analysis)*, April (in Japanese).

Ban, Kanemi (2002). "Feedback Relationship between Japan and the World Economy-some simulation results based on the Asian Link Model", the 5th Workshop on the Economic Modeling, NIESR, London; November.

CBO (2009). "Estimated Impact of the American Recovery and Reinvestment Act on Employment and Economic Output as of September 2009," *A CBO Report*, The Congress of the United States.

EPA world model team (1982). "The Structure of the EPA World Economic Model," *KEIZAI BUNSEKI (The Economic Analysis)*, (in Japanese).

Hakim Ben Hammounda and Patrick N Osakwe (2008). "Global Trade Models and Economic Policy Analysis: Relevance, Risks, and Repercussions for Africa," *Development Policy Review*, Vol. 26. Issue 2, March.

Ichimura, Shinichi and Mitsuo Ezaki (eds.) (1985). *Econometric Models of Asian Link*, Springer-Verlag.

Ichimura, Shinichi and Y Matsumoto (eds.) (1994). *Econometric Models of Asian-Pacific Countries*, Springer-Verlag.

Ichimura A Shinichi (2010). "A historic survey of macro-econometric models in Japan," in Shinichi Ichimura and Lawrence R Klein (eds.), *Macro econometric Modeling of Japan*, WSPC.

IDE (1984). *Econometric LINK System for ASEAN: Vol. I and II*, Institute of Developing Economies.

Inada, Yoshihisa, (1994). "The ICSEAD Japan-US-ROWModel." In S Ichimura and Y Matsumoto (eds.) [8].

Inada, Yoshihisa (1999). "Structure of ICSEAD World Link Model," *Working Paper Series Vol. 99-0*, ICSEAD (in Japanese).

Kamada, Koichiro and Izumi Takagawa (2005). "Policy Coordination in East Asia and across the Pacific," *BOJ Working Paper Series, No. 05-E-4.*

Kinoshita, Soshichi Y Kajino, M Saito, Y Shiina and M Yamada (1982). *Development and Application of a World Industry and Trade Model for the Analysis of International Industry and Trade Structure focusing on Japan*. ERI-EPA (in Japanese).

Kinoshita, Soshichi (1983). "Structure and Application of a World Industry and Trade Model," The Link Fall Meeting, University of Tsukuba.

Kinoshita, Soshichi and Mitsuo Yamada (1989). "The Impacts of Robotization on Macro and Sectoral Economies within a World Econometric Model," *Technological Forecasting and Social Change*, Vol. 35, No. 2–3.

Kinoshita, Soshichi (1990). "Economic Interdependence in the Pacific Basin Region and International Repercussion of Business Cycle," in Soshichi Kinoshita (ed.), *Development and Structural Adjustment in the Pacific-Basin Economies*, Nagoya University Press (in Japanese).

Kinoshita, Soshichi and Jiro Nemoto (1992). "The Changing Pattern of International Specialization and Economic Interdependence among Asia-Pacific, the US and EC economies," in Takashi Matsugi and Alois Oberhauser (eds.), *Economic Cooperation in the 1990s*, Dunker & Humblot.

Kinoshita, Soshichi (1994). "A Linked International Model for the Pacific Basin Economy," in S. Ichimura and Y. Matsumoto (1994) [8].

Kinoshita, Soshichi (1996). "Modeling the economic interdependence through trade among the Asia Pacific economies," *APEC Discussion Paper Series No. 4*, APEC Study Center, Nagoya University.

Kinoshita, Soshichi (1999). "The Japanese Approach to Econometric Modeling for Forecasting and Policy Making," in Antonio L Fernandez and NS Cooray, (eds.), *Quantitative Tools in Economic Planning: Applications and Issues in Asia.* UNCRD Research Report Series No. 30, United Nations Centre for Regional Development.

Laxton, Douglas, Peter Isard, Hamid Faruqee, Eswar Prasad, and Bart Turtleboom (1998). "MULTIMOD Mark III: The Core Dynamic and Steady-State Models," imf staff Papers, Vol. 42 (June).

Masubuchi, Katsuhiko *et al.* (1995). "EPA World Economic Model-the 5th Version," *EPA World Econometric Model Discussion Papers No. 20.*

Moriguchi, Chikashi (1973). "Forecasting and Simulation Analysis of the World Economy," *American Economic Review*, Vol. 63, No. 2, May.

Onishi, Akira (1983). "A Macroeconomic Study on the Future of Global Interdependence," in T Basar and LF Pau, (eds.), Dynamic Modeling and Control of National Ecomonies," Pergamon Press.

Onishi, Akira (2011). "A new challenge to economic science; Global model simulation," *Journal of Policy Modeling*, Vol. 32, No. 1 Jan/Feb.

Ozaki, Taiyo (1999). *Macroeconometric Analysis of the World Economy*, Koyoshobo. (in Japanese)

Ozaki, Taiyo (2011). "Econometric Evaluation of the Fiscal Expansion and Stimulus Packages in Three Asian Countries and the United States," *The Journal of Econometric Study of Northeast Asia*, Vol. 7, No. 2.

Sakurai, Norihisa (2002). "The Development of the Multi-Country Linkage Model and Simulation Analysis," *Research Reports Y01018*, Central Research Institute of Electric Power Industry.

Samuelson, L and E Kurihara (1980). "OECD Trade Linkage Methods Applied to the EPA World Economic Model," *Economic Bulletin*, No. 18, Economic Research Institute, EPA.

Sato, Kazuo (1981). "A Survey of Macroeconometric Forecasting Models of Japan: Development and Current State," *Japanese Economic Studies*, Spring.

Sato, Kazuo (1991). "Econometric models of the Japanese economy", in Ronald G. Bodkin, Lawrence R. Klein and Kanta Marwah (eds.), *A History of Macro econometric Model-Building*, Edward Elgar.

Shishido, Shuntaro, Masuo Aiso, Hironori Fujiwara and Takao Fukuchi (1981). *Tsukuba-FAIS World Econometric Model (T-FAIS V)*, U. of Tsukuba.

Shishido, Shuntaro *et al.* (1999). "A Multiregional Econometric Model for Northeast Asia (NAMIOSI): Estimation and Policy Analysis," *The Journal of Econometric Study of Northeast Asia.*

Uemura, Jinichi, (2001). "Macroeconomic Impacts under FTA Configuration in the APEC Region," in Okuda Satoru (ed.), *APEC in the 21*st *Century*, Institute of Developing Economies.

Chapter 1

The Changing Pattern of International Specialization and Economic Interdependence Among Asia-Pacific, the US and EC Economies*

Soshichi Kinoshita and Jiro Nemoto

1. Introduction

Over the last three decades since around the mid-1980s, the world economy has strengthened the economic interdependences among countries or regions. The most obvious index to measure the strength of interdependence is the ratio of merchandise exports to GDP.

As shown in Table 1, the world average of the ratio has doubled from 10.5% in 1973 to 20.5% in 2005, implying that the elasticity of world exports with respect to world GDP is greater than unity for the periods 1973–2005. As regards the ratio of individual country, while the ratio of the US and Japan in 2005 was still less than 11–16%, those of the European countries except the United Kingdom were more than 25%, significantly higher than the world average. This seems to reflect the widening of common market in the European Community.

In the process of strengthening interdependences among countries, the changes in the overall trade position of individual countries have been accompanied by shifts in their comparative advantage. Since the mid-1970s, US trade performance has continued to deteriorate in terms

*This chapter is a revised version of the original paper, which was presented at the Nagoya-Freiburg Joint Seminar in Freiburg in October 1989. We would like to thank the participants for their comments and suggestions.

Table 1 The ratio of merchandise exports to GDP.

	1950	1973	1998	2000	2005
World	5.5	10.5	17.2	18.5	20.5
United States	3.0	4.9	10.1	10.5	10.2
Canada	12.3	19.3	39.0	42.4	39.7
Mexico	3.0	1.9	10.7	12.3	12.3
France	7.6	15.2	28.7	29.9	27.6
Germany	5.0	20.6	38.9	42.1	51.1
Italy	3.5	12.5	26.1	28.7	28.8
United Kingdom	11.3	14.0	25.0	23.1	19.3
China	2.6	1.6	4.9	5.9	10.7
Japan	2.2	7.7	13.4	14.6	15.7

Note: Percentage, real trade and GDP at 1990 prices and exchange rate
Source: World Trade Report 2007, WTO

of the trade account balance and export share in comparison with the world economy. On the other hand, Japan outperformed the major industrial countries in terms of export growth and current account balance.

Also, the Asian region covering Asian NIEs and ASEAN has successfully adopted the export-led growth policy and increased their export share significantly when looked at from a collective view. As a consequence of these changes in the world trade structure, a lot of bilateral trade frictions occurred, often resulting in the serious economic issues which could only be resolved by the micro- and macroeconomic efforts of both countries.

The purpose of this chapter is two-fold in nature. The first is to examine the sectoral changes in the export share and comparative advantage to provide a background for assessing trade conflict problems. The second is to analyze quantitatively the interdependences between Japan, the US, the EC and the Asian industrializing countries. A small link model will be used for this purpose.[1]

[1]The model constructed in this paper is a crude one for an empirical study of the changing pattern of trade and industry occurred among Japan, he US and the Asian countries. A further analysis using a large scale world trade and industry model has been made in Kinoshita *et al.* (1982) and Kinoshita-Yamada (1989).

2. Changing Pattern of International Specialization

2.1. *A measure of comparative advantage*

In this section, the shifts of comparative advantage of major countries or regions are examined at the two-digit industry classification level. The indices used are the export shares in the world market and the index of comparative advantage constructed by Bela Balassa.[2] The latter index is defined as a ratio of a country's share in the exports of particular commodity category to the country's total merchandize exports, which is written as follows:

$$XRCA_{ik} = \left(X_{ik} \Big/ \sum_k X_{ik} \right) \left(\sum_i X_{ik} \Big/ \sum_i \sum_k X_{ik} \right)$$

where X stands for exports, and subscripts i and k refer to the country and commodity (industry), respectively. A value of XRCA greater than unity for a particular industry is interpreted as reflecting a comparative advantage in that industry. Likewise, a value less than unity implies a comparative disadvantage in real and nominal terms for the 1970–84 period. The classification or disaggregation of country and industry are made as follows:

The data for these indices are given by the WIT-DATA BASE developed for our world industry and trade modeling.[3] It supplies exports and imports series both in real and nominal terms for the 1970–84 period. The classification or disaggregation of country and industry are made as follows:

(1) Country grouping
Japan, the US and Korea
EC4 (France, West Germany, Italy and UK)
Asia NIEs (Taiwan, and Hong Kong)
ASEAN (Indonesia, Malaysia, Philippines, Singapore and Thailand)

---

[2] As is clearly stated in Balassa (1965), revealed comparative advantage reflects not only cost differences but also the level of technology and other non-price factors. A careful discussion should be made in evaluating the observed variations of this index as a relative competitive indicator.

[3] As for the WIT-DATA-BASE, Kinoshita *et al.* (1982) describes the data sources and detailed estimation method of individual data.

ODC (rest of OECD countries)
ROW (rest of the world)

(2) Industry classification

AG: Agriculture	MI: Mining
FD: Food and beverage	TX: Textiles
AP: Apparels	LT: Leather products
WD: Wood and furniture	PP: Pulp and paper
RB: Rubber products	CH: Chemicals
PC: Petroleum and coal	CR: Non-metallic mineral products
IS: Iron and steel	NF: Non-ferrous metals
MT: Fabricated metals	GM: General machinery
EM: Electrical machinery	TE: Transport equipment
PI: Precision instruments	MM: Miscellaneous manufacturing
AL: All industry	

2.2. *Share of exports*

Beginning with the case of Japan, in 1970, the top five industries were occupied by a combination of two light industries (textiles and apparels) and three metal-machinery industries (iron-steel, transport equipment and precious instruments). After 1980, general and electrical machinery industries surpassed textiles and apparels, and joined the top five sectors. With regard to the changing patterns of export share, a significant growing trend was observed in the five industries, that is, rubber products, iron and steel, general machinery, electrical machinery and transport equipment, while four industries in the light industry shows a declining trend.

In the US, no change occurred in the composition of the top five industries. The top five consist of agriculture, chemicals, general machinery, transport equipment and precious instruments. However, contrary to Japan, the US was losing its export share in the wood and furniture, paper and printing, metal products and machinery industries.

The EC4 showed the larger share as compared to Japan and the US in the world market. More than half of the industries have maintained over 30% share. This may reflect the comparatively high trade dependency within the EC region. The top five in 1970 were leather products, non-metallic mineral products, fabricated metals, general machinery and transport equipment. In 1984, Chemicals ranks among the top five in place of transport equipment. The decline in the export share is conspicuous in the following six industries: textiles, leather products, petroleum and coal, general machinery, electrical and transport equipment. On the other hand, the rising share of exports can be seen in mining, food products, wood and furniture, paper and printings and non-ferrous metals.

These uneven changes in the export share in the developed countries have been brought about partly by the shifts in their comparative advantage within the developed countries themselves, and partly by the export-oriented industrialization in the Asian industrializing countries or economies such as Asian NIEs and ASEAN.

2.3. *Comparative advantage and disadvantage*

Export share by industry is clearly one aspect of competitive structure of the individual economies. Revealed comparative advantage defined above takes into account the sectoral composition of world exports as well as that of individual economies.

Between 1970 and 1984, Japan lost comparative advantages in the labor-intensive industries such as textiles, apparels, leather products, nonmetallic mineral products. Rubber products and general machinery have turned into comparative advantage sectors. Among the industries with comparative advantage, electrical machinery has strengthened further its comparative advantage, but the competitive position of iron and steel industry has dropped steadily since 1975. This is due to the introduction of voluntary export restraints to the US and EC markets.

The US has kept a comparative advantage in agriculture, chemicals and four machineries over the whole period. Transport equipment, though maintaining a comparative advantage, became less competitive after the First Oil Crisis of 1973–74.

The EC4 shows comparative advantage in twelve industries in 1984. Rubber products joined the comparative advantage sector, while electrical machinery moved into a comparative disadvantage one. The decrease in the share of EC4 exports is explained by the downward trend in the revealed comparative advantage index in the major sector.

Korea, an Asian NIEs member, had a comparative advantage in the unskilled labor-intensive sectors such as food products, textiles, apparels, leather products, wood-furniture, fabricated metals. In 1984, food products, wood-furniture lost their comparative advantage, and the following four sectors moved into comparative advantage sectors: rubber products, iron and steel, electrical machinery and transport equipment (mostly ship building).

The remaining Asian NIEs (Taiwan and Hong Kong) followed roughly the same pattern as Korea, and successfully gained a competitive position in some heavy industries. The difference is that Korea has a comparative advantage in iron and steel and transport equipment (ship building), a physical capital-intensive sector, while Taiwan and Hong Kong have specialized in electrical machinery and precious instrument s, a skilled labor-intensive industry.

Comparative advantage in ASEAN is seen mostly in the natural resource industries such as agriculture, mining, food products, wood and furniture rubber products, petroleum and nonferrous metal products. In 1984, however, electrical machinery moved into comparative advantage sector. These changes in the export structure will be contrasted with the favorable results of export-oriented industrialization process.

2.4. *A product life-cycle pattern of comparative advantage*

The shift in the comparative advantage in the individual countries and region has been closely related to the process of economic development and industrialization. To confirm this, Figs. 1 to 4 show the changing patterns of comparative advantage across countries or regions in selected industries. There, the coefficient of revealed comparative advantage for four distinct years is plotted by country or region in accordance with her level of industrialization. Among the countries or regions examined, the ASEAN economy as a whole is in the lowest level of industrialization and the US ranks at the top of industrialized countries or regions.[4]

[4]As a reference of the stage of development, GDP per capita relative to the US in 1980 for each country/region was calculated as follows: EC4 = 89.4, Japan = 74.4, NIEs = 25.0, Korea = 13.7 and ASEAN = 5.4, where the figures are percentage of the US level.

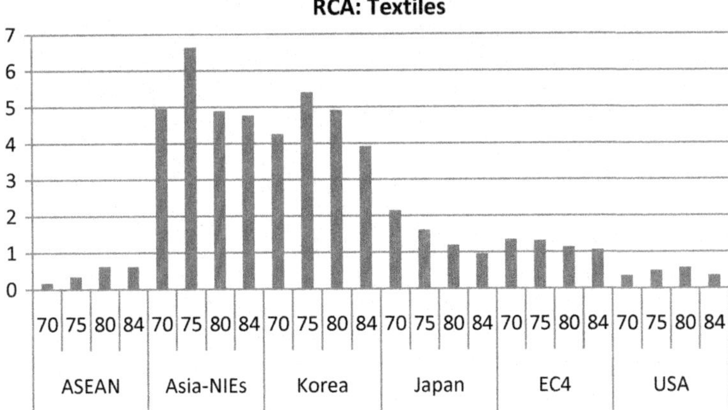

Fig. 1 International competitiveness in textiles.

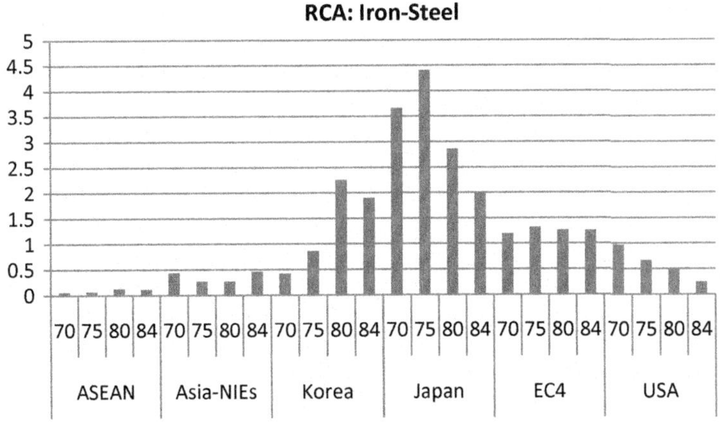

Fig. 2 International competitiveness in Iron and steel.

It is apparent that the advanced industrialized countries with a comparative advantage in a certain sector of industry tend to lose their competitive edge during the course of development, and as a result, the newly industrializing countries take over the comparative advantage in the same industry. Then various factors will cut their comparative edge gradually, shifting the comparative advantage to the newly industrializing countries. These changing patterns of comparative advantage across

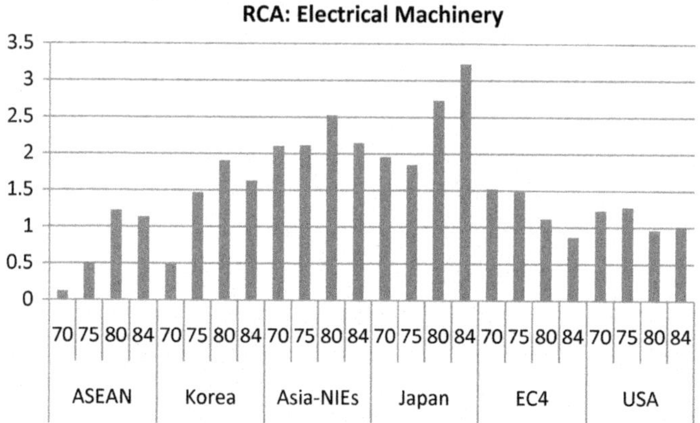

Fig. 3 International competitiveness in electrical machinery.

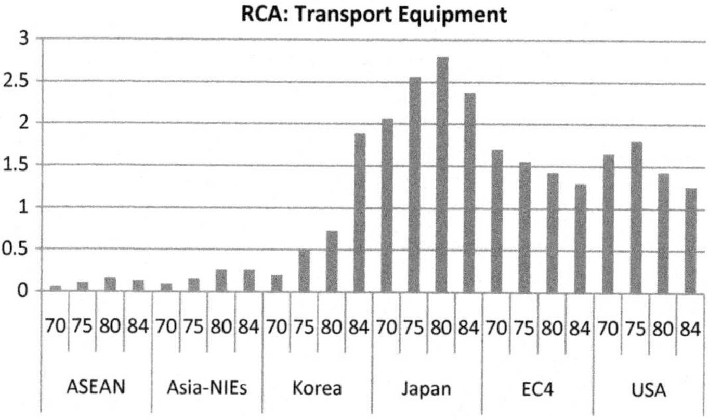

Fig. 4 International competitiveness in transport equipment.

country can be explained in the framework of "product life-cycle theory of international trade.[5]

In the case of textiles, a labor-intensive and low-technology sector, the most competitive area is Asian NIEs including Korea, followed by Japan and EC4 whose competitiveness decrease sharply over the period.

[5]Vernon's product cycle theory is basically concerned with the shift of the site located in the innovating country. From the standpoint of developing countries, it may be more appropriate to refer to the "flying-geese" theory of economic development or "catching-up product cycle" theory. See Vernon (1966) and Yamazawa (1984).

The US has already lost competitiveness in this sector. By way of contrast, ASEAN's competitiveness rises significantly in an effort to catch up with Asia NIEs.

Almost the same tendency observed above was seen in the wood and furniture. In 1984 ASEAN ranked top in her comparative advantage, while Korea saw a shift from comparative advantage to disadvantage. Also Taiwan and Hong Kong, though having it as a comparative advantage, lost competitiveness. Competitiveness in the developed countries has been quite low since 1970, and the most drastic change was seen in the case of Japan.

Comparative advantage in the heavy goods industry depicts a different picture. First, in chemicals and general machinery, the US or EC4 ranks top in the comparative advantage and maintains her competitiveness throughout the whole period. Meanwhile, Japan succeeded in catching up with Western countries, which began to lose competitiveness against Japan. A huge gap exists in the competitiveness between the developed and developing countries such as Asian NIEs and ASEAN.

Apart from the above two sectors, Asian NIEs gained a competitive edge in such industries as iron and steel, electrical machinery and transport equipment like ship building. Korea increased her comparative advantage in iron and steel, especially since 1980. The US was affected adversely and lost her comparative advantage. A comparatively weak competitiveness in Taiwan was the result of her industrialization process which laid importance on the skilled labor-intensive industry such as consumer electronics and precious instrument.

Comparative advantages across country in electrical machinery are changing over the whole period. Between 1970 and 1984, Korea and ASEAN, made remarkable progress in competitiveness. In 1984, "a geese-flying pattern" named after the Dr. Akamatsu was clearly seen in the Asian four countries or regions including Japan.[6] Both the US and EC4 lost competitiveness and showed a comparative disadvantage in 1984.

---

[6](*7) Akamatsu (1962) intended to explain the catching-up process of industrialization of latecomer economies from the three aspects: intra-industry, inter-industry and international aspects. See Kojima (2000).

Korea's sharp increase in the comparative advantage in transport equipment reflects the development of shipbuilding in this country. Within the developed countries Japan ranks top in transport equipment, followed by the US and EC4, both experiencing a declining comparative advantage.

3. Modeling the Interdependence Through Trade Among Countries

3.1. *A small macro model*

The global shift in the pattern of international specialization examined above does affect in various ways the economic performance of individual economies. The most direct channel is through exports and imports. In this section an attempt will be made to model the economic interdependence among major countries through trade.

In the first step, a small macro model is constructed for the following countries and regions: JP (Japan), US (the US), EC (EEC12), CA (Canada), AN (Korea and Asian NIEs), AS (ASEAN).

These national or regional models are then linked together with each other using the trade linkage relationships.

A prototype of national model is summarized in the following, where g(x) stands for the percentage change in X.

(Demand and Output)

(1) Y =C+IH+IF+J+G+E-M
(2) C = C(Y, g(PC), R, C(-1))
(3) IH=IH(Y, R, KH(-1))
(4) IF=IF(Y, R, KF(-1))
(5) E=E(FE)
(6) M=M(Y, PM/PGNP,M(-1))

(Wage and Prices)

(7) g(W)=W(g(PC), U/LF, PM/PGNP)
(8) PPI=PPI(PM, YW/GNP)
(9) PC=PC(PPI, W, YW/GNP)
(10) PIH=PIH(PPI, YW/GNP)

(11) PIF=PIF(PPI,YW/GNP)
(12) PE=PE(PFE, EX)
(13) PM=PM(PFI, EX)
(14) PGNP=PGNPV/GNP)

(Employment and Income)

(15) LW=LW(GNP, W/PY, LW(-1))
(16) U=LF-LW-LS
(17) YW=W*LW
(18) Y=GNPV/PC
(19) GNPV=C*PC+IH*PIH+IF*PIF+J*PPI+E*PE-M*PM

The demand and output sector includes five behavioral equations including private consumption (C), housing investment (IH), business fixed investment (IF), export (E) and import (M). Private consumption is specified using a permanent income approach with a distributed lag of income variable (Y). Interest rate (R) and inflation factors (g(PC)), if significant, are also included as additional variables. Fixed investments for housing (IH) and business fixed equipment (IF) are based on the stock adjustment principle, which relates investment to output or income and to existing capital stock (KH(-1) or KF(-1)). Interest rate is included when appropriate. Total export is directly related to the commodity exports (FE), which are determined in the trade linkage sector. Total import is a function of GNP (GDP) and relative price (PM/PGNP) with lagged responses.

The wage and price sector explains several price variables and wage earnings as a cost component of them. Wage equation (g(W)) is based on an extended Phillips curve. It includes unemployment (U/LF), rate of inflation and real input price as an indicator of ability to pay. Producer's price index (PPI), which is the key variable in this sector, is related import price and unit labor cost (YW/NP) under the markup pricing principle. Demand deflators are explained by producer price and wage variable. Export deflator (PE) is a function of producer price and exchange rate if significant. Import price (PM) is related to the export price of the countries or regions as trade partners. GNP deflator is given as the ratio of nominal GNP and real GNP.

The employment and income sector explains employment (LW), unemployment (U) and labor income (YW). Optimal employment is derived from profit maximization under the CES production function. Actual employment is determined by a partial adjustment to the optimal employment. Unemployment is defined as the difference between labor force and employment including self-employed (LS). Income variable in the consumption equation is given by deflation of nominal GNP with a consumption deflator, a proxy for real disposable income.

3.2. *Trade linkage model*

A linkage of national and regional models is realized through both trade volume and trade price relationships. As for the price relationships, import price of each country or region is a weighted average of the export prices of trade partners converted to domestic currency unit, using 1980 import share weights:

$$\mathrm{PFI} = \Sigma(w_i * PFE_i * EX_i)/\mathrm{EX}$$

where w_i is the share of i-th country (region) in the import in the home country.

Volume of commodity exports is specified as a function of the export demand variable (XFE) determined by the import volumes of each country's trading partners and a price competitive variable which reflects the relative price of home country exports in foreign markets. The export demand variable is constructed as the weighted sum of the import volumes of other countries by using the 1980's share of the home country in each of the foreign import markets. Price competitiveness (PWM) is defined as a ratio of the home country to the export price of rival countries in the foreign import markets.

3.3. *Simulation with the model*

A prototype model is fitted to the annual data for the period from 1975 to 1987, and parameter estimates of national and regional models are summarized in the Appendix.

With the estimated national models linked together, two types of simulations are made to quantify the interdependence among Japan, the US, EC and Asia-Pacific economies. They are fiscal expansion and US dollar depreciation.

Fiscal expansion is the autonomous increase in real government expenditure. To standardize the simulation, real government expenditure is increased by 1% of the real GNP and sustained over the whole period.

US dollar depreciation simulation is a 10% depreciation of US dollar against Japanese Yen and European currencies. This simulation is made to examine the impacts of exchange rate re-adjustment between US dollar and Japan–EC currencies on the macro-economy of each economy.

The results for fiscal expansion in the developed countries are shown separately in Tables 2–4.

First, the US expansion on GNP (% deviation from the base line) has the largest effects on trading partner countries, as compared to the EC and Japan. The largest is on Asia NIEs, and the smallest is on the EC. The US impacts on Japan are twice as large as those on the EC. This is due to the fact that Japan's exports to the US. amount to more than one third of the totals, and that the export dependency on the US is higher than in Japan than in the EC. Canada is affected heavily by the US expansion as can be expected.

Second, also the EC fiscal expansion affects the trading partners greatly in term of the GNP multiplier, its size being comparable to that

Table 2 Simulation of Fiscal Expansion: case of the US.

	US	JA	EC	CA	AN	AS
77	2.030	0.511	0.165	0.650	0.906	0.519
78	2.111	0.763	0.237	0.892	1.097	0.650
79	2.211	0.956	0.291	1.033	1.253	0.718
80	2.286	1.117	0.336	1.134	1.404	0.721
81	2.248	1.205	0.371	1.184	1.495	0.663
82	2.345	1.289	0.396	1.333	1.454	0.650
83	2.248	1.323	0.417	1.398	1.592	0.656
84	1.953	1.292	0.441	1.408	1.715	0.678
85	1.816	1.216	0.459	1.411	1.822	0.676
86	1.645	1.117	0.473	1.406	1.928	0.693
87	1.486	1.041	0.498	1.377	1.972	0.757

Table 3 Simulation of Fiscal Expansion: case of Japan.

	JA	US	EC	CA	AN	AS
77	1.562	0.033	0.011	0.038	0.121	0.205
78	2.063	0.058	0.022	0.067	0.179	0.290
79	2.302	0.081	0.031	0.086	0.215	0.338
80	2.453	0.095	0.045	0.100	0.245	0.343
81	2.460	0.092	0.049	0.102	0.238	0.296
82	2.475	0.093	0.052	0.113	0.224	0.282
83	2.375	0.079	0.051	0.109	0.215	0.254
84	2.038	0.061	0.048	0.095	0.191	0.221
85	1.638	0.044	0.043	0.075	0.154	0.173
86	1.270	0.027	0.034	0.049	0.086	0.120
87	0.914	0.016	0.034	0.026	0.040	0.094

Table 4 Simulation of Fiscal Expansion: case of the EC.

	EC	JA	US	CA	AN	AS
77	1.709	0.177	0.134	0.167	0.370	0.230
78	2.115	0.292	0.181	0.258	0.504	0.315
79	2.406	0.403	0.227	0.328	0.636	0.380
80	2.598	0.526	0.275	0.397	0.794	0.425
81	2.723	0.597	0.280	0.431	0.856	0.404
82	2.835	0.662	0.292	0.498	0.852	0.403
83	2.891	0.687	0.275	0.525	0.922	0.404
84	2.895	0.666	0.238	0.525	0.968	0.405
85	2.880	0.621	0.221	0.523	1.016	0.395
86	2.833	0.566	0.208	0.521	1.071	0.401
87	2.798	0.529	0.202	0.515	1.100	0.440

of the US. The EC impacts on US GNP are in the same order of the US impacts on EC GNP. As is the case of US fiscal expansion, Japan is shocked by the larger impacts from the EC than from the US.

Third, Japan's fiscal expansion has a minor impact on the trade partners as far as the estimated models are concerned. This may be explained by an inelastic behavior of Japan's imports with respect to GNP growth. Another factor responsible for the smaller impacts is the small share of exports in the final demand totals.

Comparing the impacts of respective fiscal expansion on Asia NIEs, the US and the EC show a quite large GNP multiplier, while Japan's impacts are less than one third of them respectively.

Judging from the simulation results, ASEAN economies are not as sensitive to the disturbances in the developed countries as is the case of Asia NIEs. Again the impacts of Japan on Asian economies are smaller than those of the US and the EC, partly reflecting the difference in the size of the respective domestic markets.

It is an interesting exercise to simulate the combined impacts the US federal budget cut and an offsetting fiscal expansion in Japan and the E. Simulation was made on the condition that the US decreases government expenditure by 1% of GNP, while both Japan and the EC increase government expenditure by 1% of GNP, respectively. As shown in Table 5, the negative US impacts on the Asian economies are largely offset by the positive effects of both Japan and the EC. This implies that policy coordination is indispensable among Japan, the US and the EC to resolve the US fiscal deficit with a minimum shock.

Table 6 indicates that a 10 % depreciation of the US dollar against the Japanese Yen and European currencies has a favorable impacts on the Asian NIEs. Favorable impacts on the US economy are decreasing and become negative after the fourth year. As far as export markets are concerned, the impacts are positive for the US, Asian NIEs and ASEAN, reflecting the changing price competitiveness in the world export market. The effects of US dollar depreciation on East Asian economies might be underestimated due to the missing relative price variable in the export equations of Asia NIEs and ASEAN.

Table 5 Simulation of combined fiscal shock of the US, Japan and EC.

	JA	US	EC	CA	AN	AS
77	1.244	−1.877	1.562	−0.432	−0.385	−0.069
78	1.620	−1.886	1.912	−0.548	−0.373	−0.022
79	1.786	−1.918	2.159	−0.596	−0.358	0.027
80	1.904	−1.931	2.321	−0.612	−0.317	0.075
81	1.895	−1.892	2.416	−0.625	−0.342	0.063
82	1.892	−1.979	2.507	−0.694	−0.330	0.062
83	1.782	−1.913	2.540	−0.736	−0.404	0.028
84	1.444	−1.672	2.514	−0.764	−0.508	−0.029
85	1.065	−1.568	2.472	−0.791	−0.607	−0.088
86	0.733	−1.424	2.400	−0.818	−0.728	−0.155
87	0.410	−1.280	2.338	−0.822	−0.791	−0.209

Table 6 Simulation of the US dollar depreciation Japan and European currency.

	JA	US	EC	CA	AN	AS
77	0.108	0.212	-0.122	−0.041	−0.011	−0.211
78	−0.210	0.135	-0.080	−0.134	0.061	−0.008
79	−0.528	0.007	-0.068	−0.213	0.102	−0.032
80	−0.833	−0.091	-0.021	−0.229	0.187	−0.051
81	−1.252	−0.139	0.055	−0.220	0.198	−0.077
82	−1.798	−0.158	0.125	−0.224	0.207	−0.146
83	−2.471	−0.144	0.151	−0.239	0.142	−0.258
84	−2.996	−0.130	0.147	−0.262	0.087	−0.344
85	−3.252	−0.131	0.118	−0.292	0.082	−0.397
86	−3.636	−0.079	0.021	−0.405	−0.128	−0.503
87	−3.906	−0.088	-0.094	−0.550	−0.299	−0.629

4. Concluding Remarks

It is often said that the Japanese economy has had significant structural changes since around the PLAZA agreement on the exchange rate and others in 1985. Since then the Japanese economy has followed a growth path which depends mostly on the domestic demand. Japan's import elasticity with respect to GNP seems to have increased up to over unity, and her imports from Asian economies are on the increasing trend.

The analysis in this paper does not take into account these changes occurring in Japan and trade partner countries, mostly because of the data availability.

A further study must be made to model the relation between trade position and economic performance not only at the macro level but also at the sectoral one.

References

Akamatsu, K (1962). A historical pattern of economic growth in developing countries. *Journal of Developing Economies*, No. 1.

Balassa, B (1965). Trade liberalization and "Revealed" comparative advantage. *The Manchester School of Economic and Social Study*, May.

Kinoshita, S and M Yamada (1989). The impacts of robotization on macro and sectoral economies within a world econometric model. *Technological Forecasting and Social Change*, 35(2–3).

Kinoshita, S and J Nemoto (1990). The changing pattern of international specialization and economic interdependence among Asia-Pacific, the US and the EC economies. *IEC discussion paper* No. 46, Faculty of Economics, Nagoya University.
Kinoshita, S (1994). A linked international model for the pacific basin economy. In: Ichimura Shinichi and Y. Matsumoto (eds.) *Econometric Models of Asian-Pacific Countries*, Springer-Verlag.
Kojima, K (2000). The 'Flying Geese' model of asian economic development: origin, theoretical extension, and regional policy implication. *Journal of Asian Economics*, 11(4), Autumn.
Vernon, R (1966). International investment and international trade in the product cycle. *Quarterly Journal of Economics*, May.
Yamazawa, I (1984). *Japan's Economic Development and International Division of Labor* (in Japanese), Toyokeizai, Tokyo.

Appendix: Structure of a Small linked Model

1. Values in the parenthesis indicate t-value
2. Values at the end of structural equations are R^2, standard error and D-W ratio, respectively.

(Japan Model)

(1) CJA = 21684 + 0.2059*(GNPVJA/PCJA) + 0.5373*CJA(−1)−77645*(PCJA/PCJA(−1))
(3.0016) (5.1329) (3.2274)
0.997/943/2.56

(2) IHJA = 14078 + 0.0387*GNPJA−0.0838*KHJA(−1)−824.2*RSJA + 0.9498*IHJA(−1)
(2.0475) (−3.1136) (−2.8604) (0.9498)
−5872*(PIHJA/PIHJA(-1))
(−1.9388)
0.806/808/2.10

(3) IFJA = −3912 + 0.1310*(GNPJA + GNPJA(−1)) + 0.01030*KFJA(−1)
(3.2338) (0.2461)
−43425*(YWJA/GNPJA)
(−5.007)
0.988/1062/1.40

(4) EJA = −7091 + 334.135*FEJA
(26.628)
0.985/1360/1.42

(5) MJA = exp(−0.1581 + 0.8612*log(GNPJA)−0.1935*log(PMJA/PGNPJA)
(11.879) (−2.874)
−0.2633*log(PMJA/PMJA(−1)))
(−2.9589)
0.929/0.042/2.45

(6) WPIJA = 19.635 + 0.4389*PMJA + 66.441*(YWJA/GNPJA)
(20.131) (15.003)
0.993/0.96/2.05

(7) PCJA = 2.669 + 0.1057*WPIJA + 53.264*(YWJA/GNPJA) + 0.6091*PCJA(−1)
(2.6923) 3.9787) (12.458)
0.998/0.96/1.61

(8) PIHJA = 4.157 + 0.167*WPIJA + 52.742*(YWJA/GNPJA) + 0.5058*PIHJA(−1)
(1.425) 1.1895) (2.3926)
0.974/3.10/1.59

(9) PIFJA = 23.344 + 0.5057*WPIJA + 44.785(YWJA/GNPJA)
(5.9154) (3.5880)
0.969/2.26/0.46

(10) YWJA = WJA*LWJA

(11) WJA = (0.3640 + 0.8476*(PCJA/PCJA(−1))−0.0627*(PMJA/PGNPJA)
(8.797) (−2.931)
−3.9341*(UJA/LWJA)−0.03682*D80)*WJA(−1)
(−4.7279) (−2.8802)
0.973/0.11/1.53

(12) LWJA = exp(1.60485 + 0.3272*log(GNPJA + GNPJA(−1)) + 0.2838*log(LWJA(−1))
(4.6745) (1.692)
−0.0581*log(WJA/PGNPJA))
(−1.2078)
0.994/0.006/1.97

(13) UJA = exp(−2.652 + 0.7114*log(LFJA)−2.5483*log(GNPJA/GNPJA(−1))
(0.6007) (−2.7226)
+ 0.3383*log(UJA(−1))−2.4693*log(WJA/WJA(−1)))
(1.3312) (−3.120)
0.942/0.072/1.65

(14) PEJA = 67.172 + 76.95*PFEJA−0.5709*TIME
(17.684) (−4.947)
0.967/1.37/1.19

(15) KFJA = −354 + 0.9519*KFJA(−1) + IFJA
(276.04)

(16) KHJA = 380.8 + 0.9173*KHJA(−1) + IHJA
(125.4)

(17) PMJA = 1.613 + 82.66*PM$*EXJA + 0.1323*PGNPJA
(35.081) (2.322)
0.992/1.53/1.57

(18) GNPJA = CJA + IHJA + IFJA + JJA + GJA + EJA−MJA

(19) GNPVJA = CJA*PCJA + IHJA*PIHJA + IFJA*PIFJA + GJA*PGJA
+ EJA*PEJA−MJA*PMJA + JJA*WPIJA

(20) PGNPJA = GNPVJA/GNPJA

(US Model)

(21) CUS = 75.52 + 0.2717*(GNPVUS/PCUS)−2.5027*RCBUS
(4.2826) (−1.6923) (−8.077)
−1136.4*(PCUS/PCUS(1−)) + 0.6045*CUS(−1)
(−8.077) (7.3534)
0.998/9.77/2.85

(22) IHUS = 34.795 + 0.2085*(GNPVUS/PCUS)−0.1159*KHUS(−1)−4.7289*RCBUS
(6.3566) (−4.548) (−3.2277)
0.910/8.35/1.40

(23) IFUS = −220.4 + 0.2235*GNPUS−0.040*KFUS(−1) + 63.857*(PMUS/PGNPUS)
(6.0941) (−2.2163) (1.8993)
0.958/13.47/1.32

(24) EUS = 589.7 + 1.6331*FEUS + 7.7582*TIME
(13.752) (12.562)
0.982/6.64/1.53

(25) MUS = exp(−11.07 + 2.0969*log(GNPUS)−0.4783*log(PMUS/PGNPUS)
(34.491) (−7.2366)
0.994/0.019/2.87

(26) PPIUS = exp(0.1183 + 0.4365*log(PMUS) + 0.1782*log(YWUS/GNPUS)
(10.586) (2.3082)
+ 0.3*log(PPIUS(−1)))
(3.5277)
0.998/0.015/2.12

(27) PCUS = 13.295 + 2.088*PPIUS + 4.3077*WUS − 363.2*(GNPUS/LWUS)
(13.390) (36.429) (−1.607)
0.999/0.25/2.87

(28) PIHUS = −10.637 + 0.4136*PPIUS + 0.1422*(YWUS/GNPUS)
(4.6265) (8.277)
0.995/1.93/0.68

(29) PIFUS = 6.9497 + 0.8904*PPIUS
(35.960)
0.988/2.31/1.52

(30) PEUS = 9.4928 + 0.863*PPIUS + 4.087*OPPFE$
(37.289) (4.076)
0.997/0.022/1.04

(31) PGUS = −4.0446 + 0.1376*PPIUS + 0.1051*(YWUS/GNPUS) + 0.4105*PGUS(−1)
(5.6959) (6.1348) (6.2979)
0.991/0.45/1.77

(32) GNPUS = CUS + IHUS + IFUS + JUS + GUS + EUS − MUS
(33) GNPVUS = CUS*PCUS + IHUS*PIHUS + IFUS*PIFUS + GUS*PGUS
+ UUS*PPIUS + EUS*PEUS − MUS*PMUS
(34) PGNPUS = GNPVUS/GNPUS
(35) YWUS = WUS*LWUS
(36) WUS = exp(−0.8065 + 0.50215*log(PCUS) − 0.1807*(UUS/LWUS)
(11.513) (−2.5413)
+ 0.5015*log(WUS(−1)))
(12.244)
0.999/0.0044/1.49

(37) LWUS = exp(3.7258 + 0.6408*log(GNPUS) − 0.2324*log(WUS/PGNPUS)
(10.619) (−2.2635)
+ 0.1828*log(LWUS(−1)))
(2.5106)
0.995/0.0069/1.49

(38) KHUS = −14.465 + 0.9938*KHUS(−1) + IHUS
(39) KFUS = 75.995 + 0.9493*KFUS(−1) + IFUS
(40) UUS = 2535 + 0.6806*LFUS − 0.7796*LWUS
(31.601) (−27.816)
0.987/203/1.61

(EC Model)
(41) CEC = −17.92 + 0.3310*GDPEC*(PGDPEC/PCEC) − 328.3*(PCEC/PCEC(−1))
(11.258) (−4.346)
+ 0.4847*CEC(−1)
(13.120)
0.999/3.69/1.86

(42) INVEC = 801.65 + 0.5585*GDPEC − 0.1324*GDPEC(−1) − 21.089*TIMR
(9.555) (−1.2569) (3.4521)
+ 0.3361*INVEC(−1)
(1.5004)
0.956/4.01/1.23

(43) EEC = −10.819 + 1.3246*FEEC
(83.043)
0.998/4.79/1.21

(44) MEC = exp(−6.2112 + 1.6118*log(GDPEC)−0.174*log(PMEC/PGDPEC))
(17.454) (−2.3703)
0.981/0.016/1.97

(45) GDPEC = CEC + INVEC + GCEC + EEC−MEC

(46) PCEC = −219.81 + 0.1796*PMEC + 3.182*TIME + 0.5195*PCEC(−1)
(9.1195) (4.743) (7.0677)
0.999/0.98/1.44

(47) PEEC = −129.999 + 86.01*PFEEC + 1.809*TIME
(22.67) (7.0097)
0.999/0.95/0.59

(48) PMEC = PM$EC*EXEC

(49) PGDPEC = −237.44 + 0.0998*PMEC + 3.4755*TIME + 0.5457*PGDPEC (−1)
(4.69186) 4.6186) (5.3593)
0.999/0.78/2.08

(Canada Model)

(50) CCA = 21.853 + 0.29392*GDPCA*(PGDPCA/PCCA) + 0.6207*CCA(−1)
(2.0646) (2.8763)
0.862/3.53/1.87

(51) MCA = exp(−6.747 + 1.9418*log(GDPCA))
(21.373)
0.976/0.032/1.67

(52) ECA = −5.1197 + 1.1765*FECA + 0.64*(ECA(−1)−FECA(−1)
(19.21) (4.2121)
0.995/1.42/1.33

(53) GDPCA = CCA + GDICA + GCCA + ECA−MCA

(54) PCCA = −4.2837 + 0.3939*PMCA + 0.06194*TIME
(1.8063) (6.2922)
0.984/0.036/1.28

(55) PECA = 0.1362 + 0.8756*PFECA
(69.773)
0.998/0.008/1.26

(56) PMCA = PM$CA*EXCA

(57) PGDPCA = 0.1128 + 0.8789*PCCA
(47.286)
0.995/0.018/2.30

(Asia NIEs Model)

(58) CAN = 16.800 + 0.1837*GDPAN*(PGDOAN/PCAN) + 0.6675*CAN(−1)
(4.8359) (8.542)
−10.349*(PCAN/PCAN(−1)
(−1.8124)
0.9810.98/1.59

(59) MAN = exp(−1.066 + 0.8665*log(GDPAN) + 0.2684*log(MAN(−1)))
(4.3223) (1.6715)
0.981/0.046/1.40

(60) EAN = 14.568 + 0.8889*FEAN
(26.622)
0.985/4.43/1.64

(61) INVAN = 62.618 + 0.05768*HDPAN + 0.6367*INVAN(−1)
(1.8914) (6.0826)
−55.797*(PMAN/PGDPAN)
(−4.1054)
0.990/0.108/2.44

(62) GDPAN = CAN + INVAN + GCAN + EAN−MAN

(63) PCAN = −0.01964 + 0.68*PMAN + 0.4038*PCAN(−1)
(6.876) (5.0286)
0.995/0.021/0.82

(64) PEAN = −2.1489 + 0.9689*PFEAN + 0.02718*TIME
(5.8181) (3.3727)
0.982/0.035/0.92

(65) PMAN = PM$an*EXAN

(66) PGDP = −0.0797 + 0.5916*PMAN + 0.5489*GDPAN(−1)
(3.0244) (4.0661)
0.991/0.030/1.57

(ASEAN Model)

(67) CAS = 18.372 + 0.3358*GDPAS*(PGDPAS/PCAS)−17.524*(PCAS/PCAS(−1))
(4.6483) (−1.2529)
+ 0.5006*CAS(−1)
(4.760)
0.998/1.68/1.57

(68) INVAS = −32.6644 + 0.2026*GDPAS + 46.994*(PFEAS/PMAS)
(6.066) (4.2726)
0.876/3.25/1.13

(69) MAS = exp(−3.6445 + 1.5235*GDPAS))
(15.737)
0.957/0.056/0.74

(70) EAS = 7.823 + 0.8979*FEAS + 0.8172*(EAS(−1)−FEAS(−1))
(19.090) (3.2461)

(71) GDPAS = CAS + INVAS + GCAS + EAS−MAS

(72) PCAS = −0.1289 + 0.4568*PMAS + 0.7841*PCAS(−1)
(3.5253) (10.616)
0.992/0.036/2.15

(73) PGDPAS = 0.1816 + 0.633*PMAS + 0.6949*PGDPAS(−1)
(3.8855) (6.2339)
0.989/0.038/1.58

(74) PMAS = PM$AS*EXAS

(Trade Linkage Sector))

(75) XFEJA = 0.128*MUS + 0.0242*MEC + 0.0391*(MCA/1.1692) + 0.2553*MAN
+ 0.2184*MAS

(76) XFEUS = 0.17404*(MJA/226.74) + 0.0846*MEC + 0.6754*(MCA/1.692) + 0.1907*MAN
+ 0.1538*MAS

(77) XFEEC = 0.0593*(JAM/226.74) + 0.128*MUS + 0.5035*MEC + 0.0776*(MCA/1.1692)
+ 0.0934*MAN + 0.1882*MAS

(78) XFECA = 0.0416*(MJA/226.74) + 0.1701*MUS + 0.0213*MEC + 0.0122*MAN
+ 0.0087*MAS

(79) XFEAN = 0.0416*(MJA/226.74) + 0.0657*MUS + 0.0154*MEC + 0.0217*(MCA/1.1692)
+ 0.0582*MAN + 0.0601*MAS

(80) XFEAS = 0.1514*(MJA/226.4) + 0.0508*MUS + 0.0136*MEC + 0.0054*(MCA/1.1692)
+ 0.0816*MAN + 0.1504*MAS

(81) PFIUS = 0.128*PFEJA + 0.1522*PEE$EC + 0.1701*PEE$CA + 0.0657*PEE$AN
+ 0.0508*PEE$AS

(82) PFI$JA = 0.174*PEEUS + 0593*PEE$EC + 0.0335*PEE$CA + 0.0416*PEE$AN
+ 0.1514*PEE$AS

(83) PFI$EC = 0.0242*PEE$JA + 0.0846*PEEUS + 0.5035*PEE$EC + 0.0123*PEE$CA
+ 0.0154*PEE$AN + 0.0136*PEE$AS

(84) PFI$CA = 0.391*PEE$JA + 0.6854*PEEUS + 0.0776*PEE$EC + 0.0217*PEE$AN
+ 0.0054*PEE$AS

(85) PFI$AN = 0.2553*PEE$JA + 0.1907*PEEUS + 0.0934*PEE$EC + 0.0122*PEE$CA
+ 0.0582*PEE$AN + 0.0816*PEE$AS

(86) PFI$AS = 0.2184*PEE$JA + 0.1538*PEEUS + 0.1882*PEE$EC + 0.0087*PEE$CA
+ 0.0601*PEE$AN + 0.1505*PEE$AS

(87) PM$JA = −0.2384 + 2.3382*PFI$JA + 0.16298*OPPFE$
(7.1851) (2.1923)
0.976/0.029/1.32

(88) PMUS = −14.597 + 117.042*PFIUS + 9.0468*OPPFE$ + 0.4321*PMUS(−1)
(11.102) (3.5665) (10.528)
0.993/1.42/1.99

(89) PM$EC = −13.11 + 170.24*PFI$EC + 2.071*OPPFE$
(40.822) (1.5863)
0.995/1.42/1.54

(90) PM$CA = 0.5733 + 0.4258*PFI$CA + 0.08078*OPPFE$
(13.335) (5.2216)
0.982/0.013/1.67

(91) PM$AN = 0.0449 + 1.1155*PFI$AN + 0.17121*OPPFE$
(19.602) (8.8128)
0.991/0.13/1.08

(92) PM$AS = 1.7019 + 0.44328*PFI$AS + 0.40658*OPPFE$ − 0.0179*TIME
(2.4924) (10.255) (−4.2262)
0.952/0.027/1.65

(93) PFE$JA = (0.3826 + 0.00993*WPIJA + .1437*EXJA − 0.00625*TIME)/EXJA

(94) PFEUS = 0.05993 + 0.01087*PPIUS − 0.02786*EXEC

(95) PFE$EC = (−1.7358 + 0.7142*PFI$EC*EXEC + 0.06013*OPPFE$EXEC
+ 0.02752*TIME)/EXEC

(96) PFE$CA = (2.4831 + 1.5521*PFI$CA*EXCA − *TIME)/EXCA*PFEAN)/EXAN

(97) PFE$AN = (0.3326 + 0.5399*PMAN + 0.1186*TIME)/EXAN

(98) PFE$AS = (0.2518 + 0.5864*OPPFE$*EXAS + 0.000994*PMUS*EXAS)/EXAS

(99) PWMUS = 0.168*PM$JA + 0.3989*PM$EC/100) + 0.2824*PM$CA
+ 0.0837*PM$AN + 0.0666*PM$AS

(100) PWMJA = 0.3855*(PMUS/100) + 0.2081*(PM$EC/100) + 0.0298*PM$CA
+ 0.2042*PM$AN + 0.1723*PM$AS

(101) PWMEC = 0.1236*PM$JA + 0.5424*(PMUS/100) + 0.0699*PM$CA + 0.0884*PM$AN
+ 0.1756*PM$AS

(102) PWMCA = 0.0853*PM$JA + 0.7385*(PMUS/100) + 0.1521*(PM$EC/100)
+ 0.0141*PM$AN + 0.0100*PM$AS

(103) PWMAN = 0.1570*PM$JA + 0.2504*(PMUS/100) + 0.2825*(PM$EC/100)
+ 0.0353*PM$CA + 0.1014*PM$AS

(104) PWMAS = 0.4964*PM$JA + 0.2504(PMUS/100) + 0.1567*(PM$EC/100)
+ 0.005*PM$CA + 0.0912*PM$AN*(PM$EC/)

(105) FEJA = FEJA0 + exp(−2.1273 + 1.4260*log(XFEJA) − 0.4667*log(PFE$JA/PWMJA))
(20.386) (−2.249)
0.972/0.059/1.18

(106) FEUS = FEUS0 + exp(0.4515 + .8590*log(XFEUS) − 0.8772*log(PFEUS/PWMUS))
(18.642) (−7.7849)
0.969/0.023/1.56

(107) FEEC = FEEC0 + exp(−1.837 + 1.259*log(XFEEC) − 0.1406*log(PEE$EC/PWMEC))
(33.741) (−3.0432)
0.990/0.020/1.06

(108) FECA = FECA0 + exp(−1.0552 + 1.1408*log(XFECA) + 0.1365*log(PEE$CA/PWMCA))
(15.862) (0.7614)
0.981/0.033/1.03

(109) FEAN = FEAN0 + exp(−4.6672 + 2.1497*log(XFEAN)−0.8285*log(PEE$AN/PWMAN))
(17.975) −4.4796)
0.989/0.057/1.14

(110) PEAS = PEAS0 + exp(−1.6048 + 1.3164*log(XFEAS)−0.1765*log(PEE$AS/PWMAS))
(16.896) (−1.7602)
0.980/0.040/1.84

(111) PFEJA = PFE$JA*EXJA
(112) PFEEC = PFE$EC*EXEC
(113) PFECA = PFE$CA*EXCA
(114) PFEAN = PFE$AN*EXAN
(115) PFES = PFE$AS*EXAS

List of Variables

1 Defined for individual country and region in the following: JA = Japan, the US = United States, EC = European Community, CA = Canada, AN = Asian NIEs, AS = ASEAN

3 Values for Japan and Canada are expressed in domestic currency unit, while those for others in US dollar

Variable	Description	Unit
C	Private final consumption	billion in 1980 prices
IH	Private housing investment	billion in 1980 prices
IF	business investment	billion in 1980 prices
INV	Gross fixed investment	billion in 1980 prices
J	Changes in inventories	billion in 1980 prices
GDI	Gross investment	billion in 1980 prices
GDI	Government expenditure	billion in 1980 prices
GC	Government consumption	billion in 1980 prices
E	Exports of goods and services	billion in 1980 prices
M	Imports of goods and services	billion in 1980 prices
GNP	Gross national product	billion in 1980 prices
GNPV	Gross national product, nominal	billion in current prices
GDP	Gross domestic product	billion in 1980 prices
GDPV	Gross domestic product, nominal	billion in current prices
KH	Year-end private housing capital stock	billion in 1980 prices
KF	Year-end private fixed business capital stock	billion in 1980 prices
PC	Deflator for C	1980 = 100
PIH	Deflator for IH	1980 = 100
PIF	Deflator for IF	1980 = 100
PPI	Producer price index (WPI)	1980 = 100
PG	Deflator for G	1980 = 100
PGC	Deflator for GC	1980 = 100
PE	Deflator for E	1980 = 100
PM	Deflator for M	1980 = 100
PGNP	Deflator for GNP	1980 = 100

(*Continued*)

(*Continued*)

Variable	Description	Unit
PGDP	Deflator for GDP	1980 = 100
W	Wage earning per employee	million
YW	Compensation of employee	billion in current prices
LW	Number of employee	thousands of persons
LS	Self-employed persons	thousands of persons
LF	Labor force	thousands of persons
U	Unemployed persons	thousands of persons
EX	Exchange rate	per US dollar
FE	Commodity exports	US dollar in 1980 prices
XFE	Potential export demands	US dollar in 1980 prices
PFE$	Export unit value index	1980 = 100 in US dollar
PM$	Import unit value index	1980 = 100 in US dollar
PFI$	Import unit value index (excl. from ROW)	1980 = 100 in US dollar
PWM	Rivals' export price indices in the world market	1980 = 100 in US dollar
OPPFE$	OPEC export price index	1980 = 100 in US dollar
TIME	Time trend	year

Data Source

Country	Title	Source
USA	National Income and Product Account	Department of Commerce
	Fixed Reproducible Tangible Wealth in the United States 1925–85	Department of Commerce
	Business Statistics	Department of Commerce
Japan	Annual Report on National Accounts	Economic Planning Agency
	Gross Capital Stock of Private Business	Economic Planning Agency
	Annual Report on Labor Force Survey	Somusho
Canada $EC	National Accounts, Vol. 1 and 2	OECD
Asia NIEs & ASEAN	World Table 1988–1989	World Bank
Taiwan	Taiwan Statistical Data	National Statistics
	Quarterly National Economic Trend	National Statistics
Foreign Trade	Direction of Trade	IMF
	International Financial Statistics	IMF
	Taiwan Statistical Data	National Statistics

Chapter 2

Structure and Application of a World Industry and Trade Model*

Soshichi Kinoshita

1. Introduction

During the past ten years or so since the first oil-crisis, Japan and the developed countries have been facing the various complex economic issues arising from both internal and external sources. One of these issues is centered on the macroeconomic adjustments to slower economic growth, higher inflation and balance of payment imbalance in these countries. Another important issue is related to the industrial restructuring problem that has been caused by two global oilcrisis, trade frictions among developed economies and rapid industrialization of newly and semi-newly industrializing countries.

With the background of these economic difficulties, most developed countries have been greatly concerned with the way how they should enhance and maintain the structural adaptability of domestic economy to the changing economic environment.

This chapter intends to study quantitatively the impacts of changing international economic environments, especially the export promotion policies of developing countries and the protectionism in the US and

*This is based on the paper presented at the Link Fall Meeting, which was held at the University of Tsukuba on September 12~16, 1983. The study for this paper was the outcome of the three-year project of developing a world model of trade and industry at the Research Economic Institute of former EPA. The detailed report was published in Kinoshita *et al.* (1982).

EC countries upon sectoral productions, foreign trades, employments in Japan and her closely related countries.

2. Construction of a World Industry and Trade Model

In order to accomplish the above-mentioned purpose properly, we construct an econometric model of world industry and trade, which can be used to evaluate the interdependence between Japan and her major trading partners through inter-industry relations and commodity trade linkages.

The world industry and trade model to be constructed here consists of the following four elements:

(1) Multi-sectoral models of seven individual countries,
(2) Regional models dealing mainly with import volume and export price of remaining countries or regions,
(3) Trade linkage model of major commodity group which links country and regional models through trade flow in a consistent way, thus determining world trade volume and trade price by commodity group,
(4) Interfaces transferring and/or transforming relevant variables among different models.

The countries whose multi-sectoral models are to be constructed are selected based on the importance in the world market and that as a Japan's trade partner of individual country, as well as the availability of input-output table and related sectoral data. These countries are Japan, the US, Korea, four EC country (France, West Germany, Italy, and the UK). The construction of multi-sectoral model has been completed for Japan, the US and Korea. Models for remaining four EC countries have not yet completed, and as a result simple macro models will be included in the linkage simulation.

The regional model has been constructed for the following four regions:

(1) Asia NIEs including Singapore,
(2) ASEAN excluding Singapore,

(3) Other developed countries,
(4) The rest of the world economy including other developing countries and socialist economies.

Sectoral disaggregation of the whole economy was made on the basis of the importance of individual sector in industrial restructuring and international comparability of sectoral classification adopted in compiling national input-output tale. Individual sectors are as follows:

(1) Agricultural, forestry and fishing,
(2) Crude oil, coal and other mining,
(3) Food, beverages and tobacco,
(4) Textiles,
(5) Apparels,
(6) Leather product and foot wear,
(7) Wooden products and furniture,
(8) Pulp, paper and printing products,
(9) Rubber and plastic products,
(10) Chemicals,
(11) Petroleum and coal products,
(12) Non-metallic, mineral products,
(13) Iron and steel products
(14) Non-ferrous mineral products,
(15) Fabricated metals,
(16) General machinery
(17) Electrical machinery,
(18) Transport equipment,
(19) Professional goods
(20) Miscellaneous manufacturing products,
(21) Construction, electricity and gas, transportation and other tertiary industries.

3. Structure of the Model

The basic idea of modeling for world industry and trade analysisis, assuggested above, to link individual country and regional model

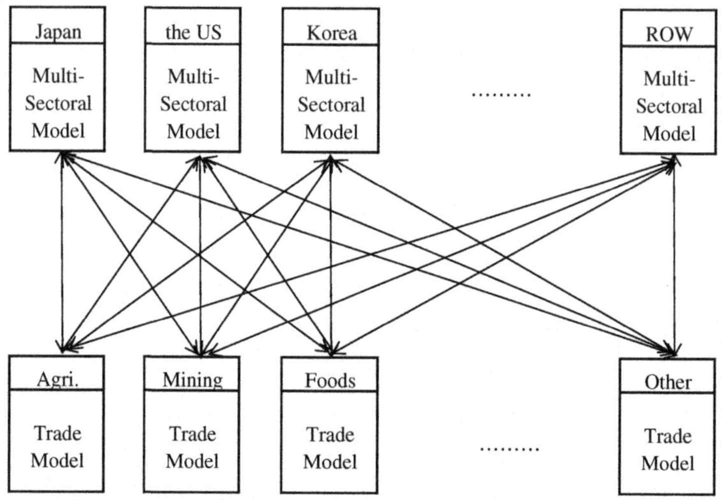

Fig. 1 Linkage of country and regional models with trade models.

with each other using trade linkage sub-model. Figure 1 shows how the individual model should be linked together to study the interdependence among individual country and region.

3.1. *Structural features of multi-sectoral model*

The multisectoral model for major countries is a large scale equation system that attempts to analyze the input-output relation and the national income and products behaviors simultaneously. The basic structure of the model is depicted in Fig. 2.

This model has several features. First, domestic demands and imports are explicitly specified as a function of relevant demand variable and relative price. Specifically, domestic demands are derived from input-output model based on price dependent input-output coefficients and final demand converters. Sectoral outputs are assumed to be determined so as to meet the demands for domestic outputs, which are the sum of domestic and foreign demands minus imports. Inventory changes are included in domestic demands, mostly due to the lack of sectoral data. The sectoral outputs thus determined affect investment and employment behavior in each sector.

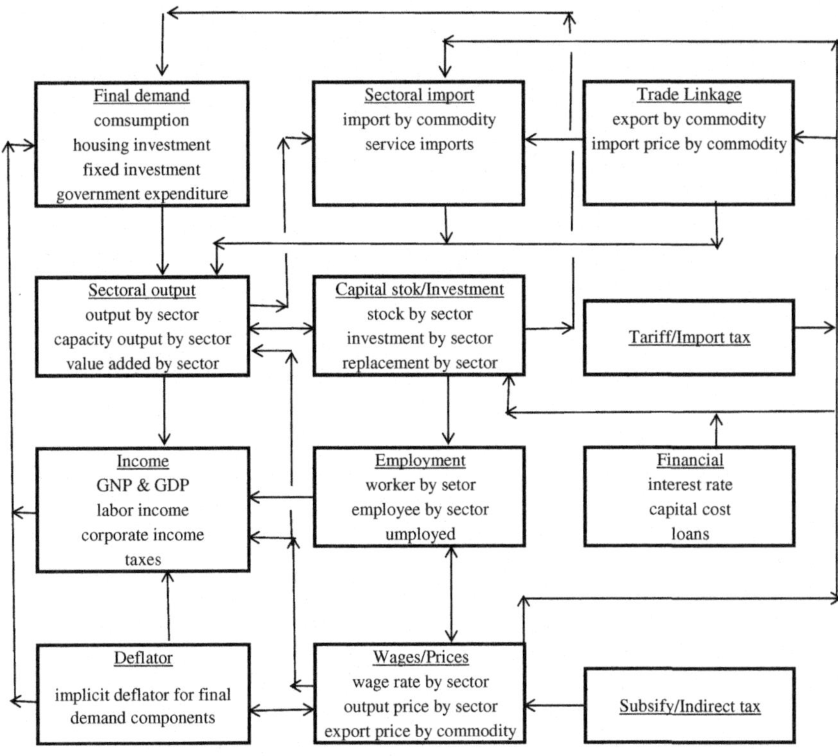

Fig. 2 Structure of a multi-sectoral model.

Secondly, as regards the demands fir primary factor inputs, sectoral investments are expressed as a distributed lag function of the gap between the desired capital stock and the existing one, and the desired stock is assumed to depend basically on expected output and real cost of capital. Sectoral changes in employment are also specified to fill the gap between the desired or required employment and the initial one. The desired or required level of employment is derived either from profit maximization as a function of output and real wage rate or from the solution of production function with given output and capital stock.

Thirdly, sectoral output prices are determined by both market conditions and cost factors, and the latter include costs for intermediate inputs, labor and indirect tax. Further, costs for intermediate inputs are derived from input side of input-output model, as shown below,

$$\sum a_{ji}(1 - mj)^{*} PO_j + \sum a_{ji} m_j {}^{*} PM_j$$

where a_{ji} is input-output coefficient, m_j is import ratio, PO_j is domestic output price and PM_j is import price.

As for demand deflator, implicit deflator for final demand component is explained by commodity price for domestic use and final demand converter, the latter of which specifies the commodity contents of individual final demand component.

Lastly, only a few points need to be mentioned about income distribution block. First, labor incomes are given by the product of employment and wage earning. Secondly, wage earning by sector reflects the difference in labor productivity as well as the general wage rate. Thirdly, non-wage incomes are determined by the balance between value added and labor incomes.[1]

It is easily understood that the model is basically of demand-determined type, assuming the flexible supply response to changes in the demand side of the economy. Structural equations are specified so as to take accounts of the lagged responses that have been observed in the adjustment mechanism in both demand and supply side.

The size and structural features of the multisectoral models of Japan, the US and Korea is summarized in Table 1.

And estimated parameters of the equations for sectoral investment, employment and import demands are shown the subsequent three Tables 2~4. We can see in these tables the differences and similarities between different sectors as well as those between individual economies.

Sectoral investments, which work as a price mover in restructuring industrial economies, have been explained by expected output, existing capital stock and financial variables such as user cost of capital defined by D.W. Jorgenson and real interest rate. The results imply that the average time lags between investment and output changes are shorter

---

[1] Structural equations of the national and trade linkage model are listed in the Appendix with the definition of variables.

		Japan		USA		Korea	
		Bahavioral	Idendity	Bahavioral	Idendity	Bahavioral	Idendity
Final demand	consumption	1	—	1	—	1	—
	housing investment	1	—	1	—	1	—
	change in Stock	1	—	1	—	—	—
	fixed investment	1	1	1	—	1	2
	exports	3	—	2	2	2	—
	imports	22	—	22	4	21	—
Sectoral output	final demand conversion	—	22	—	21	—	22
	domestic demand	22	—	—	—	22	—
	output	—	22	21	—	—	22
	value added I/O	—	22	—	21	—	22
	value added NIPA	22	—	21	—	22	—
	capacity output	20	—	—	—	—	—
	capacity utilization	20	—	—	—	—	—
Sectoral investment & capital stock	fixed investment	21	—	21	—	21	—
	replacement	21	—	—	—	—	—
	capital stock	—	21	1	22	—	21
	inventory	—	1	—	1	—	—
	housing stock	1	—	1	—	—	—
Employment	worker	22	1	22	1	20	1
	employee	22	1	—	—	21	1
	enemployed	1	1	—	2	—	1
Sectoral wage & prices	Wage rate	22	—	21	—	21	—
	unit labor cost	—	—	—	21	—	21
	unit material cost	—	—	—	21	—	21

(*Continued*)

Table 1 (*Continued*)

		Japan		USA		Korea	
		Bahavioral	Idendity	Bahavioral	Idendity	Bahavioral	Idendity
	unit main cost	22	—	—	—	—	—
	output price	43	1	21	—	21	—
	(commodity & industry)			8			
Income	personal income	1	1	7	—	—	1
	tax revenue	1	24	6	4	—	1
	national income account	1	3	—	—	—	2
	income aggregate	—	1	1	1	1	—
Final expenditure price	consumption I/O	—	1	—	1	—	1
	investment I/O	—	1	—	1	—	1
	public expenditure I/O	—	—	—	1	—	—
	inventory I/O	—	—	—	—	—	—
	consumption	1	—	2	—	1	—
	housing investment	1	—	2	—	1	—
	fixed investment	1	—	2	—	1	—
	public expenditure	—	—	2	—	—	—
	producer price	—	—	2	—	1	—
	construction	—	—	2	—	—	—
	plant & equipment	—	—	2	—	—	—
	export price	23	—	20	2	22	—
	import price	1	22	2	1	1	—
Financial	interest rate	1	—	—	—	—	—
	capital cost	—	—	—	23	—	—
		319	147	200	157	202	140

Table 2a Estimates of sectoral investment function: Japan.

		Output	Non-wage income	Interest rate	Capital Stock	Lagged Investment	R
3	Food	0.1377	0.1332	−3.0950	−0.1750	—	0.976
4	Textiles	0.0676	—	—	−0.0905	0.765	0.938
5	Apparel	0.0327	—	−0.3570	−0.0422	—	0.977
6	Leather	0.0624	—	−0.7420	—	—	0.904
7	Wood = Furniture	0.0499	0.1196	−2.3380	−0.0368	—	0.968
8	Pulp = Paper	0.0625	0.3716	—	−0.0206	—	0.985
9	Rubber	0.1120	—	−1.3000	−0.0786	0.593	0.965
10	Chemicals	1.1851	—	—	−0.4296	—	0.921 log
11	Petroreum	2.0154	—	—	−0.6705	—	0.922 log
12	Non-metalic minerals	0.1412	—	−2.6430	−0.0796	0.213	0.983
13	Iron = Steels	0.1090	—	−6.1680	−0.0342	—	0.946
14	Non = ferrous metals	1.0639	—	—	−0.4414	0.511	0.930 log
15	Fabricated metals	0.1026	—	−2.1443	−0.0207	—	0.951
16	Machinery	0.0517	0.2109	—	−0.0320	0.219	0.962
17	Electrical machinery	0.0411	0.1020	−3.8359	−0.0856	—	0.948
18	Transport equipment	0.0675	0.2996	−9.6674	−0.1574	—	0.975
19	Instruments	0.0725	—	—	−0.1854	—	0.961
20	Miscellaneous	0.1013	—	—	—	—	0.973

in Japan than in the US and investment in Korea is highly affected by the availability of investment funds.

Employment behaviors in Japan and Korea are specified as the partial adjustment process to the desired employment level that is determined by expected output and real wage rate, while employment in the US. is determined to fill the gap between short-run labor requirement and actual employment in the preceding year. Short-run employment requirements are derived from given output, capital stock and the level of technology under the Cobb=Douglas production function. Estimated results suggest that the partial adjustment coefficients are different among individual sectors. The US has a larger adjustment coefficient for most sectors compared to Japan and Korea.

Table 2b Estimates of sectoral investment function: USA.

	Desired capital	Output	Real cost of capital	Capital stock	RR	Mean lag	
	pX/uc	X	uc/p	K		X	uc/p
3 Food	—	0.0830	−27.2320	−0.2306	0.974	2.02	2.43
4 Textiles	—	0.1107	−58.1100	−0.2004	0.948	1.38	1.72
5 Apparel	—	0.0568	—	−0.2181	0.847	1.24	—
6 Leather	—	0.0598	−4.8380	−0.2011	0.765	1.41	1.23
7 Wood = Furniture	—	0.0835	—	−0.0823	0.829	1.32	—
8 Pulp = Paper	1.7483	—	—	−0.0059	0.902	1.82	—
9 Rubber	—	0.1516	−55.0700	−0.2056	0.987	1.11	2.26
10 Chemicals	—	0.2181	−279.1200	−0.2612	0.968	2.17	2.54
11 Petroleum	—	0.1751	−99.6640	−0.3345	0.942	1.77	2.27
12 Non-metalic minerals	—	0.2548	—	−0.2940	0.933	1.73	—
13 Iron = Steels	—	0.1546	−74.8570	−0.1658	0.971	1.96	2.28
14 Non = ferrous metals	—	0.1612	—	−0.2176	0.902	2.06	—
15 Fabricated metals	1.1097	—	—	−0.0196	0.962	1.87	—
16 Machinery	—	0.1236	—	−0.1849	0.987	1.83	—
17 Electrical machinery	—	0.0608	−226.9400	−0.1575	0.981	1.61	2.34
18 Transport equipment	1.1056	—	—	0.0954	0.875	1.89	—
19 Instruments	—	0.0687	−23.0490	−0.0850	0.934	1.00	2.44
20 Miscellaneous	0.7027	—	—	−0.1120	0.898	1.35	—

Import demands by commodity are explained by the traditional specification, which relates import volume to domestic demand variable, relative price and lagged imports. The estimated results show that import demands are significantly influenced by relative price, reflecting the effects of changes in the comparative advantage of individual country in the world market. Estimated elasticities with respect to domestic demand variable are larger in the US for most commodity groups than in Japan. This implies that as the domestic market for individual commodity grows, the share of foreign-produced product in the US market become larger, possibly due to the poor performance of the US manufactures in terms of quality and delivery condition.

Table 2c Estimates of sectoral investment function: Korea.

		Output	Capital stock	Interest rate	Loans	R
3	Food	0.0585	−0.0900	—	1.0857	0.984
4	Textiles	0.2753	−0.6361	—	1.5884	0.937
5	Apparel	0.0253	—	—	5.8351	0.984
6	Leather	0.0540	—	—	6.7183	0.970
7	Wood = Furniture	0.0318	—	—	0.0490	0.889
8	Pulp = Paper	0.0792	−0.1013	—	1.3579	0.974
9	Rubber	0.0665	—	—	1.2221	0.966
10	Chemicals	0.0584	—	−0.1701	—	0.866
11	Petroleum	0.0390	—	—	—	0.841
12	Non-metalic minerals	0.2081	−0.2324	—	0.7979	0.984
13	Iron = Steels	0.2347	−0.5705	—	4.1711	0.932
14	Non = ferrous	0.0708	−0.0983	—	0.0458	0.945
15	Fabricated metals	0.0500	—	—	0.6961	0.971
16	Machinery	0.1460	—	—	1.1297	0.947
17	Electrical machinery	0.0758	−0.0501	−0.0530	—	0.997
18	Transport equipment	0.1526	—	−0.1626	—	0.803
19	Instruments	0.1849	−0.5148	—	—	0.856
20	Miscellaneous	0.0296	—	—	—	0.870

3.2. *Structure of trade linkage model*

The trade linkage models are constructed to determine export volumes and import prices by commodity for each country and region in a consistent way, given imports volumes and export prices by commodity for each country and region. The idea of achieving the consistencies in export-import relationships in the world market is briefly explained below.

Let the trade linkage matrix, m_i^{kl} be defined as,

$$m_i^{kl} = M_i^{kl} \Big/ \sum M_i^{kl} = M_i^{kl} / M_i^l$$

where M_i^{kl} is export volume of the i-th commodity from the k-th country to the l-th country and Mil is the total import volume of the i-th commodity in the l-th country.

Thus, milk is the commodity's market share of the k-th country exports in the l-th country imports. Then the total export volume of

Table 3a Estimates of labor demand function: Japan-log.

	Output	Real wage	Lagged employment	Capital stock	R	Adjustment coeff.
3 Food	0.2101	−0.1334	0.5184	—	0.954	0.4816
4 Textiles	0.5867	−0.4033	0.2371	—	0.990	0.7629
5 Apparel	0.1954	—	0.4241	—	0.977	0.5759
6 Leather	—	−0.1859	—	0.4518	0.979	1.0000
7 Wood = Furniture	0.2966	−0.2191	0.2401	—	0.968	0.7599
8 Pulp = Paper	0.2881	−0.1717	0.3783	—	0.977	0.6217
9 Rubber	0.4766	−0.2857	0.5240	—	0.986	0.4760
10 Chemicals	0.2293	−0.2212	0.8334	—	0.893	0.1666
11 Petroleum	—	−0.0467	—	0.1852	0.988	1.0000
12 Non-metalic minerals	0.3306	−0.1700	—	–	0.980	1.0000
13 Iron = Steels	0.2056	−0.1864	0.7217	—	0.968	0.2783
14 Non = ferrous metals	0.2104	−0.2229	0.8661	—	0.970	0.1339
15 Fabricated metals	0.3095	−0.2299	0.4269	—	0.981	0.5731
16 Machinery	0.2343	−0.1835	0.5937	—	0.974	0.4063
17 Electrical machinery	0.3442	−0.2649	0.5424	—	0.996	0.4576
18 Transport equipment	0.3574	−0.2488	0.3634	—	0.994	0.6366
19 Instruments	0.4817	−0.4861	0.5890	—	0.988	0.4110
20 Miscellaneous	0.4348	−0.2782	0.1329	—	0.997	0.8671

the i-th commodity of the k-th country is given by

$$E_i^k = \sum M_i^{kl} = \sum m_i^{kl*} M_i^l.$$

Likewise, import price of i-th commodity of l-th country is given by a weighted average of the export prices of supplying countries as follows:

$$PM_i^l = \sum m_i^{kl*} PE_i^{kl}$$

and if there is no price discrimination in export market, the above relation is rewritten as

$$PM_i = \sum m_i^{kl*} PE_i^k.$$

Table 3b Estimates of labor demand function: USA.

		Man base		Man-hour base	
		Adjustment coeff.	Time trend	Adjustment coeff.	Time trend
3	Food	0.5350	−0.0564	0.5755	−0.0140
4	Textiles	0.5182	−0.0136	0.6717	−0.0199
5	Apparel	0.5984	−0.0168	0.6959	0.0200
6	Leather	0.6791	−0.0109	0.7080	−0.0125
7	Wood = Furniture	0.7669	−0.0022	0.8983	−0.0054
8	Pulp = Paper	0.3734	−0.0061	0.4743	−0.0079
9	Rubber	0.4913	−0.0141	0.5632	−0.0167
10	Chemicals	0.1363	−0.0266	0.1511	−0.0293
11	Petroleum	0.3126	0.0106	0.3934	0.0126
12	Non-metalic minerals	0.5323	−0.0069	0.6584	−0.0091
13	Iron = Steels	0.5164	−0.0054	0.6903	−0.0067
14	Non = ferrous metals	0.5225	−0.0048	0.6125	−0.0064
15	Fabricated metals	0.7518	−0.0019	0.8625	0.0005
16	Machinery	0.5099	−0.0061	0.6148	−0.0081
17	Electrical machinery	0.6945	−0.0061	0.7426	−0.0104
18	Transport equipment	0.4114	−0.0074	0.4790	−0.0087
19	Instruments	0.5758	−0.0036	0.6309	−0.0023
20	Miscellaneous	0.9419	−0.0066	0.7861	−0.0084

Thus if we could know he trade linkage matrix m_i^{kl}, then given the vector of import volumes M_i, the vector of export volumes E_i is uniquely determined by the above relation. Likewise, given the export price PE_i, then the import price PM_i is uniquely determined.

In trade linkage model, alternative methods of estimating the trade linkage matrix have been proposed so far, and the comparison of alternative methods has been done at the highly aggregate level. The comparison of alternative method at the disaggregated level was confined to the following three methods:

(1) Moriguchi method,
(2) Samuelson-Kurihara method,
(3) Hichman-Lau method.

Moriguchi method assumes that the period to period variation of M_i^{kl} depends on relative price and the relative size of export capacity

Table 3c Estimates of labor demand function: Korea-log.

		Output	Real wage	Lagged employment	Capital stock	R	Adjustment coeff.
3	Food	0.7201	−0.2161	—	—	0.973	1.0000
4	Textiles	0.1980	—	0.7031	—	0.961	0.2969
5	Apparel	0.2235	—	—	0.7364	0.853	1.0000
6	Leather	0.3072	—	0.7458	—	0.854	0.2542
7	Wood = Furniture	0.1743	—	0.6642	—	0.919	0.3358
8	Pulp = Paper	0.3717	—	—	0.5557	0.988	1.0000
9	Rubber	0.6809	−0.2745	0.2374	—	0.991	0.7626
10	Chemicals	—	—	—	—	—	—
11	Petroleum	—	−0.0849	0.6689	0.0305	0.734	0.3311
12	Non-metalic minerals	0.6717	−0.4197	—	—	0.947	1.0000
13	Iron = Steels	—	—	0.2989	0.2390	0.937	0.6011
14	Non = ferrous metals	0.4574	−0.2025	—	—	0.903	1.0000
15	Fabricated metals	0.2075	−0.1039	0.6979	—	0.987	0.3021
16	Machinery	0.5046	−0.2416	0.1921	—	0.932	0.8079
17	Electrical machinery	0.5676	−0.2992	0.3351	—	0.996	0.6649
18	Transport equipment	—	—	0.7635	0.1857	0.956	0.2365
19	Instruments	0.5742	−0.7613	0.4470	—	0.805	0.5530
20	Miscellaneous	0.0973	—	0.5854	—	0.953	0.4146

to import market. Real export share function is estimated by pooling cross section and time series data for each exporting country.

Hichman-Lau method is based on the assumption that an index of the quantity of imports for l-th country is a CES function of trade flow to that country, and that quantities of bilateral import flow M_i^{kl} is derived from cost minimization for given total imports M_i. A real trade flow function is estimated for each importing country by pooling cross section and time series data. Here, estimated elasticity of substitution and other parameters satisfy the world trade consistency requirement.

Table 4a Estimates of import demand function: Japan-log.

		Domestic demand	Relative price	Lagged import	R	Price elasticity long-run
1	Agriculture	1.7899	−0.0679	—	0.974	−0.0679
2	Mining	1.1449	—	0.0672	0.999	—
3	Food	1.6082	−0.4954	—	0.990	−0.4954
4	Textiles	1.1890	−1.8398	0.6788	0.990	−5.7279
5	Apparel	2.0969	−4.4702	—	0.988	−4.7279
6	Leather	1.6314	−0.4911	0.5148	0.991	−1.0122
7	Wood = Furniture	1.2844	−1.2192	0.4303	0.983	−2.1401
8	Pulp = Paper	0.8811	−0.9962	—	0.969	−0.9962
9	Rubber	0.7096	−1.9995	0.5994	0.993	−4.9913
10	Chemicals	0.9490	−1.1652	—	0.991	−1.1652
11	Petroleum	0.8527	−0.1676	—	0.977	−0.1676
12	Non-metalic minerals	0.5892	−1.5158	0.2835	0.963	−2.1156
13	Iron = Steels	—	—	—	—	—
14	Non = ferrous metals	1.0981	—	—	0.973	—
15	Fabricated metals	0.7596	−0.8726	0.2143	0.991	−1.2379
16	Machinery	1.5005	−0.2304	0.3110	0.954	−0.3344
17	Electrical machinery	0.7768	−0.4622	0.3429	0.993	−0.7034
18	Transport equipment	0.6332	−1.1921	0.2876	0.942	−1.6734
19	Instruments	1.1699	−1.7810	—	0.993	−1.7810
20	Miscellaneous	1.2323	−0.3936	—	0.989	−0.3936

Samuelson-Kurihara method explains the total real reports of the i-th commodity for each country as a log-linear function of activity variable and relative price. The bilateral trade flows are then computed by the RAS method to meet the world trade consistency condition.

We applied three methods to the common set of disaggregated trade matrix data covering the period 1973–76, and used Moriguchi method tentatively for the simulation experiments with the linked system. It may be appropriate to explain briefly the basic idea behind Moriguchi method.

First, we assume that for each commodity group the market for exports of the k-th country is described by the following two equations:

$$\text{Demand function } M_i^{kl} = M\left(PM_i^{kl}/PM_i^{l},\ M_i^{l}\right)$$

$$\text{Supply function } E_i^{kl} = E\left(PE_i^{kl}/PE_i^{k},\ E_i^{k}\right)$$

Table 4b Estimates of import demand function: USA-log.

		Domestic demand	Relative price	Lagged import	R	Price elasticity long-run
1	Agriculture	0.9838	−1.0053	−0.6989	0.970	−0.592
2	Mining	0.8022	—	0.6361	0.995	—
3	Food	1.3432	−1.1715	0.4391	0.874	−2.088
4	Textiles	1.0296	−1.3442	0.1938	0.868	−1.666
5	Apparel	0.9925	−1.0939	0.7116	0.995	−3.793
6	Leather	3.9702	−1.1144	0.3800	0.615	−1.797
7	Wood = Furniture	2.1139	−1.0831	0.0989	0.969	−1.202
8	Pulp = Paper	0.8135	−0.2772	−0.2681	0.878	−0.219
9	Rubber	1.7759	−0.8706	0.3758	0.990	−1.395
10	Chemicals	1.7853	−0.4205	−0.0649	0.997	−0.395
11	Petroleum	0.6999	−0.4797	0.3876	0.964	−0.783
12	Non-metalic minerals	1.8501	−1.4288	0.4358	0.969	−2.532
13	Iron = Steels	1.1951	−0.4799	0.6122	0.822	−1.237
14	Non = ferrous metals	1.3816	−1.2029	0.2109	0.858	−1.505
15	Fabricated metals	1.0818	−0.0257	0.6328	0.872	−0.070
16	Machinery	0.9930	−0.2266	0.6337	0.992	−0.619
17	Electrical machinery	1.2196	−1.1224	0.7550	0.976	−4.581
18	Transport equipment	1.0137	−1.2348	0.8423	0.991	−7.829
19	Instruments	1.5879	−0.5170	−0.0026	0.973	−0.516
20	Miscellaneous	0.7417	−0.6594	0.5969	0.921	−1.636

These functions can be approximated by the log-linear form as

$$ln(M_i^{kl}) = a_i^{kl} - d_i^{kl}\,ln(PM_i^{kl}/PM_i^{l}) + e_i^{kl}\,ln(M_i^{l})$$
$$ln(E_i^{kl}) = b_i^{kl} - s_i^{kl}\,ln(PE_i^{kl}/PE_i^{k}) + c_i^{kl}\,ln(E_i^{k})$$

where d_i^{kl} = demand elasticity with respect to relative price,
e_i^{kl} = demand elasticity with respect to total imports,
s_i^{kl} = supply elasticity with respect to relative price,
c_i^{kl} = supply elasticity with respect to export capacity.

Then, from the equilibrium conditions for this market, we have

$$E_i^{kl} = M_i^{kl}$$
$$PE_i^{kl} = PM_i^{kl}$$

Table 4c Estimates of import demand function: Korea-log.

		Domestic demand	Relative price	Lagged import	R	Price elasticity long-run
1	Agriculture	—	−2.1280	0.4331	0.996	−3.7537
2	Mining	2.5898	—	—	0.928	—
3	Food	0.4661	−5.1708	—	0.966	−5.1708
4	Textiles	0.6727	−1.8167	0.3766	0.973	−2.9142
5	Apparel	0.3906	−5.1454	—	0.952	−5.1454
6	Leather	0.6167	—	–	0.919	—
7	Wood = Furniture	0.3820	−2.7168	0.1764	0.913	−3.2987
8	Pulp = Paper	0.5293	−1.8235	0.5824	0.954	−4.3666
9	Rubber	0.7658	−3.9299	0.3687	0.966	−6.2251
10	Chemicals	0.4948	−1.0673	0.1826	0.983	−1.3056
11	Petroleum	1.6376	−3.0753	—	0.903	−3.0753
12	Non-metalic minerals	0.2589	−0.3747	0.5445	0.946	−0.8226
13	Iron = Steels	0.5397	−0.7912	—	0.986	−0.7912
14	Non = ferrous metals	1.0949	−0.6559	—	0.921	−0.6559
15	Fabricated metals	0.5259	—	0.1012	0.936	—
16	Machinery	1.3119	−0.7949	0.2248	0.908	−1.0254
17	Electrical machinery	0.9157	−1.0266	—	0.930	−1.0266
18	Transport equipment	0.5724	−0.8769	0.1672	0.745	−1.0529
19	Instruments	1.0722	−0.3322	—	0.985	−0.3322
20	Miscellaneous	0.8809	−3.4021	0.3560	0.975	−5.2828

The equilibrium price PE_i^{kl} and equilibrium export volumes M_i^{kl} will be derived as follows:

$$\begin{aligned} ln(PE_i^{kl}) &= 1/(d_i^{kl}+s_i^{kl})[s_i^{kl}ln(PE_i^k)+d_i^{kl}ln(PM_i^l) \\ &\quad + e_i^{kl}ln(M_i^l) - c_i^{kl}ln(E_i^{kl}) + a_i^{'kl}] \\ ln(M_i^{kl}) &= 1/(d_i^{kl}+s_i^{kl})[d_i^{kl}s_i^{kl}ln(PM_i^{kl}/PE_i^k)+e_i^{kl}s_i^{kl}ln(M_i^l) \\ &\quad + c_i^{kl}d_i^{kl}ln(E_i^k) + b_i^{'kl}] \end{aligned}$$

Considering the definition of export share m_i^{kl} and substituting the above equation, we write the export share function as

$$\begin{aligned} ln(m_i^{kl}) &= 1/(d_i^{kl}+s_i^{kl})[d_i^{kl}s_i^{kl}ln(PM_i^l/PE_i^k) \\ &\quad - ((e_i^{kl}-1)s_i^{kl}-d_i^{kl})ln(M_i^l) + c_i^{kl}d_i^{kl}ln(E_i^k) + b_i^{'kl}]. \end{aligned}$$

Further, assuming that elasticities e_i^{kl} and c_i^{kl} are unity, we have

$$ln(m_i^{kl}) = 1/(d_i^{kl} + s_i^{kl})[d_i^{kl} s_i^{kl} ln(PM_i^l/PE_i^k) + d_i^{kl} ln(E_i^k/M_i^l) + b_i'^{kl}].$$

This equation is the trade share function based on Moriguchi method. To simplify the model and increase the degree of freedom, Moriguchi has proposed to drop the superscript l from d_i^{kl}, s_i^{kl} and $b_i'^{kl}$ and then introduce dummy variables D_i^l for importing countries.

The final specification for estimating trade share matrix by Moriguchi method is accordingly written as

$$ln(m_i^{kl}) = A_i + B_i ln(PE_i^k/POPM_i^{kl}) + c_i^{kl} ln(E_i^k/M_i^l) + \sum F_i^{kl} D_i^l$$

where $POPM_i^{kl}$ is the price index of exports that are competitive with the k-th country's exports in the l-th country's import market.

Table 5 shows the estimated elasticities for Japan, the US and Korea. In the estimation total export capacity E_i^k is replaced by the actual export of the previous year, and if appropriate, additional dummy variables are introduced to explain the irregularities over the sample period. We may conclude from this table that price elasticities of Japanese exports are higher for heavy industry products than for light industry ones, and in most cases become higher than unity in the long-run. On the other hand, the US exports are largely less elastic to the changes in relative prices than the Japanese exports. Considerably high price elastisities for the Korean exports may reflect the effects of omitted variables which could promote Korean exports in addition to the ration of export capacity to the size of exporting market. It is interesting to note that in all three countries, their export shares have been affected significantly by the non-price factors for all products.

4. Simulation Analyses with the Linked System

Having finished the estimation of individual models comprising our world model, we can proceed to make simulation with the whole system. First, we need to link multisectoral models and regional models together by using the trade linkage model based on Moriguchi method.

The regional model includes one total import function, 20 commodity import demands equations and 20 commodity export price

Table 5 Estimates of trade linkage sub-model: 1968–76.

		Elasticity with respect to					
		Price factor			Non-price factor		
		Japan	USA	ROK	Japan	USA	ROK
1	Agriculture	−0.340	−0.261	−0.775	0.693	0.045	0.702
2	Mining	−0.075	−0.470	−0.349	0.129	0.494	—
3	Food	—	−0.435	−1.683	0.837	0.540	0.471
4	Textiles	−0.123	−1.763	−1.254	0.191	0.018	0.211
5	Apparel	—	−0.341	−3.311	0.459	0.357	0.225
6	Leather	−0.345	−0.002	−5.448	0.287	0.389	0.204
7	Wood = Furniture	−0.891	−0.603	−6.087	0.540	0.015	0.462
8	Pulp = Paper	—	—	−7.373	—	—	0.630
9	Rubber	−0.745	−0.048	−3.231	0.095	0.153	0.195
10	Chemicals	−1.859	−0.343	−2.355	0.289	0.507	0.742
11	Petroleum	−1.224	−0.092	−3.491	0.403	0.673	0.010
12	Non-metalic minerals	−0.678	—	−0.118	0.305	0.140	—
13	Iron = Steels	−0.304	−0.401	−5.491	0.742	0.148	0.258
14	Non = ferrous metals	−3.056	−0.657	−2.158	0.189	0.325	—
15	Fabricated metals	−0.817	−0.316	−2.350	0.467	0.258	0.814
16	Machinery	−0.488	−0.024	−3.730	0.841	0.085	0.735
17	Electrical machinery	−1.561	−0.312	−5.199	0.549	0.117	0.325
18	Transport equipment	—	—	−5.409	0.668	0.169	0.242
19	Instruments	−1.772	—	−2.816	0.577	0.280	0.722
20	Miscellaneous	—	−0.451	−5.404	—	0.143	0.915

equations. The total import demand function determines total import of each region by lagged imports and purchasing power of the total export earnings and the latter is defined by total nominal exports deflated by aggregate import price index. The real import of individual commodity is a function of total import, relative price and lagged import. Dummy variable is also included in the import equation of each commodity, if it is significant. The export price of each commodity for each region is specified as a function of domestic price and export prices of developed countries, both of which are assumed to be approximated by import price of each commodity to each region.

The linked system for world trade and industry analysis involves direct linkage among foreign trade variables belonging to different sub-models. Since most of these variables is explained endogenously somewhere in different models, exogenous foreign variables are foreign exchange rate indices and export prices of primary commodities, and the latter will be explained by the demand-supply relationship s in the world market of individual commodities.

In the simulation shown below, however, real imports and export prices of the EC countries are treated as exogenous, due to the incompletion of multisectoral models.

We report here on the five kinds of simulation experiment based on our world industry and trade model. They are as follows:

SIM1 — interdependency of trade among Japan, the US and EC,
SIM2 — restrictive trade policies in the US and EC,
SIM3 — export promotion by Asia NIEs,
SIM4 — oil price hike by OPEC
SIM5 — import promotion by Japan.

The first simulation experiment SIM1 based only on trade linkage sub-model has been done to examine how Japan and Korea are competitive on their exports to the US market and to the world market.

In this experiment, import volume or export price is raised for each commodity by 10% in one country at a time and is sustained in the entire simulation period. The control path is the within sample dynamic solution for the period 1968–76. The results for the case of higher export price are shown in Table 6 in matrix form. From this table, we can say that Korea has become a strong competitor of Japan in the world market and that the relative rise of Japan's export price has caused a sharp uprising of Korean export share in the world market, especially in the US market. This tendency has been observed not only in the light industry products such as textiles, apparels and wooden products but also in the heavy industry products such as fabricated metals, electrical machinery and professional goods. Another interesting point is that

Table 6 Impact of increased export prices in trade linkage model.

Increase in Export prices in		Impact on											
		Total exports in			Textiles in			Apparel in			Wooden product in		
		JA	US	KR	JA	US	KR	JA	US	KR	JA	US	KR
	Year												
Japan	1	−5.6	0.1	3.3	−2.5	1.3	1.4	−0.8	−0.5	4.5	−8.0	0.2	6.3
	2	−7.6	0.3	4.9	−2.9	1.2	1.7	−1.2	−0.7	5.2	−12.0	0.2	8.8
	4	−9.4	0.5	6.6	−2.9	1.1	1.6	−1.7	−0.9	4.8	−15.4	0.2	10.1
	8	−11.9	0.7	11.7	−2.8	0.9	1.0	−2.9	−1.0	2.8	−18.2	0.1	5.9
US	1	0.4	−3.0	1.3	0.3	−15.2	1.0	−0.2	−3.7	0.5	0.5	−5.2	1.8
	2	0.5	−3.6	1.7	0.2	−15.6	1.0	−0.2	−5.0	0.6	0.7	−5.5	2.3
	4	0.6	−3.9	2.2	0.2	−15.6	1.0	−0.3	−5.7	0.6	0.7	−5.5	2.4
	8	0.6	−3.9	3.7	0.8	−15.0	1.4	−0.3	−5.4	0.4	0.7	−5.7	3.3
Korea	1	0.0	0.0	−20.3	0.0	0.1	−11.3	0.4	0.1	−26.6	0.7	0.1	−43.8
	2	0.1	0.0	−26.3	0.1	0.2	−13.4	0.9	0.2	−31.1	1.3	0.1	−56.8
	4	0.4	0.0	−30.7	0.1	0.2	−13.6	2.2	0.5	−30.9	2.8	0.2	−63.1
	8	1.3	0.3	−35.7	0.5	0.5	−11.9	7.9	2.2	−23.9	17.5	1.1	−55.2

(Continued)

Table 6 (*Continued*)

		Impact on								
		Iron-steel			Electricals			Instrument		
		JA	US	KR	JA	US	KR	JA	US	KR
	Year									
Japan	1	−4.9	−0.4	19.1	−12.1	0.8	27.0	−13.4	1.0	8.0
	2	−6.7	0.3	24.6	−17.2	1.1	38.6	−19.4	1.6	14.9
	4	−7.6	0.9	30.8	−21.1	1.5	40.0	−23.4	2.1	25.0
	8	−10.0	0.8	31.7	−25.4	2.2	28.0	−25.3	1.7	32.2
US	1	−0.3	−5.3	5.9	1.3	−4.6	5.4	2.4	−1.2	5.9
	2	−0.3	−5.8	8.2	1.8	−5.3	7.2	3.6	−1.5	10.4
	4	−0.2	−5.6	6.0	2.1	−5.0	8.6	4.5	−1.5	16.2
	8	−0.1	−5.3	4.6	2.2	−4.4	6.0	4.1	−1.4	17.4
Korea	1	0.0	0.0	−40.8	0.1	0.0	−39.1	0.0	0.0	−23.5
	2	0.0	0.0	48.2	0.2	0.0	−48.2	0.0	0.0	−37.0
	4	0.1	0.0	−50.4	0.4	0.1	−51.4	0.1	0.0	−50.4
	8	1.8	0.5	49.4	3.8	1.0	−48.5	0.8	0.5	−58.3

Note: Figures in the table are percentage changes in the corresponding exports against control simulations.

because Japan is a major supplier of intermediate goods and machineries for Korea as well as a major importer of her products, higher Japan's export price has a negative effect on the competitiveness of Korean exports in the world market through raising input prices of industrial products from Japan.

We also learn from Table 7 that an expansion of US real imports has a considerable impact on exports from Japan and Korea, while changes in the real imports of Japan and Korea have relatively small impacts on the US exports. As is expected from the trade linkage and difference in market size, an expansion of real imports of Japan exerts a large effect on Korean exports.

The second simulation is concerned with the restrictive trade policies in the US and the EC countries. In this simulation, we assumed that import control measures were introduced by the US and/or the EC countries against foreign produced steels, electrical machinery, transport equipment and apparels. We introduced two kinds of import restrictive measures. One of them is to cut the import volumes to the US or the EC countries by 10% below the control path. The other is to impose a special import tariff of 10% on the imports to these countries.

The results of simulation experiment based on Japan-US linkage system are shown in Table 8, in which impacts on total employment of the US import control are summarized for each case. The table indicates that the impacts of import controls on the US economy differ in size and direction among four commodities on the kind of adopted control measures as well as on the importance of each commodity in the whole economy. Significant differences are observed for the case of steel import control. Import control by tariff measure produced a negative effect on steel-consuming industries such as machineries and transport equipment by raising the input prices for these industries, and as a result, net effect of import control for steel industry has become negative for the economy as a whole.

The comparison of the results on two-country (Japan-US) linkage system with the one based on multiregional linkage system has shown in Table 9 that the negative impact of import control by the US and the EC was amplified through simultaneous reduction of export volume in the world economy.

Table 7 Impact of increased real imports in trade linkage model.

Increase in Real Imports prices in		Impact on											
		Total exports in			Textiles in			Apparel in			Wooden product in		
		JA	US	KR	JA	US	KR	JA	US	KR	JA	US	KR
	Year												
Japan	1	0.0	0.9	2.8	0.0	0.3	2.9	0.0	0.1	0.9	0.0	2.1	0.7
	2	0.0	1.0	3.0	0.0	0.3	3.6	0.0	0.2	1.3	−0.1	2.1	0.6
	4	−0.1	1.0	2.9	−0.1	0.4	4.1	−0.1	0.3	1.9	−0.2	2.2	0.5
	8	−0.1	0.9	2.6	−0.1	0.4	4.6	−0.2	0.2	2.4	−0.3	3.2	0.8
US	1	3.2	0.1	3.0	2.0	0.0	1.5	6.7	0.0	6.3	6.4	0.0	8.8
	2	3.3	−0.2	3.6	1.9	−0.2	1.3	7.3	−0.5	6.6	7.1	−0.9	10.7
	4	3.4	−0.2	4.4	2.0	−0.2	1.2	7.7	−0.6	6.3	7.3	−0.7	12.0
	8	2.5	−0.3	4.7	0.9	−0.1	0.7	5.1	−0.5	5.1	5.3	−0.6	10.3
Korea	1	0.4	0.1	0.0	0.7	0.0	0.0	0.0	0.1	0.0	0.1	0.1	0.0
	2	0.5	0.1	0.0	0.7	0.0	0.0	0.0	0.0	0.0	0.1	0.1	0.0
	4	0.6	0.1	0.0	0.8	0.0	0.0	0.0	0.1	0.0	0.1	0.1	0.0
	8	0.7	0.1	0.0	0.9	0.0	0.0	0.0	0.0	0.0	0.1	0.0	0.0

(*Continued*)

Table 7 (*Continued*)

Increase in Real Imports prices in		Impact on								
		Iron-steel			Electricals			Instrument		
		JA	US	KR	JA	US	KR	JA	US	KR
	Year									
Japan	1	0.0	1.5	2.2	0.0	0.5	1.4	0.0	0.8	2.2
	2	0.0	1.5	2.5	0.0	0.6	1.7	−0.1	0.9	2.7
	4	0.0	0.8	1.3	−0.1	0.7	2.0	−0.1	1.0	3.3
	8	0.0	0.6	0.6	−0.1	0.7	1.9	−0.2	1.2	3.5
US	1	4.3	0.0	5.0	4.8	0.0	7.0	4.8	0.0	2.8
	2	4.1	−0.8	5.4	5.5	−0.4	8.3	4.9	0.0	2.4
	4	4.1	−0.9	7.2	5.2	−0.6	7.6	4.9	0.0	1.8
	8	2.6	−0.7	6.1	3.4	−0.7	6.3	5.0	0.0	1.7
Korea	1	0.3	0.2	0.0	0.3	0.1	0.0	0.2	0.1	0.0
	2	0.5	0.3	−0.1	0.3	0.2	−0.1	0.2	0.1	0.0
	4	0.6	0.3	−0.2	0.4	0.2	−0.1	0.3	0.1	0.0
	8	0.6	0.3	−0.2	0.5	0.3	−0.1	0.3	0.1	−0.1

Note: Figures in the table are percentage changes in the corresponding exports against control simulations

Table 8 Impact of the US import controls on total employment of the US and Japan.

		Impact on							
		Controls by tax measures				Controls by Quota system			
	Case	1	2	3	4	1	2	3	4
	Year								
US	1	−4.6	10.1	20.1	−1.7	17.3	23.2	42.7	25.3
	2	−5.5	36.4	77.7	19.1	15.4	29.0	54.2	30.9
	3	−4.0	62.2	119.7	36.1	12.6	29.8	48.6	28.0
	4	−2.3	77.4	151.2	43.9	14.4	30.1	46.6	26.5
	5	−0.7	91.4	168.6	48.2	15.4	31.1	42.5	26.0
	6	−8.8	102.8	192.3	41.2	10.3	33.4	44.7	22.2
	7	−13.7	100.7	190.2	27.2	8.0	30.4	40.3	16.7
	8	−17.3	93.0	154.2	46.9	3.9	26.1	30.1	22.8
	9	−17.5	111.2	133.9	72.4	2.4	30.8	24.8	32.1
	AV.	−8.3	76.1	134.2	37.0	9.4	29.3	41.6	25.6
Japan	1	−7.8	−24.6	−23.1	−3.6	−18.2	−23.9	−19.7	−2.7
	2	−12.9	−58.0	−48.0	−5.8	−21.8	−38.3	−24.7	−2.7
	3	−17.3	−88.1	−60.7	−5.7	−21.8	−42.9	−20.5	−1.9
	4	−14.4	−105.8	−66.5	−5.0	−13.9	−39.6	−14.5	−1.2
	5	−8.3	−93.5	−55.4	0.3	−4.3	−26.6	−6.6	0.8
	6	0.1	−59.5	−43.2	3.2	5.1	−9.9	−1.5	1.7
	7	3.8	−52.4	−36.6	4.2	8.2	−4.7	0.6	1.8
	8	9.0	−49.4	−28.2	3.2	11.7	−4.1	1.3	1.2
	9	10.2	−58.0	−19.9	2.7	11.4	−8.1	1.3	0.9
	AV.	−4.2	−65.4	−42.4	−0.7	−4.8	−22.0	−9.4	−0.2

Note: Unit of the figure in this table is 1,000 persons.
The case numbers correspond to specific industries as follow; 1 = Ireon-steel, 2 = Electrical machinery, 3 = transport industry and 4 = Textiles and apparels.

The third simulation experiment SIM3 has been done to study the impacts on the Japanese and the US economies of the export-oriented development policies adopted by Asia NIEs including Singapore. In this experiment, export prices of his region are lowered by 10% for the entire simulation period. The results shown in Table 10 indicate that short-run effects of export-oriented industrialization policy are relatively small, while in the long-run, the impacts on employment in specific industries has become larger in both Japan and the US The impact on the US electrical machinery industry is striking.

Table 9 Impact of depressed real imports to the US and EC on total exports from each country and region: the case of electrical machinery.

		Impact on											
		Japan	US	Korea	Asia NIEs	ASEAN	France	Germany	Italy	UK	Other DC	ROW	World
	Year												
Japan-US linakge	1	−0.7	−0.1	−0.2	−0.6	0.0	−0.1	−0.2	−0.3	−0.2	−0.2	−0.1	−0.2
	2	−0.8	−0.1	−0.2	−0.9	0.0	−0.2	−0.2	−0.4	−0.2	−0.2	−0.1	−0.2
	3	−0.9	−0.1	−0.2	−1.2	0.0	−0.2	−0.2	−0.4	−0.1	−0.2	−0.1	−0.3
	4	−0.9	−0.2	−0.5	−1.4	−0.1	−0.2	−0.2	−0.3	−0.1	−0.2	−0.1	−0.3
	5	−0.9	−0.2	−1.0	−1.6	0.0	−0.2	−0.2	−0.3	−0.1	−0.2	−0.2	−0.3
	6	−0.7	−0.2	−1.6	−2.0	0.0	−0.2	−0.3	−0.3	−0.1	−0.2	−0.2	−0.3
	7	−0.7	−0.2	−1.3	−2.2	0.0	−0.2	−0.3	−0.3	−0.1	−0.3	−0.2	−0.3
	8	−0.7	−0.2	−1.4	−1.7	−0.1	−0.2	−0.2	−0.3	−0.1	−0.2	−0.2	−0.3
	9	−0.7	−0.2	−1.5	−1.5	−0.1	−0.2	−0.2	−0.3	−0.1	−0.2	−0.2	−0.3
Multi-region linkage	1	−0.8	−0.2	−0.2	−0.7	−0.1	−0.2	−0.3	−0.4	−0.3	−0.2	−0.1	−0.3
	2	−1.0	−0.3	−0.3	−1.2	−0.2	−0.2	−0.4	−0.4	−0.3	−0.3	−0.2	−0.3
	3	−1.2	−0.4	−1.0	−1.7	−0.3	−0.3	−0.4	−0.5	−0.3	−0.3	−0.2	−0.4
	4	−1.2	−0.4	−0.6	−2.0	−0.3	−0.3	−0.4	−0.4	−0.4	−0.3	−0.3	−0.4
	5	−1.2	−0.5	−1.2	−2.4	−0.4	−0.4	−0.4	−0.4	−0.4	−0.3	−0.3	−0.5
	6	−1.2	−0.6	−1.9	−2.6	−0.4	−0.4	−0.5	−0.4	−0.4	−0.4	−0.3	−0.5
	7	−1.1	−0.6	−1.5	−2.5	−0.4	−0.4	−0.5	−0.5	−0.4	−0.4	−0.3	−0.5
	8	−1.1	−0.6	−1.5	−2.1	−0.4	−0.4	−0.5	−0.5	−0.4	−0.3	−0.3	−0.5
	9	−1.1	−0.5	−1.5	−1.8	−0.4	−0.4	−0.6	−0.5	−0.4	−0.3	−0.3	−0.5

Note: Figures in the table are percent changes in the total exports against control simulation path.

Table 10 Impact on employment of industrializing policies focused on specific industries.

	Impact on					
	Japan			US		
	Textile	Apparel	Total	Textile	Apparel	Total
Year						
1	−1.7	−0.8	−5.5	−0.8	−1.6	−2.0
2	−3.4	−1.1	−9.1	−2.0	−4.7	−8.2
4	−30.4	−3.4	−27.9	−4.2	−11.3	−19.4
8	−28.0	−19.1	−67.4	−11.5	−31.8	−53.0

	Impact on							
	Japan				US			
	Machinery	Electrical machinery	Transport equipment	Total	Machinery	Electrical machinery	Transport equipment	Total
Year								
1	−0.2	−0.6	−0.2	−5.6	−0.1	−1.4	−0.1	−2.1
2	−0.6	−1.7	−0.7	−12.9	−0.4	−3.9	−0.3	−5.9
4	−2.5	−5.7	−4.6	−46.7	−1.0	−10.4	−0.5	−15.3
8	−7.5	−12.8	−4.9	−77.6	−6.1	−57.4	−4.4	−84.8

Note: Unit of figure is 1,000 persons.

The fourth experiment is to analyze the impacts of oil price hike by the OPEC. In this experiment, we introduced the OPEC's oil price hike by raising the export price of ASEAN and Rest of the World, and assume that the price of domestic produced mining products in the US is regulated by the government at the historical level. As is understood, the impacts of oil price hike by the OPEC depend on how the OPEC countries spend their increased export earnings to the purchase of industrial products of Japan and other developed countries. We hypothesize that the OPEC's spending would be determined by the following import functions:

$$\text{ASEAN } lnM = 0.7398 + 0.3637 ln \times \left(\sum (PE_i E_i / PM) + 0.5937 lnM(-1)\right)$$
$$(4.1787) \qquad (5.3259)$$
$$R^2 = 0.928 \quad S = 0.393 \quad D.W. = 0.901$$

$$\text{ROW } lnM = 0.0172 + 0.4525 ln \times \left(\sum (PE_i E_i / PM) + 0.5648 lnM(-1)\right)$$
$$(4.2884) \qquad (4.5856)$$
$$R^2 = 0.944 \quad S = 0.285 \quad D.W. = 1.790$$

These functions are the estimated relations that reflect the historical spending pattern of each region for the period 1963–76.

The simulation experiments have been done in two cases, one of which used Japan-US linkage system where no spending was assumed, and the other of which was based on multi-regional linkage system with the OPEC's re-spending.

The results reported in Table 11 indicate that 10% hike in the oil price by the OPEC will decrease the real GNP by $0.2 \sim 1.3\%$ in Japan and $0.026 \sim 0.07\%$ in the US in no re-spending case, and that in the case of OPEC re-spending, it will decrease the real GNP by $0.0 \sim 0.8\%$ in Japan and increase by 0.025% in the fourth year in the US. These results imply that the OPEC re-spending has positively affected both Japanese and US economies. The examination of sectoral export structure depicted in Tables 12-1 and Table 12-2 confirm this point,

Table 11 Impact of increased oil price on GNP, inflation and employment.

		Impact on											
		Real GNP in		PPI in		PC in		L in		Real exports in		Real imports in	
	Year	JA	US	JA	US	JA	US	JA	US	JA	US	JA	US
Japan-US linkage	1	−0.2	−0.026	0.6	0.1	0.5	0.0	−12	−10	−0.5	0.1	0.1	−0.1
	2	−0.6	−0.021	1.0	0.2	0.9	0.0	−60	−11	−0.9	0.2	−0.2	−0.1
	4	−1.0	−0.016	1.4	0.2	1.3	0.1	−92	−4	−1.4	0.2	−0.3	−0.3
	8	−1.3	−0.070	2.2	0.2	1.9	0.2	−95	−26	−2.2	0.2	−0.3	−0.3
Multi-regional linkage	1	0.0	−0.006	0.6	0.1	0.5	0.0	2	−1	−0.1	0.4	0.2	−0.1
	2	−0.4	0.010	1.0	0.1	0.9	0.0	−31	6	−0.2	0.7	0.1	−0.1
	4	−0.7	0.025	1.5	0.1	1.4	0.1	−57	22	−0.5	0.9	0.0	−0.1
	8	−0.8	0.012	2.4	0.3	2.2	0.2	−55	29	−0.7	1.5	0.3	−0.2

Note: Figures in the table are per cent changes in the variables. The exception is employment, L, which is 1,000 persons.

Table 12-1 Impacts of increased oil price on sectoral exports of Japan and the US: the case of no re-spending.

		Impact on											
		Iron = Steel		Non-ferrous metals		Metal products		General Machinery		Electrical Machinery		Transport Equipment	
		JA	US	JA	US	JA	US	JA	US	JA	US	JA	US
	Year												
Japan-US linkage	1	−0.8	−0.1	−2.3	−0.1	−0.8	0.0	−0.1	0.0	−0.5	0.0	0.0	0.0
	2	−1.2	−0.1	−2.3	−0.1	−1.3	0.0	−0.2	0.0	−1.2	0.0	−0.1	0.0
	4	−1.9	0.1	−4.0	−0.2	−1.9	0.0	−0.4	0.0	−2.4	0.1	−0.2	0.0
	8	−3.1	−0.1	−6.2	−0.3	−3.2	0.1	−0.7	0.0	−3.3	0.4	−0.3	0.1
Multi-regional linkage	1	−0.1	0.4	−1.9	0.1	−0.4	0.1	0.3	0.5	−0.2	0.4	0.6	0.3
	2	−0.2	0.9	−1.8	0.1	−0.8	0.3	0.4	0.7	−0.5	0.8	0.9	0.6
	4	−0.4	1.5	−3.2	0.2	−1.1	0.6	0.2	0.9	−1.4	1.3	1.3	0.9
	8	−0.5	2.4	−5.3	0.5	−1.8	1.1	0.3	1.6	−1.8	2.2	2.0	1.6

Table 12-2 Impacts of increased oil price on sectoral exports of Japan and the US: the case of re-spending.

	Impact on											
	Iron = Steel		Non-ferrous metals		Metal products		General Machinery		Electrical Machinery		Transport Equipment	
	JA	US	JA	US	JA	US	JA	US	JA	US	JA	US
Year												
1	0.7	0.5	0.4	0.2	0.4	0.3	0.4	0.5	0.3	0.4	0.6	0.3
2	1.0	1.0	0.5	0.2	0.5	0.3	0.6	0.7	0.7	0.8	1.0	0.6
4	1.5	1.4	0.8	0.4	0.8	0.6	0.6	0.9	1.0	1.2	1.5	0.9
8	2.6	2.5	0.9	0.8	−3.2	1.2	1.0	1.6	1.5	1.8	2.3	1.5

Note: Figures in the table are the difference between Japan-US linkage and Multi-regional linkage

showing relatively large effects of OPEC re-spending on the exports of iron and steel, general machinery, electrical machinery and transport equipment.

The impacts on the Japan's total exports have been negative even in the case of OPEC re-spending, while exports of general machinery and transport equipment would be increased by the re-spending. The positive effects of the re-spending have an increasing trend which may be caused by the lagged response of the OPEC re-spending to foreign produced industrial products.

The last simulation experiment has been done to see the impacts of the Japan's import promotion policies upon the world trade structure. In this experiment, we assumed that the tariff and tax on imported commodities to Japan was cut by 50% evenly for all commodities. The results shown in Tables 13~14 indicate that the increased imports of Japan

Table 13 Impact of 50% tariff cut on world exports.
(Percentage changes from the control path)

	Commodity	1	2	4	8 year
3	Food	0.3	0.3	0.3	0.2
4	Textiles	0.1	0.3	0.7	0.8
5	Apparel	0.5	0.5	0.8	1.4
6	Leather	0.0	0.1	0.1	0.1
7	Wood = Furniture	0.0	0.0	0.1	0.1
8	Pulp = Paper	0.0	0.0	0.0	0.0
9	Rubber	0.0	0.1	0.1	0.2
10	Chemicals	0.1	0.1	0.1	0.1
11	Petroleum	0.0	0.0	0.0	0.0
12	Non-metalic minerals	0.1	0.2	0.2	0.1
13	Iron=Steels	0.0	0.0	0.0	0.0
14	Non=ferrous metals	0.0	0.0	0.0	0.0
15	Fabricated metals	0.0	0.0	0.0	0.0
16	Machinery	0.0	0.0	0.0	0.0
17	Electrical machinery	0.1	0.1	0.3	0.2
18	Transport equipment	0.1	0.1	0.1	0.1
19	Instruments	0.2	0.3	0.3	0.3
20	Miscellaneous	0.1	0.1	0.1	0.1
	Total including primary commodities	0.1	0.1	0.2	0.1

Table 14 Impact of 50% tariff cut on sectoral outputs in Japan. (Percentage changes from the control path)

	Sectors	1	2	4	8 year
3	Food	−0.2	0.1	0.2	0.2
4	Textiles	−0.1	0.0	−0.8	−1.3
5	Apparel	−0.2	0.5	0.4	−1.0
6	Leather	0.1	0.2	0.2	−0.5
7	Wood = Furniture	0.1	0.4	0.5	0.0
8	Pulp = Paper	0.0	0.4	0.5	0.0
9	Rubber	0.0	0.3	0.2	−0.6
10	Chemicals	−0.3	0.6	0.9	0.2
11	Petroleum	0.1	0.6	0.9	0.3
12	Non-metalic minerals	0.3	0.6	0.7	0.2
13	Iron = Steels	0.0	0.4	0.5	0.0
14	Non = ferrous metals	−0.1	0.3	0.4	−0.1
15	Fabricated metals	−0.1	0.3	0.2	−0.2
16	Machinery	−0.2	0.5	0.7	0.0
17	Electrical machinery	−0.1	0.8	1.2	0.4
18	Transport equipment	−0.2	0.1	0.2	−0.7
19	Instruments	−1.4	−0.9	−0.1	−0.2
20	Miscellaneous	0.0	0.6	0.8	0.2
	Total including primary commodities	0.0	0.4	0.5	0.1

will expand the world exports of apparels, electrical machinery and professional goods, which have become the major export commodities of Asia NIEs to the developed countries. As regards the effects of tariff reduction on the Japanese industrial structure, chemicals, petroleum products, general machinery and electrical machinery increase their share in the whole economy, while textiles, apparels, leather and rubber and professional goods lose their shares. The decreased share in the light industry has been caused by the penetration of foreign produced products to the Japanese market. The reduction of tariff and tax on imports decreases the input cost of imported raw materials and fuels, which in turn improves the competitiveness of heavy industry products and increase their shares.

5. Concluding Remarks

As mentioned before, the estimated parameters and linked simulation experiments discussed above represent some tentative results of our efforts to model the world industry and trade structure in a global way. A more complete integration of various economies with multi-sectoral and trade linkage models will be done in the future. This is conducted through estimating the multi-sectoral models for the four EC countries and through modeling the world commodity markets. These efforts will produce a useful framework for studying the international economic frictions among developed and developing countries.

References

Hickman, BG and LJ Lau (1973). "Elasticities of Substitution and Export Demands in a World Trade Model," *European Economic Review*, vol.

Kinoshita, S, Y Kajino, M Saito, Y Shiina and M Yamada (1982). *Development and Application of a World Industry and Trade Model for the Analysis of International Trade and Industry Structure Focusing on Japan, (in Japanese)*, Economic Research Institute, EPA, July.

Moriguchi, C (1973). "Forecasting and Simulation Analysis of the World Economy," *The American Economic Review*, Vol. 63 No. 2.

Samuelson, L and E Kurihara (1980). "OECD Trade Linkage Method Applied to the EPA World Econometric Model," *Economic Bulletin*, No. 18.

Yamada, M (1983). "Measurement of Export Price Elasticities with Disaggregated Trade Data," (in Japanese), *Saga University Economic Review*, Vol. 16 No. 1.

Appendix: Structure of a World Industry and Trade Model

Equations of the Model

A. National Multi-sectoral Model

(1) Gross domestic product

$$GDP = C + CG + I + IG + ED - MD + J$$

(2) Private final consumption

$$C = f\left(\frac{YDV}{pc}, \frac{pc}{pc_{-1}}, C_{-1}\right)$$

(3) Private fixed investment

$$I = IE + IH$$

(4) Private non-residential investment

$$IE = IE_1 + IE_2 + \cdots + IE_{21}$$

(5) Private housing investment

$$IH = f\left(\frac{YDV}{pc}, \frac{pih}{pc}, rlb - pih\right)$$

(6) Private inventory investment

$$J = f\left(GDP, KJ_{-1}, \frac{p}{p-1}\right)$$

(7) Total exports

$$ED = E_1 + E_2 + \cdots + E_{21}$$

(8) Total imports

$$MD = M_1 + M_2 + \cdots + M_{21}$$

(9) Domestic demand by sector

$$D_i = f\left(\sum_j a_{ij}X_j, \sum_j f_{ij}Y_j, \frac{p_i}{p}, t\right)$$

(10) Imports by sector

$$M_i = f\left(D_i, \frac{pm_i}{p_i}, M_{-1}\right)$$

(11) Output by sector

$$X_i = D_i + E_i - M_i$$

(12) Total output

$$X = X_1 + X_2 + \cdots + X_{21}$$

(13) Private non-residential investment by sector

$$IE_i = f(X_i, K_{i-1}, GP_i, (V_i - w_iLW_i + IDT_i + SUB_i)$$

(14) Capital stock by sector

$$K_i = K_{i-1} + IE_i - REP_i$$

(15) Replacement investment by sector

$$REP_i = f(K_{i-1})$$

(16) Capacity output by sector

$$X_i^c = f(QR_i, K_{i-1}, LH_i LE_i, t)$$

(17) Capacity utilization rate

$$GP_i = f(X_i, X_i^c, GP_{i-1})$$

(18) Employment by sector

$$LE_i = f\left(X_i, \frac{w_i}{p_i}, LE_{i-1}, K_{i-1}\right)$$

(19) Employee by sector

$$LW_i = f(LE_i, t)$$

(20) Total employment

$$LED = LE_1 + LE_2 + \cdots + LE_{21}$$

(21) Total employee

$$LWD = LW_1 + LW_2 + \cdots + LW_{21}$$

(22) Unemployment rate

$$UR = \frac{LF - LED}{LF}$$

(23) Hours worked by sector

$$LH_i = f\left(GP_i, \frac{w_i}{p_i}, LH_{i-1}\right)$$

(24) Wage income per employee

$$w = f\left(UR, \frac{pc}{pc_{-1}}, \frac{GDPV}{LWD}, w_{-1}\right)$$

(25) Wage income by sector

$$w_i = f\left(w, \frac{V_i/LW_i}{GDPV/LWD}, w_{i-1}\right)$$

(26) Output price

$$P_i = f\left(\sum_j a_{ji}(1 - m_j)p_j, \sum_j a_{ji} m_j pm_j, \frac{w_i LW_i}{X_i}, idt_i, GP_i\right)$$

where $m_j = M_j/D_j$

(27) Average output price

$$p = \sum_i \frac{x_i}{\Sigma_i X_i} p_i$$

(28) Export price

$$pe_i = f(p_i, GP_i, EX, pe_{i-1})$$

(29) Import price

$$pm_i = (1 + tr_i)pmm_i$$

(30) Private final consumption deflator

$$pc = f\left(\sum_i f_{i1}\left(\frac{p_i X_i + pm_i M_i - pe_i E_i}{D_i}, t\right)\right.$$

(31) Private non-residential investment deflator

$$pip = f\left(\sum_i f_{i3}\left(\frac{p_i X_i + pm_i M_i - pe_i E_i}{D_i}, t\right)\right.$$

(32) Private housing investment deflator

$$pih = f\left(\sum_i f_{i4}\left(\frac{p_i X_i + pm_i M_i - pe_i E_i}{D_i}, t\right)\right.$$

(33) Value added by sector

$$v_i = f\left(p_i X_i, \sum_j p_j a_{ji} X_i, t\right)$$

(34) Nominal GDP

$$GDPV = f\left(\sum_i V_i\right)$$

(35) Nominal GNP

$$GNPV = GDPV + TAPV$$

(36) Total indirect tax

$$IDTV = \sum_i IDT_i + \sum_i pm_i M_i \frac{tr_i}{1 + tr_i}$$

(37) Indirect tax by sector

$$IDT_i = idt_i X_i$$

(38) Capital consumption

$$DEPV = f\left(pip \sum_i K_{i-1}\right)$$

(39) Total direct tax

$$DTV = f(w_i LW_i (GDPV - ITDV + SUBV + TGPV - EPSV - w_i LW_i))$$

(40) Total subsidies

$$SUBV = \sum_i SIB_i$$

(41) Private disposable income

$$YDV = GNPV - DEPV - IDTV + SUBV + TGPV - DTV - EPSV$$

(42) Inventory stock

$$KJ = KJ_{-1} + J$$

(43) Average interest rate on bank loan

$$rlb = f(rb)$$

(44) Current account surplus

$$BRT = ED - MD + TAP$$

B. International Trade Linkage Model

(45) Trade share by sector

$$m_i^{kl} = f\left(\frac{pe_i^k}{pcom_i^{kl}}, \frac{SE_i^k}{M_i^l}, DMY_i^k\right)$$

(46) k-th county's export competitive in l-th country's market

$$pcom_i^{kl} = \sum_{s \neq k,l} \left(\frac{pe_i^s M_i^{sl}}{m_i^l}\right)\left(\frac{EX^k}{EX^s}\right)$$

(47) k-th country's exports by sector

$$E_i^k = \sum_i m_i^{kl} M_i^l$$

(48) k-th country's import price by sector

$$pmm_i^k = \sum_i m_i^{kl} pe_i^l \left(\frac{EX^k}{EX^l}\right)$$

Definition of Variable ad Parameter

BRT = surplus on current account in 1970 prices
C = private final consumption in 1970 prices
CG = government final consumption in 1970 prices
$DEPV$ = capital consumption allowance
DTV = total direct tax
D_i = domestic demands by sector in 1970 prices
ED = exports of goods and services in 1970 prices
$EPSV$ = statistical discrepancy
EX = exchange rate per dollar
E_i = exports of goods by sector in 1970 prices
GDP = gross domestic product in 1970 prices
$GDPV$ = nominal GDP
GNP = gross national product in 1970 prices
$GNPV$ = nominal GNP

GP_i = rate of capacity utilization by sector
I = private fixed investment in 1970 prices
$IDTV$ = total indirect tax
IDT_i = indirect tax payment by sector
idt_i = indirect tax rate by sector
IE = private non-residential fixed investment in 1970 prices
IG = government fixed investment in 1970 prices
IH = private housing investment in 1970 prices
IE_i = private non-residential fixed investment by sector
I = inventory investment in 1970 prices
K_j = inventory stock
K_i = private fixed capital stock by sector in 1970 prices
LED = total employment
LF = total labor force
LWD = total employee
LE_i = employment by sector
LH_i = hours worked by sector
LW_i = employee by sector
MD = imports of goods and services in 1970 prices
M_i = imports of goods by sector in 1970 prices
p = average output price index, 1970 = 100
pc = private final consumption deflator, 1970 = 100
pih = private housing investment deflator, 1970 = 100
pip = private non-residential fixed investment deflator, 1970 = 100
p_i = output price index by sector, 1970 = 100
pe_i = export price index by sector, 1970 = 100
pm_i = import price index by sector, 1970 = 100
pmm_i = import price index by sector (FOB), 1970 = 100
QR_i = quality index of fixed capital stock
rb = official discount rate (%)
REP_i = replacement investment by sector
rlb = average interest rate on bank loans by all banks (%)
$SUBV$ = total subsidies
SUB_i = subsidies by sector

t = time trend, 1960 = 60
TAP = net receipts of factor income abroad in 1970 prices
$TGPV$ = nominal TAP
$TAPV$ = net government transfer to private sector
tr_i = import tax duties by sector
UR = unemployment rate
V_i = gross value added by sector
w = average labor income per employee
w_i = labor income per employee by sector
X = total output in 1970 prices
X_i = output by sector in 1970 prices
X_i^c = capacity output by sector in 1970 prices
YDV = private disposable income
Y_j = domestic final demands by component,
j = 1 for private final consumption (C),
= 2 for government final consumption (CG),
= 3 for private fixed investment (I),
= 4 for government fixed investment (IG),
= 5 for inventory investment (J)
a_{ij} = input coefficient of i-th output in j-th sector in 1970
f_{ij} = sectoral distribution coefficient of j-th domestic final demand component in 1970 prices

Chapter 3

The Impacts of Robotization on Macro and Sectoral Economies within a World Econometric Model*

Soshichi Kinoshita and Mitsuo Yamada

1. Introduction

In the past decades, especially since the early 1980s, the world has seen a strong trend toward robotization with the introduction of industrial robots in the manufacturing industry. Table 1 summarizes the estimated operational stock of industrial robots in selected countries and regions. As is clear here, Japan is predominantly a big country of industrial robots in the world and her share is more than 50% up to 2000.

A number of studies on the impacts of robotization have been conducted based on modeling and non-modeling approaches. A study by W. Leontief and F. Duchin (1986) is a recent one based on the modeling approach.[1] This chapter addresses the same basic issue as these studies and analyzes globally the probable impacts of robotization on the macro and sectoral economies within a world model of industry and trade.

The global model we use in this study makes it possible to evaluate two important impacts: (1) the domestic impacts through inter-industry relationships in the dynamic input-output model, and

*This is taken, after a slight revision, from "The Impacts of Robotization on Macro and Sectoral Economies within a World Econometric Model," in *Technological Forecasting and Social Changes*, 1986 (vol., No. 2–3).

[1]W. Leontief and F. Duchin (1986) analyze the impacts of automation, including robot, on workers for the US economy.

Table 1 Stock of multipurpose robots at year-end. (Number of units)

Area	1985	1990	1995	2000	2005
Japan	93,000	274,210	387,290	389,442	373,481
North America	20,000	34,090	56,945	89,880	139,984
Europe	24,655	134,509	130,542	211,298	296,918
Africa				90	634
World	138,457	450,988	604,786	750,508	922,838

*North America = Canada, Mexico and USA
Source: *World Robotics 2008*, International Federation of Robotics.

(2) the international impacts through trade relationships among trade partners specified in the trade linkage model.

This chapter is organized as follows. Section 2 is concerned with the main structure of the global model. In Section 3 we explain the specification and some estimates of international interdependence through commodity trade. Section 4 summarizes the diffusion process of the impacts of robotization. Section 5 is concerned with the assumptions used in the simulation experiments. Section 6 provides some simulation experiments on robotization in the machinery industries. The last section provides a summary and conclusions.

2. Overview of the World Industry and Trade Model

As explained in the preceding chapter, the world model used in this study is based on a decomposition of the world economy into several multi-sectoral models for countries and regions. The system is closed by the international trade linkage model by sector, which determines the export volume and import prices of individual countries and regions. This is to ensure world accounting consistency for the international trade flow.

The current version of the model subdivides the world economy into the following countries or country groups:

- Japan
- United States
- Korea

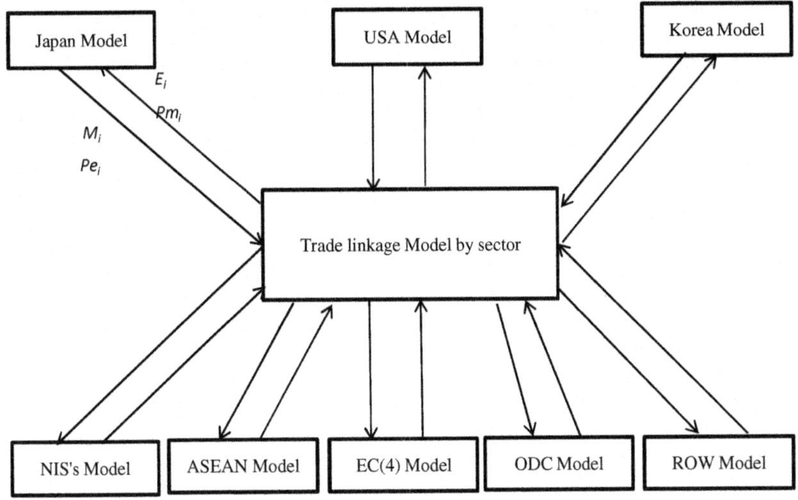

Fig. 1 Linkage of country and regional models.

- EC(4) (France, Italy, West Germany, and UK)
- ODC (OECD countries excluding Japan, the United States, and EC(4))
- ANIEs (Taiwan and Hong Kong)
- ASEAN (Indonesia, Malaysia, Philippines, Singapore, and Thailand)
- ROW (rest of the world)

Figure 1 shows how the individual country and regional model could be linked with each other within a world industry and trade model.

Domestic economy in the individual country or group of countries is disaggregated into 21 sectors as shown in Table 2.

With regard to national and regional modeling, the model for Japan, the US, and Korea is a large-scale equation system that attempts to simultaneously explain the input-output relation and Keynesian macro-economic behaviors.[2] Modeling for groups of countries, on the other hand, is based on a rather simplified formula, in which the sectoral

[2]The current version of the national model contains about 470 equations for Japan, 360 for the United States, and 350 for Korea.

Table 2 Sectoral classification of the model.

1. Agriculture, forestry, and fishing	12. Nonmetallic mineral products
2. Mining	13. Iron and steel products
3. Food, beverage, and tobacco	14. Nonferrous metals
4. Textiles	15. Fabricated metal products
5. Apparel	16 Machinery, except electrical
6. Leather products and footwear	17. Electrical machinery
7. Wooden products and furniture	18. Transport equipment
8. Pulp, paper, printing, and publishing	19. Precision instruments
9. Rubber and plastic products	20. Miscellaneous manufacturing products
10. Chemicals	21. Construction and tertiary industry
11. Petroleum and coal products	

import volumes and export prices are related directly with aggregate economic variables and not with sectoral input-output relations. This simplification is due mostly to the availability of I-O sectoral time-series data.

Figure 2 shows the basic structure of the multi-sectoral model.

It can be seen that the model includes the basic elements of an economy-wide model, i.e. (1) a final demand block, (2) an input-output block, (3) a factor demand block, (4) an income generation block, (5) an input cost and price block, (6) a wage and unemployment block, and (7) en export-import block.

3. International Interdependence Through Commodity Trade

To evaluate the international impacts of robotization, it is a prerequisite to model the trade-dependent relations among countries in the model. The trade linkage model is thus developed as a submodel of the world model. This was done in order to determine consistently the export volumes and import prices by sector for each country or region, given the import volumes and export prices determined in the national or regional model.

The idea of achieving consistency in export-import relationships in the world market is briefly explained below. Let the trade linkage

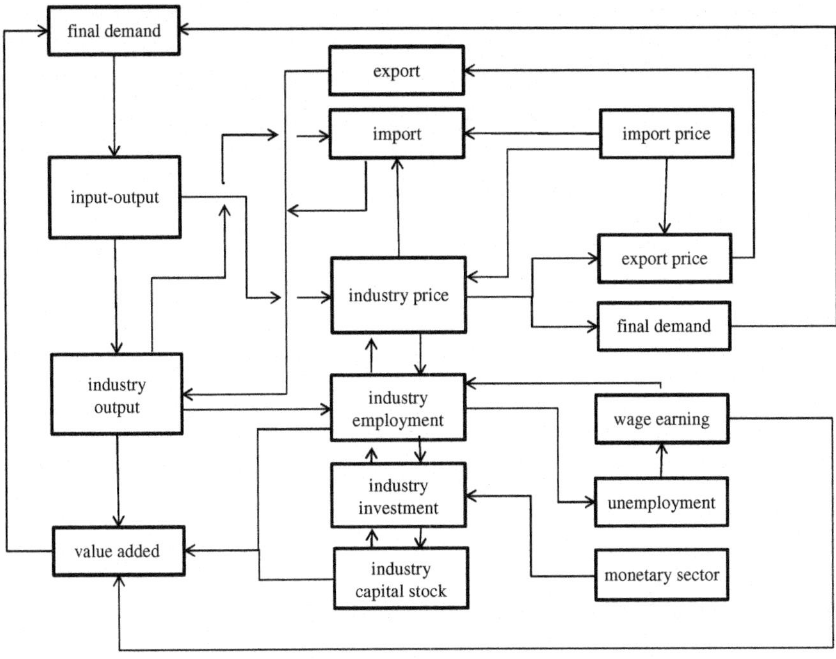

Fig. 2 Structure of a multi-sectoral model.

matrix, m^{rs} be defined as

$$m^{rs} = \frac{M^{rs}}{\Sigma_r M^{rs}} = \frac{M^{rs}}{M^s},$$

where M^{rs} is export from country r to country s, and M^s is the total import of country s.

Thus, m^{rs} is the market share of country r's export in country s's imports. Then, by definition, the total export of country $r(E^r)$ is given by

$$E^r = \Sigma_s M^{rs} = \Sigma_s m^{rs} M^s. \tag{1}$$

Since summation of M^{rs} over r is unity, we see that the export volume determined above satisfies the world identity in real trade flow,

$$\Sigma_r E^r = \Sigma_s M^s.$$

Likewise, if there is no price discrimination in the export market, import price of country $s(Pm^s)$ is given by the weighted average of the export prices of supplying countries (Pe^r) as follows:

$$Pm^s = \Sigma_r m^{rs} Pe^r. \tag{2}$$

This import price guarantees that a companion world identity,

$$\Sigma_s Pm^s M^s = \Sigma_r Pe^r E^r$$

holds.

Thus, if the trade share matrix is given, export volumes and import prices are jointly determined so as to preserve the world trade accounting identities in both current and constant prices.

Our specification of the trade linkage model is based on Moriguchi method. The advantage this method has over alternative methods lies in the fact that it includes both demand and supply factors in the bilateral trade flow equation [see Moriguchi (1983) 6].

Trade share matrix, m^{rs} in the Moriguchi approach, is written as

$$\ln(m^{rs}) = a^r + b^r \ln(Pe^r / Pcom^{rs}) + c^r \ln(Ec^r / M^s) + \Sigma_s d^{rs} D^s \tag{3}$$

where $Pcom^{rs}$ is the export prices of country r's rivals in country s's market, Ec^s is the export capacity of country r, and D^s is the dummy variable(s) by which import country s takes into account geographic and other trade linkage factors. This equation implies that the export share of country r in country s is determined through demand-supply interaction by price competitiveness, $Pe^r / Pcom^{rs}$, and non-price factor, $\Sigma_s d^{rs} D^s$.

In estimating this equation by sector, we assumed that the market share elasticities with respect to price and non-price variables are equal across the import markets and pooled time series of m^{rs} for each export country r. Furthermore, export capacity variable Ec^r is approximated by the realized exports in the previous year, and if appropriate, additional dummy variables are introduced to adjust irregularities over the sample period 1970–1984.

Table 2 summarizes the estimated results for the electrical machinery industry. From this table we first find the direct impacts of export price changes as follows:

1. A 10% decrease in Japan's export price raises her export volume by 4.1% in the first year and 7.7% in the fifth year. The impacts on

Table 3 Estimates for the electrical machinery industry.

	Export price increase in			Import volume increase in		
Impact on	Japan	United States	Korea	Japan	United States	Korea
Export volumes in						
Japan	−0.41	0.05	0.02	—	0.11	0.02
	−0.77	0.0	0.03	—	0.24	0.03
United States	0.09	−0.39	0.01	0.06	—	0.02
	0.10	−0.43	0.01	0.05	—	0.06
Korea	0.24	0.09	−0.99	0.06	0.18	—
	0.42	0.20	−2.17	0.12	0.41	—
EC(4)	0.06	0.05	0.00	0.00	0.01	0.00
	0.06	0.08	0.01	0.00	0.02	0.00
Asia NIEs	0.23	0.06	0.03	0.03	0.33	0.01
	0.24	0.09	0.04	0.04	0.42	0.01
ASEAN	0.47	0.10	0.06	0.00	0.02	0.00
	1.04	0.32	0.20	0.00	0.05	0.00
ODC	0.02	0.01	0.00	0.00	0.03	0.00
	0.03	0.02	0.00	0.00	0.06	0.00
Import price in						
Japan	—	0.35	0.17			
	—	0.80	0.21			
United States	0.37	—	0.07			
	0.62	—	0.07			
Korea	0.44	0.17	—			
	0.74	0.28	—			
EC(4)	0.11	0.10	0.01			
	0.19	0.09	0.02			
Asia NIEs	0.42	0.14	0.00			
	0.68	0.14	0.00			
ASEAN	0.29	0.13	0.01			
	0.69	0.24	0.01			
ODC	0.11	0.18	0.01			
	0.20	0.14	0.01			

Note: Figures in the table are elasticities, and for each country or group of countries the upper number indicates the impact in the forst year and the lower one is that the fifth year.

exports of other country or groups of countries are all negative. In the fifth year, impacts are −10.4% for ASEAN and −4.2% for Korea. Import prices are affected favorably, and significant decreases are seen in the US, Korea, and Asia NIEs.

2. A 10% reduction of US export prices increases her own export by 3.9% in the first year and 4.3% in the fifth year. The favorable

impacts on US exports are small as compared with the case of Japan. The impact on exports of other economies in the fifth year are −1.0%, −2.0%, and −3.2% for Japan, Korea, and ASEAN, respectively. The impacts on import prices of the trade partners are quite small compared with those of Japan.

3. A 10% decrease in Korean export prices raises her own exports by 9.9% in the first year and 21.7% in the fifth year. This reflects the high price elasticity of Korean exports. The impacts on other economies are rather modest, except for ASEAN.

Turning to the impacts of increased import volumes on the trade partners' exports, we see a slight increase in the impact from Japan and Korea. The reason for the small impact from Korea may be because of the relative size of the Korean import market to total exports from Japan and the US. The impacts from the US are relatively strong because of her large import volumes and high dependency on exports from Japan and Korea. A 10% increase in US imports raises exports in the fifth year by 2.4%, and 4.2% for Japan and Asia NIEs, respectively.

4. Diffusion Process of the Impacts of Robotization in the Model

Before discussing the simulation experiments, it is convenient for us to look at, based on the specification of the model, the diffusion mechanism through which robot investment in a specific industry affects aggregate and sectoral behaviors of other industries, both domestically and internationally.

According to the report of the Japan Industrial Robot Association (JIRA), wage cost pressure is the most important factor that encourages robot investment [see JIRA (1985)]. This means that the impact of robotization is initially observed in the form of labor displacement or increased labor productivity in the robot-using industry. This then tends to induce associated changes in the following ways. First, output price will be depressed as a result of wage cost reduction by increased labor productivity. Second, wage cost reduction will improve profitability, which may induce additional investment.

The lower output price in the robotized industry will not only increase price competitiveness of this industry in the export market, but also decrease intermediate input price of related industries through input-output relations. Accordingly, the initial price decrease in the robot-using industry influences output prices of all industries to a varying degree. Further decline will be expected in the prices of output and exports if the wage pressure in the labor market is reduced by the labor displacement effects of robotization.

On the demand side, investment for robotization will increase production in the robot-producing (capital goods) industry, and it in turn will require additional employment and fixed investment.

These impacts on price, production, and factor demands will diffuse gradually into the income distribution block and affect private consumption and housing investment expenditures. Thus, the initial impact will be multiplied domestically through the interdependent relations of the model.

The domestic interplays initiated by robotization are transmitted to foreign countries through the international trade linkage. This is because changes in the export prices and import volumes generated in the domestic economy are assumed to influence import prices and export volumes of all countries. Specifically, an export price decrease in the transmitting robotized country will depress exports from rival countries and decrease import prices in transmitting countries. In addition, import increases caused by the demand-side effect of robotization in the transmitting country will increase exports from partner countries and affect production there.

These effects in foreign countries will be fed back with a certain time lag to the domestic economy through the channels of trade flow.

The intensity and scope of the impacts of robotization on individual sectors depends mostly on the estimated parameters and lag patterns in the world model, the details of which are given in a separate paper.

5. Assumption on the Demand-Supply Effect of Robotization

As is clearly stated in the JIRA report (1985), business firms will make a decision regarding robotization depending on the labor displacement effect of robot investment. The larger the labor cost saving relative to the robot price, the higher the probability of introducing robots in the production process in place of workers.

Then, a question arises. What is the critical level of the real price of robots in terms of per capita employment cost? Again, according to the JIRA report (1985), the maximum amount of money that business firms can afford to invest in robots is about twice as much as the annual employment cost per worker. This implies that, given an industrial robot fully displacing one worker in the net term, this robot will become profitable when the price of the robot becomes less than twice the annual employment cost.

Thus, assuming that annual employment cost per worker is 4 million yen in 1980 prices, business firms will plan to spend 8 million yen or less for robots. Since the actual robot investment has to cover both core and peripheral equipments, the total amount is estimated to be at least in the order of 10 million yen in 1980 prices.

In analyzing the overall impacts of robotization, the critical point is how to feed the direct impacts of them into the model. Our procedure is such that the labor displacement effect of robot use is given by a downward shift of labor demand function, and the investment demand for robotization is represented by the upward shift of investment function of a given industry. Five assumptions are introduced on the shifting patterns of two functions in the individual industries as follows:

A1: Based on the sectoral distribution of robot stock in Japan, robotization in the simulation is confined to the four machinery industries. These are machinery except electrical, electrical machinery, transport equipment, and instruments. Robotization in other industries is disregarded.

A2: Magnitude of the downward shift of labor demand function in Japan is set by 10,000 per year for three machinery industries and 5,000 for the instrument industry. These figures are based on estimates by JIRA and Saito(1988).

A3: The same magnitude of direct labor displacement is introduced in the United States,whereas the shift in Korea is reduced to one-fourth of that in Japan. These differences in magnitude are justified by the relative size of each economy and are needed to make our comparison between the US and Korea more realistic.

A4: Upward shift of the investment function is determined by per capita annual labor cost and labor displacement effect of robot investment. The required robot investment to displace 10,000 workers is estimated to be 65 billion yen at 1980 prices, and 32.5 billion yen is needed to decrease employment by 5,000 workers. Additional investment is made on the order of 10% of initial investment from the second year and afterward.

A5: Two types of simulation are made in order to evaluate the relative importance of labor displacement effect and demand-side effect. The first simulation (Si-1) disregards demand-side effects, and the second simulation (Si-2) includes both effects of robot investment.

6. Simulation Results on Robotization in Japan, the US, and Korea

The procedure of robotization simulation with the estimated global model first involves the establishment of control solutions for the whole system. The control solutions in this experiment were given by solving the model without robotization assumptions for the period 1979–1983.

The second step is to derive disturbed solutions based on the alternative robotization scenario. Given these two solutions, the impacts of robotization on the macro and sectoral economies are measured by the differences between the two.

We computed disturbed solutions for the following three scenarios:

S1: Robotization in the Japanese machinery industry.
S2: Robotization in the US machinery industry.
S3: Robotization in the Korean machinery industry.

In scenarios 1 and 2, two types of simulation (Si-1 or Si-2), as described in A5 above, are conducted to compare the relative importance of demand-side and supply-side effects of robotization.

The results of simulation in each country are presented first as the macro-economic impacts on the domestic economy, second on the external economies, and third on the sectoral impacts in the domestic economy.

Table 4 Impacts on macro-economy-S1: Robotization in Japan (unit: %).

	S1-1		S1-2	
	Period 1	Period 5	Period 1	Period 5
Real GNP				
Japan	0.02023	0.37454	0.16357	0.36157
United States	−0.00399	−0.03175	−0.00373	−0.03015
Korea	−0.00495	0.00853	0.00514	0.01401
Nominal GNP				
Japan	−0.11831	−0.63053	−0.06367	−0.57934
United States	−0.00017	−0.02985	0.00045	−0.02871
Korea	−0.02190	−0.12473	−0.02460	−0.11234
Consumption				
Japan	0.00686	0.15176	0.05504	0.16539
United States	0.00068	0.01740	0.00133	0.01791
Korea	−0.00012	0.01293	0.00236	0.01894
Housing investment				
Japan	−0.12008	0.28680	0.00001	0.28766
United States	0.00558	0.07257	0.00919	0.07325
Korea	−0.00071	0.03139	0.01183	0.04150
Business investment				
Japan	0.09522	0.95958	0.92503	0.88230
United States	−0.00282	−0.03279	−0.00257	−0.03218
Korea	0.00862	0.11591	0.02869	0.11927
Export				
Japan	0.07132	0.74230	0.10946	0.71651
United States	−0.01683	−0.06254	−0.01183	−0.05284
Korea	−0.03130	−0.06536	−0.00406	−0.05648
Import				
Japan	−0.00584	0.03220	0.13731	0.06275
United States	0.02257	0.30009	0.03072	0.29828
Korea	−0.00015	0.04120	0.01428	0.04651
Employment				
Japan	−0.07467	−0.12189	−0.04800	−0.11182
United States	−0.00100	−0.00161	−0.00084	−0.00051
Korea	0.00205	0.02480	0.00650	0.02814
Rate of unemployment				
Japan	0.24543	0.33396	0.15775	0.35164
United States	0.02669	0.18568	0.02627	0.17548
Korea	0.00499	−0.02009	−0.00518	−0.02462
GNP deflator				
Japan	−0.13851	−1.00132	−0.22688	−0.93752
United States	0.00383	0.00206	0.00418	0.00143
Korea	−0.01695	−0.13245	−0.02974	−0.12634

(*Continued*)

Table 4 (*Continued*)

	S1-1		S1-2	
	Period 1	Period 5	Period 1	Period 5
Wage rate				
Japan	−0.06307	−0.70312	−0.07498	−0.63126
United States	−0.00120	−0.03769	−0.00154	−0.03681
Korea	−0.02381	−0.16571	−0.03349	−0.15757

Note: S1-1 disregards demand-side effects, and S1-2 include both effects of robot investment.

6.1. *The case of robotization in Japan*

The impacts of robotization on the macro-level are shown in Table 4. For Japan, the results are an improvement in the GNP amounting to 0.35–0.37% over the control solutions in the fifth year. Contributing factors for this are the downward shift of the price trend and the resulting increases in exports and domestic investments.

The impacts on the US economy as a whole are small but negative. This is because the negative impacts on net exports and investment are not fully cancelled out by the positive effects on private consumption and housing investment.

For Korea, changes in the comparative advantage affect her exports negatively, as is the case in the US. However, since the induced investment growth offsets most of the export decline, the negative impacts on the GNP are negligible. Slight but positive impacts are observed in labor demands.

The observed differences in the investment response between the US and Korea are explained by the fact that Korea depends heavily on Japan for her supply of capital goods — specifically the products of the machinery industry. Cheaper capital goods imported from Japan significantly decrease the cost of capital in Korea and, as a result, stimulate domestic investment.

At the sectoral level, labor displacement effects of robotization in Japan are concentrated in the robotized industries, as shown in Table 5 and amount to 36.9 thousand jobs in the first year and 62.3 thousand jobs in the fifth year when disregarding the demand-side effects of

Table 5 Effects on Employment –S1: Robotization in Japan (unit: 1000 persons).

	S1-1		S1-2	
	Period 1	Period 5	Period 1	Period 5
Employment in Japan				
1. Agri., forestry, fishing	0.434	6.663	3.684	6.674
2. Mining	0.000	0.000	0.000	0.000
3. Food, beverage, tobacco	0.026	0.694	0.129	0.677
4. Textiles	0.361	5.175	0.823	4.878
5. Apparel	0.087	1.198	0.307	1.179
6. Leather prod., footwear	0.005	0.061	0.023	0.068
7. Wooden prod., furniture	0.030	1.432	0.368	1.469
8. Paper and pulp, printing	0.762	0.348	0.743	
9. Rubber and plastics	0.019	0.200	0.052	0.182
10. Chemicals	1.786	0.181	1.851	
11. Petroleum and coal prod.	0.005	0.036	0.036	0.035
12. Nonmetallic mineral prod.	0.115	1.920	0.379	1.935
13. Iron and steel product	0.036	0.793	0.109	0.787
14. Nonferrous metals	0.033	0.592	0.083	0.575
15. Fabricated metal product	0.063	0.754	0.409	0.682
16. Machinery ex. Elect.	−10.837	−34.790	−9.610	−33.885
17. Electrical machinery	−10.265	−16.344	−8.762	−16.278
18. Transport equipment	−12.358	−38.079	−11.567	−37.779
19. Precision instruments	−9.966	−4.783	−9.947	
20. Miscellaneous manuf.	0.059	0.658	0.357	0.652
21. Tertiary industry	0.193	14.162	3.713	18.389
Industry Total	−36.900	−62.291	−23.721	−57.145

robot investment. The results in Table 4 also show that the demand-side effects of robot investment have worked to decrease the labor displacement effects by about 10 thousand jobs in the short run. It should be noted here that, in both cases, the workers displaced in robotized industries tend to be partially absorbed by other industries, and the negative impacts on jobs are reduced over time.

The impacts on sectoral output prices are shown in Table 6, where the significant price decreases in the robotized sectors have diffused to all sectors through declining input prices and wage cost. After 5 years, price reductions from the control solutions are over 1% for the robotized sectors and at least 0.5% for the remaining sectors. The

Table 6 Effects on output price and investment-S1: Robotization in Japan (unit:%).

	S1-1		S1-2	
	Period 1	Period 5	Period 1	Period 5
Output price in Japan				
1. Agri., forestry, fishing	−0.07365	−0.05845	−0.13103	−0.54771
2. Mining	−0.09963	−0.64210	−0.15518	−0.63375
3. Food, beverage, tobacco	−0.06242	−0.63147	−0.12130	−0.59488
4. Textiles	−0.05164	−0.42623	−0.09609	−0.39324
5. Apparel	−0.04909	−0.46159	−0.09058	−0.41254
6. Leather prod., footwear	−0.05961	−0.65006	−0.11920	−0.30168
7. Wooden prod., furniture	−0.06355	−0.54100	−0.11867	−0.50475
8. Paper and pulp, printing	−0.07793	−0.66299	−0.15081	−0.61699
9. Rubber and plastics	−0.05850	−0.52149	−0.11515	−0.48485
10. Chemicals	−0.05596	−0.47977	−0.10872	−0.44574
11. Petroleum and coal prod.	−0.05118	−0.35787	−0.10615	−0.33739
12. Nonmetallic mineral prod.	−0.07305	−0.60091	−0.14591	−0.55051
13. Iron and steel product	−0.04594	−0.40924	−0.08812	−0.38055
14. Nonferrous metals	−0.03787	−0.31211	−0.07279	−0.29151
15. Fabricated metal product	−0.05621	−0.49940	−0.12521	−0.45807
16. Machinery ex. Elect.	−0.23841	−1.15077	−0.34385	−1.08986
17. Electrical machinery	−0.26149	−1.08271	−0.38880	−1.01652
18. Transport equipment	−0.46800	−2.05712	−0.54830	−1.99141
19. Precision instruments	−0.61287	−1.76206	−0.71259	−1.71436
20. Miscellaneous manuf.	−0.07645	−0.69036	−0.15904	−0.63678
21. Tertiary industry	−0.08146	−0.76884	−0.16318	−0.71432
Business investment in Japan				
1. Agri., forestry, fishing	0.00139	0.04714	0.01184	0.06022
2. Mining	0.00000	0.00000	0.00000	0.00000
3. Food, beverage, tobacco	−0.03772	0.08943	0.00094	0.11338
4. Textiles	0.15441	1.86747	0.45129	1.62519
5. Apparel	0.03125	0.53687	0.10274	0.49232
6. Leather prod., footwear	0.04009	0.54051	0.10700	0.53939
7. Wooden prod., furniture	−0.19092	1.21076	0.21114	1.00402
8. Paper and pulp, printing	0.00583	0.17096	0.05827	0.20101
9. Rubber and plastics	−0.16538	0.63519	−0.11450	0.61417
10. Chemicals	0.00631	0.40058	0.03591	0.41246
11. Petroleum and coal prod.	0.05316	0.46815	0.38153	0.37905
12. Nonmetallic mineral prod.	0.01456	0.17703	0.11899	0.16956
13. Iron and steel product	−0.03570	0.11292	−0.18303	0.18325
14. Nonferrous metals	0.14262	1.35272	0.57484	1.29815
15. Fabricated metal product	0.01820	0.03900	0.15457	0.05943

(*Continued*)

Table 6 (*Continued*)

	S1-1		S1-2	
	Period 1	Period 5	Period 1	Period 5
16. Machinery ex. Elect.	0.53908	2.77369	6.63774	2.73649
17. Electrical machinery	0.18967	1.52322	5.71329	1.33214
18. Transport equipment	0.29968	2.75685	6.13869	0.22879
19. Precision instruments	0.52652	1.75907	15.74241	5.24865
20. Miscellaneous manuf.	0.09824	0.77956	0.29902	0.72956
21. Tertiary industry	0.11274	1.14197	0.31482	1.09544

cumulative effects on output prices are considerable in the transport equipment and precision instruments industries.

The effects on sectoral investments are positive for almost all sectors, although the magnitude of the effects varies among individual sectors. In the first year, over 40% of the increases are concentrated in the robotized sectors. But in the fifth year the share of the robotized sectors declines to around 33%, and that of remaining sectors as a whole amounts to 67%.

The positive impacts on sectoral exports, as shown in Table 7, fall heavily on particular sectors, that is, electrical machinery and transport equipment. This is because of the combined effects of significant price decreases and the high price elasticity of exports in these sectors.

6.2. *The case of robotization in the US*

The next simulation represents the impacts of robotization in the US on aggregate and sectoral economies. It can be seen in Table 8 that when the demand-side effect are disregarded, the effects on GNP are negative not only in Japan and Korea but also in the United States. These results are contrary to those of Japan, since the robotization in Japan has a positive impact on the GNP.

The following four factors are responsible for these contrasting results.

1. Price decreases from robotization are relatively small.
2. The resulting impacts on export expansion from price reductions are weak.

Table 7 Effects on foreign trade-S1: Robotization in Japan (unit:%).

	S1-1		S1-2	
	Period 1	Period 5	Period 1	Period 5
Real export in Japan				
1. Agri., forestry, fishing	0.02238	0.35554	0.04250	0.34073
2. Mining	0.08684	1.28767	0.15518	1.28441
3. Food, beverage, tobacco	0.04900	0.55249	0.08514	0.52699
4. Textiles	0.00650	0.01388	0.00483	0.00483
5. Apparel	0.00000	1.19008	0.17278	1.08112
6. Leather prod., footwear	0.09040	0.02556	0.00826	0.02401
7. Wooden prod., furniture	0.00281	0.35122	0.04920	0.33901
8. Paper and pulp, printing	0.02373	0.03259	0.00793	0.02990
9. Rubber and plastics	−0.00048	0.18305	0.02801	0.17056
10. Chemicals	0.01174	0.16897	0.02729	0.16568
11. Petroleum and coal prod.	0.00726	0.15254	0.07568	0.14380
12. Nonmetallic mineral prod.	0.02907	0.37764	0.08518	0.35344
13. Iron and steel product	0.03919	0.17485	0.03962	0.16148
14. Nonferrous metals	0.01945	0.26717	0.08522	0.24759
15. Fabricated metal product	0.03555	0.16717	0.03025	0.16129
16. Machinery ex. Elect.	0.00882	0.46797	0.08328	0.45132
17. Electrical machinery	0.05660	1.26204	0.33050	1.19954
18. Transport equipment	0.21831	1.46185	0.21211	1.43659
19. Precision instruments	0.18133	0.37399	0.12885	0.37008
20. Miscellaneous manuf.	0.11118	−0.03364	−0.00434	−0.03298
Real import in Japan				
1. Agri., forestry, fishing	0.00261	0.07827	0.02249	0.09118
2. Mining	0.00181	−0.00592	0.15842	−0.00399
3. Food, beverage, tobacco	−0.00929	0.04349	0.01813	0.08307
4. Textiles	−0.01656	0.22084	0.08283	0.33253
5. Apparel	0.01464	−0.03616	0.11493	−0.02561
6. Leather prod., footwear	−0.01710	−0.39888	−0.00771	−0.35343
7. Wooden prod., furniture	0.03410	0.93530	0.35482	0.99134
8. Paper and pulp, printing	−0.04343	−0.47898	−0.02638	−0.43242
9. Rubber and plastics	0.02338	−0.26348	0.18110	−0.15492
10. Chemicals	−0.01922	0.00001	0.10224	0.02631
11. Petroleum and coal prod.	0.01443	0.13896	0.10635	0.14652
12. Nonmetallic mineral prod.	−0.10986	−1.13712	−0.13643	−1.01853
13. Iron and steel product	−0.00400	−0.18255	0.06960	−0.12945
14. Nonferrous metals	0.03636	0.44273	0.20664	0.45841
15. Fabricated metal product	0.00870	−0.08032	0.13955	−0.04134
16. Machinery ex. Elect.	−0.10189	−0.41611	−0.04344	−0.39277
17. Electrical machinery	−0.12953	−0.31911	0.07527	−0.25732
18. Transport equipment	−0.26121	−0.50588	0.04808	−0.48856
19. Precision instruments	0.15613	0.42049	0.36524	0.47292
20. Miscellaneous manuf.	0.03764	0.49937	0.26472	0.51996

Table 8 Impacts on macro-economy-S2: Robotization in the US (unit:%).

	S2-1		S2-2	
	Period 1	Period 5	Period 1	Period 5
Real GNP				
Japan	−0.00223	−0.03369	0.01074	−0.02193
United States	−0.00257	−0.00418	0.06592	−0.00488
Korea	−0.00178	−0.01411	0.01524	0.00020
Nominal GNP				
Japan	−0.00146	−0.02173	0.00341	−0.00974
United States	−0.05700	−0.19607	−0.00295	−0.15382
Korea	−0.00721	−0.05147	0.00751	−0.03527
Consumption				
Japan	−0.00024	−0.01141	0.00387	−0.00393
United States	−0.00328	−0.02296	0.00441	−0.02536
Korea	−0.00016	−0.00440	0.00422	0.00615
Housing investment				
Japan	−0.00196	−0.04879	0.00764	−0.02636
United States	−0.07557	−0.12517	−0.03878	−0.13193
Korea	−0.00087	−0.015171	0.02144	0.00149
Business investment				
Japan	−0.00290	−0.05356	0.01431	−0.03575
United States	0.00531	0.03700	0.59929	0.08578
Korea	0.00348	0.01318	0.03962	0.03291
Export				
Japan	−0.01122	−0.10859	0.06116	−0.07318
United States	0.01186	0.06009	0.02077	0.07032
Korea	−0.01001	−0.05938	0.04825	−0.03304
Import				
Japan	0.00001	−0.01748	0.01453	0.00001
United States	−0.00814	−0.04210	0.08839	0.00744
Korea	0.00035	−0.01235	0.03018	0.00470
Employment				
Japan	−0.00047	−0.00953	0.00206	−0.00430
United States	−0.03752	−0.08497	−0.01729	−0.08089
Korea	0.00009	−0.00013	0.00674	0.00665
Rate of unemployment				
Japan	0.00155	0.02609	−0.00678	0.01178
United States	0.08019	0.12620	−0.37447	0.12945
Korea	0.00180	0.00743	−0.01535	−0.00173
GNP deflator				
Japan	0.00077	0.01196	−0.00733	0.01219
United States	−0.05442	−0.19191	−0.06882	−0.14895
Korea	−0.00543	−0.03737	−0.00773	−0.03547

(*Continued*)

Table 8 (*Continued*)

	S2-1		S2-2	
	Period 1	Period 5	Period 1	Period 5
Wage rate				
Japan	−0.00030	−0.00751	−0.00128	−0.00127
United States	−0.01608	−0.09943	−0.00559	−0.05268
Korea	−0.00726	−0.04986	−0.00354	−0.04110

Note: S2-1 disregards demand-side effects, and S2-2 includes both effects of robot investment.

Table 9 Effects on employment –S2: Robotization in the US (unit: 1000 persons).

	S2-1		S2-2	
	Period 1	Period 5	Period 1	Period 5
Employment in the United States				
1. Agri., forestry, fishing	−0.005	−0.020	−0.005	−0.014
2. Mining	0.000	0.000	0.000	−0.006
3. Food, beverage, tobacco	0.005	−0.057	0.001	0.026
4. Textiles	0.076	0.088	0.007	0.059
5. Apparel	0.022	0.141	0.018	0.033
6. Leather prod., footwear	−0.001	−0.001	−0.003	−0.004
7. Wooden prod., furniture	0.000	0.006	0.027	0.000
8. Paper and pulp, printing	−0.001	−0.012	0.001	−0.048
9. Rubber and plastics	0.003	0.036	0.023	0.028
10. Chemicals	0.000	0.007	0.007	−0.004
11. Petroleum and coal prod.	0.000	−0.002	0.000	−0.002
12. Nonmetallic mineral prod.	0.002	0.014	0.022	0.016
13. Iron and steel product	0.014	0.062	0.082	0.062
14. Nonferrous metals	0.002	0.013	0.007	0.012
15. Fabricated metal product	0.013	0.039	0.071	0.057
16. Machinery ex. Elect.	−1.473	−3.800	−1.168	−3.789
17. Electrical machinery	−1.064	−1.594	−0.741	−1.584
18. Transport equipment	−0.894	−1.783	−0.812	−1.750
19. Precision instruments	−0.656	−2.632	−0.582	−2.595
20. Miscellaneous manuf.	0.003	0.028	0.010	0.026
21. Tertiary industry	0.358	0.690	1.344	1.230
Industry Total	−3.666	−8.662	−1.689	−8.246

Table 10 Effects on output price and investment-S2: Robotization in the US (unit:%).

	S2-1		S2-2	
	Period 1	Period 5	Period 1	Period 5
Output price in the United States				
1. Agri., forestry, fishing	−0.01944	−0.06411	−0.02419	−0.04516
2. Mining	−0.01874	−0.06678	−0.02178	−0.05233
3. Food, beverage, tobacco	−0.02132	−0.07087	−0.02707	−0.04889
4. Textiles	−0.01266	−0.02358	−0.01900	−0.00712
5. Apparel	−0.00957	−0.03503	−0.01201	−0.02534
6. Leather prod., footwear	−0.02772	−0.08925	−0.03295	−0.05643
7. Wooden prod., furniture	−0.01852	−0.06095	−0.02363	−0.04373
8. Paper and pulp, printing	−0.03211	−0.11304	−0.04093	−0.08277
9. Rubber and plastics	−0.01777	−0.07400	−0.02285	−0.05506
10. Chemicals	−0.01313	−0.06449	−0.01656	−0.04883
11. Petroleum and coal prod.	−0.02039	−0.07741	−0.02433	−0.05370
12. Nonmetallic mineral prod.	−0.03051	−0.11156	−0.04144	−0.07058
13. Iron and steel product	−0.02423	−0.08718	−0.04171	−0.05544
14. Nonferrous metals	−0.01706	−0.05605	−0.02071	−0.04233
15. Fabricated metal product	−0.03091	−0.11757	−0.04130	−0.08960
16. Machinery ex Elect.	−0.24417	−0.80624	−0.23755	−0.78444
17. Electrical machinery	−0.07201	−0.27780	−0.09465	−0.25419
18. Transport equipment	−0.05840	−0.37143	−0.07281	−0.34955
19. Precision instruments	−0.30539	−2.31872	−0.40603	−2.28692
20. Miscellaneous manuf.	−0.02679	−0.10729	−0.03384	−0.08331
21. Tertiary Industry	−0.04470	−0.13079	−0.05768	−0.08242
Business investment in the United States				
1. Agri., forestry, fishing	0.01979	0.49354	0.02484	0.49616
2. Mining	−0.00010	0.42003	0.00240	0.37066
3. Food, beverage, tobacco	−0.01228	−0.03924	0.00263	−0.05328
4. Textiles	−0.00579	−0.05989	0.00734	−0.03727
5. Apparel	−0.01788	0.02830	−0.01796	0.03856
6. Leather prod., footwear	−0.02239	0.04693	−0.08722	−0.02287
7. Wooden prod., furniture	−0.00305	−0.20894	0.08811	−0.23323
8. Paper and pulp, printing	−0.03244	−0.10116	0.04868	−0.08951
9. Rubber and plastics	−0.00396	0.06137	0.15536	0.02136
10. Chemicals	−0.01944	−0.26577	0.27020	−0.30430
11. Petroleum and coal prod.	−0.00449	−0.05427	−0.00369	−0.03904
12. Nonmetallic mineral prod.	−0.01795	0.03540	0.04116	0.08263
13. Iron and steel product	0.00924	0.28964	−0.05787	0.27030
14. Nonferrous metals	−0.00050	0.02124	−0.01759	−0.00801

(*Continued*)

Table 10 (*Continued*)

	S2-1		S2-2	
	Period 1	Period 5	Period 1	Period 5
15. Fabricated metal product	0.00107	0.12819	0.05024	0.16851
16. Machinery ex Elect.	0.15039	0.24838	5.05146	1.45291
17. Electrical machinery	0.01167	0.06727	5.82752	0.41193
18. Transport equipment	−0.00381	−0.13647	3.76654	0.76087
19. Precision instruments	0.54729	3.61899	13.60921	4.45478
20. Miscellaneous manuf.	0.02231	0.20284	0.08737	0.20609
21. Tertiary Industry	−0.00455	−0.04744	0.03012	−0.11010

3. Sectoral investments are less sensitive to increased profitability.
4. Wage rate response is less sensitive to the labor market condition.

The negative impacts on economic growth are larger in Japan than in Korea. This is explained by the larger impacts of decreased US imports on Japanese exports, especially on her machinery exports. The positive effects on Korean investment, which were derived from the cheaper imported capital goods, have partially offset the initial negative effects.

As shown in Table 9, the total sum of labor displacements in the US are approximately 37,000 in the first year, 69,000 in the second year, and 87,000 in the fifth year. Whereas the labor displacements in Japan peak in the fourth year and decrease afterward, the effect in the United States shows an increasing trend and exceeds that in Japan. Regarding the sectoral distribution of labor displacements, magnitude of the robotized sectors shows little difference between the US and Japan. The larger labor displacements in the US are because of the smaller compensating increases in the tertiary industry employment.

For output prices, the effects in the US shown in Table 10 are negative and comparable in size to those in Japan for general machinery and precision instruments. The effects on electrical machinery and transport equipment, however, are considerably less than those in Japan. As a result of this and the small impacts on wage rates, the total effects on output prices in non-robotized sectors are quite small when compared with those in Japan.

Table 11 Effects on foreign trade –S": Robotization in the US (unit:%).

	S2-1		S2-2	
	Period 1	Period 5	Period 1	Period 5
Output price in the United Sates				
1. Agn., forestry, fishing	0.00144	−0.00281	0.00552	−0.00128
2. Mining	−0.00380	−0.01790	0.00709	−0.01462
3. Food, beverage, tobacco	0.00267	−0.00826	0.01000	−0.00431
4. Textiles	0.00910	−0.00494	0.02251	−0.00904
5. Apparel	−0.00166	−0.03708	0.00790	−0.01733
6. Leather prod., footwear	0.00818	−0.02157	0.02800	−0.02046
7. Wooden prod., furniture	−0.00357	−0.05432	0.01477	−0.02477
8. Paper and pulp, printing	−0.00066	−0.03368	0.00612	−0.03641
9. Rubber and plastics	−0.00179	−0.03612	0.00810	−0.02336
10. Chemicals	−0.00790	−0.04719	0.00082	−0.04071
11. Petroleum and coal prod.	0.00075	−0.00568	0.00842	−0.00255
12. Nonmetallic mineral prod.	0.00607	0.01200	0.02094	0.01175
13. Iron and steel product	0.02077	0.09545	0.04257	0.06099
14. Nonferrous metals	0.02662	0.11057	0.04573	0.09356
15. Fabricated metal product	0.00836	0.01327	0.02042	0.01871
16. Machinery ex Elect.	0.04426	0.15603	0.04833	0.17078
17. Electrical machinery	0.01605	0.05518	0.03528	0.07081
18. Transport equipment	0.01604	0.08217	0.03409	0.09735
19. Precision instruments	0.04481	0.49321	0.07708	0.52232
20. Miscellaneous manuf.	−0.00078	−0.04626	0.02117	−0.01660
Industry total	0.01472	0.06477	0.02077	0.07032
Business investment in the United States				
1. Agri., forestry, fishing	−0.01144	−0.05209	−0.00563	−0.04403
2. Mining	0.00006	0.10529	0.00123	−0.15773
3. Food, beverage, tobacco	−0.02837	−0.10370	−0.01988	−0.08618
4. Textiles	−0.03889	−0.11839	−0.01209	−0.08022
5. Apparel	−0.04149	−0.35698	−0.04192	−0.33869
6. Leather prod., footwear	−0.06260	−0.22056	−0.18762	−0.31826
7. Wooden prod., furniture	−0.03453	−0.14123	0.17109	−0.09382
8. Paper and pulp, printing	−0.03158	−0.12601	0.01648	−0.10884
9. Rubber and plastics	−0.00772	−0.03259	0.14336	0.02446
10. Chemicals	−0.01254	−0.05626	0.07769	−0.03881
11. Petroleum and coal prod.	−0.00885	−0.05765	−0.00573	−0.04908
12. Nonmetallic mineral prod.	−0.02801	−0.16195	0.08384	−0.10919
13. Iron and steel product	−0.02107	−0.09390	0.04517	−0.05038
14. Nonferrous metals	−0.00113	0.02238	0.20800	0.07153
15. Fabricated metal product	−0.01800	−0.11149	0.14449	−0.02428

(*Continued*)

Table 11 *(Continued)*

	S2-1		S2-2	
	Period 1	Period 5	Period 1	Period 5
16. Machinery ex Elect.	−0.01730	−0.39648	0.35871	0.04631
17. Electrical machinery	−0.06634	−0.41454	0.38651	−0.32507
18. Transport equipment	−0.02570	−0.46016	0.06522	−0.32759
19. Precision instruments	0.33454	4.24052	1.19235	4.57997
20. Miscellaneous manuf.	0.03323	0.19808	0.13467	0.14214
Industry total	−0.01058	−0.05096	−0.11489	−0.00081

The impacts on foreign trade in the US, as seen in Table 11, are more pronounced in the import substitution than in the export expansion. For example, after 5 years, the effects on electrical machinery and transport equipment are a 0.06–0.08% increase in exports and 0.4–0.5% decrease in imports.

It is clear from the data in Tables 8–11 that the demand-side effects of robot investment partially or fully compensate for the negative impacts they have on key economic variables in the US. The impacts on economic growth become positive, and the labor displacements in the first year are reduced by around 20,000 jobs. In the fifth year, however, because of the declining demand-side effects, labor displacements, as a whole, differ little from those in the case where demand-side effects are disregarded.

6.3. *The case of robotization in Korea*

The impacts of robotization in Korea are summarized in Tables 12 and 13. The international impacts are considerably small, as anticipated by taking into account her relative size in the world economy.

For the domestic impacts, the effects on GNP growth in Korea are positive, as is the case in Japan. Increased productivity by robotization tends to depress output prices, which in turn expand exports and encourage domestic investments. But the positive impacts on the Korean economy tend to spill over to other countries, especially Japan, which is a major exporter of capital goods to Korea.

Table 12 Impacts on macro-economy@S3: Robotization in Korea (unit:%).

	Period 1	Period 5
Real GNP		
Japan	0.00003	0.00071
United States	−0.00080	−0.00024
Korea	0.02699	0.07222
Nominal GNP		
Japan	−0.00009	−0.00006
United States	0.00001	−0.00023
Korea	−0.03730	−0.02203
Consumption		
Japan	0.00007	0.00050
United States	0.00003	0.00017
Korea	−0.00496	0.02306
Housing investment		
Japan	−0.00004	0.00136
United States	0.00017	0.00063
Korea	−0.02552	0.06700
Business investment		
Japan	0.00008	0.00139
United States	−0.00009	−0.00033
Korea	0.07927	0.13284
Export		
Japan	0.00106	0.00259
United States	−0.00024	−0.00047
Korea	0.05552	0.10245
Import		
Japan	0.00094	0.00203
United States	0.00057	0.00600
Korea	0.01530	0.05074
Employment		
Japan	−0.00001	0.00016
United States	−0.00005	0.00000
Korea	−0.07172	−0.04267
Rate of unemployment		
Japan	0.00003	−0.00044
United States	0.00056	0.00130
Korea	−0.02718	−0.03914

(*Continued*)

Table 12 (*Continued*)

	Period 1	Period 5
GNP deflator		
Japan	−0.00012	−0.00077
United States	0.00009	0.00002
Korea	−0.06427	−0.09419
Wage rate		
Japan	−0.00007	−0.00035
United States	−0.00004	−0.00033
Korea	−0.02777	−0.04984

For employment, the net effects of robotization are 9,900 job decreases in the first year and 6,200 job decreases in the fifth year. In the robotized sectors, the figures are 10,200 and 9,600, respectively. Thus in the fifth year, about one-third of the job losses in the robotized sectors are absorbed by job increases in the non-robotized sectors.

The effects on output prices are rather small, because the wage cost share in the production cost is not as high in Korea as it is in Japan or the United States. As a result, the positive impact on exports through price effect becomes limited.

6.4. *A Comparison of the impacts of robotization in Japan and the US on Korea*

Korea, which is one of the NIEs, has close economic ties with Japan and the US through international trade. It is interesting to compare the impact on the Korean economy that is the result of robotization in these two countries.

Table 14 presents a comparison of the macro-economic impacts of robotization. Disregarding demand-side effects, the impacts on economic growth in Korea are negative for both countries in the first 2 years. However, from the third year onward, the effects of Japan become positive, whereas those of the United States continue to be negative with an increasing trend.

The differences in the impacts of these two countries emerge for the following reasons: first, the effects of Japan are growth promoting, whereas those of the US are deflationary in nature; second, the larger

Table 13 Effects on sectoral economies-S3: Robotization in Korea.

	Employment in Korea (unit: thousand persons)		Output price in Korea (unit: %)	
	Period 1	Period 5	Period 1	Period 5
Output price in Japan				
1. Agri., forestry, fishing	0.534	1.040	−0.00918	−0.02188
2. Mining	0.005	−0.037	−0.01738	−0.03950
3. Food, beverage, tobacco	−0.003	0.048	−0.01329	−0.03336
4. Textiles	0.072	0.252	−0.02827	−0.06210
5. Apparel	0.009	0.094	−0.03218	−0.06915
6. Leather prod., footwear	−0.001	0.025	−0.01077	−0.04525
7. Wooden prod., furniture	0.021	0.038	−0.02266	−0.04112
8. Paper and pulp, printing	0.017	0.042	−0.03217	−0.05298
9. Rubber and plastics	0.042	0.109	−0.03445	−0.06147
10. Chemicals	0.012	0.060	−0.03197	−0.05192
11. Petroleum and coal prod.	0.020	0.003	0.00482	0.00614
12. Nonmetallic mineral prod.	0.002	0.037	−0.03670	−0.05313
13. Iron and steel product	0.016	0.050	−0.03949	−0.05394
14. Nonferrous metals	0.034	0.022	−0.03724	−0.04716
15. Fabricated metal product	0.013	0.057	−0.07069	−0.12195
16. Machinery ex Elect.	0.033	−2.211	−0.82718	−0.67544
17. Electrical machinery	−2.212	−2.287	−0.01671	−0.23880
18. Transport equipment	−2.377	−1.956	−0.08558	−0.12600
19. Precision instruments	−2.401	−1.239	−0.95062	−1.04424
20. Miscellaneous manuf.	−1.240	0.071	−0.04580	−0.09811
21. Tertiary industry	0.058	1.915	−0.04103	−0.05768
Industry total	0.240	−6.243		
	Real export in Korea (unit: thousand persons)		**Real import in Korea (unit: %)**	
	Period 1	Period 5	Period 1	Period 5
Business investment in Japan				
1. Agri., forestry, fishing	0.00911	0.10015	−0.00035	0.02001
2. Mining	0.00180	0.00315	0.03882	0.05941
3. Food, beverage, tobacco	0.00683	0.03628	−0.00445	0.05765
4. Textiles	0.01926	0.04987	−0.03460	−0.06310
5. Apparel	0.03730	0.13128	−0.00404	0.02884
6. Leather prod., footwear	0.00219	0.02599	−0.02444	−0.02658
7. Wooden prod., furniture	0.02821	0.04735	0.01072	0.03103
8. Paper and pulp, printing	0.00982	0.03397	−0.00025	0.01828

(*Continued*)

Table 13 (*Continued*)

	Employment in Korea (unit: thousand persons)		Output price in Korea (unit: %)	
	Period 1	Period 5	Period 1	Period 5
9. Rubber and plastics	0.01131	0.04100	0.03029	0.06694
10. Chemicals	0.02476	0.10250	0.02174	0.05603
11. Petroleum and coal prod.	−0.00271	−0.00691	0.08199	0.14604
12. Nonmetallic mineral prod.	0.02372	0.03937	0.02051	0.06718
13. Iron and steel product	0.04464	0.13204	0.02539	0.03783
14. Nonferrous metals	0.02544	0.02594	0.06838	0.10046
15. Fabricated metal product	0.06550	0.07532	0.00301	0.04114
16. Machinery ex Elect.	0.15211	0.18051	−0.09163	−0.01493
17. Electrical machinery	0.01281	0.03517	0.05903	0.08825
18. Transport equipment	0.26467	0.34151	0.03482	0.07003
19. Precision instruments	−0.00038	0.00316	0.06367	0.10287
20. Miscellaneous manuf.	0.30501	0.18764	0.34574	0.51560

Table 14 Impacts of robotization in Japan and the US on the Korean economy.

	S-1		S-2	
	Period 1	Period 5	Period 1	Period 5
Real GNP (10 mil. Won)				
Effect of Japan	−1.976	3.778	2.074	6.683
Effect of United States	−0.702	−6.516	6.103	0.230
Consumption (10 mil. Won)				
Effect of Japan	−0.027	3.735	0.585	5.656
Effect of United States	−0.039	−1.290	1.043	1.937
Housing investment (10 mil. Won)				
Effect of Japan	−0.016	0.948	0.272	1.206
Effect of United States	−0.019	−0.419	0.492	0.103
Business investment (10 mil. Won)				
Effect of Japan	0.691	10.803	2.306	11.114
Effect of United States	0.281	1.080	3.177	3.009
Export (10 mil. Won)				
Effect of Japan	−3.696	−11.295	−0.447	−9.442
Effect of United States	−1.171	−10.667	5.734	−5.823

(*Continued*)

Table 14 (*Continued*)

	S-1		S-2	
	Period 1	Period 5	Period 1	Period 5
Import (10 mil. Won)				
Effect of Japan	−0.018	8.131	2.163	9.143
Effect of United States	0.058	−2.539	4.545	0.896
Employment (1,000 persons)				
Effect of Japan	0.285	3.735	0.901	4.199
Effect of United States	0.014	−0.036	0.932	0.995
GNP deflator (1980 = 100)				
Effect of Japan	−0.012	−0.182	−0.021	−0.073
Effect of United States	−0.004	−0.051	−0.005	−0.047
Investment deflator (1980 = 100)				
Effect of Japan	−0.037	−0.391	−0.053	−0.371
Effect of United States	−0.014	−0.133	−0.0171	−0.127
Wage rate(%)				
Effect of Japan	−0.024	−0.167	−0.034	−0.151
Effect of United States	−0.007	−0.051	−0.004	−0.041

Note: S-1 disregards demand-side effects, and S-2 includes both effects of robot investment.

impacts on output prices in Japan contribute to lower the price of capital goods in Korea and lead to a larger investment.

In the fifth year, the decreases in investment deflator in Korea are 0.37% point in the case of Japan and 0.13% point for the US. The resulting investment increases are 11.1 billion won in 1980 prices in the case of Japan and 3.01 billion won in the case of the US.

Comparing the case of S-1 with that of S-2, we see that the demand-side effects of robot investments promote economic growth in Korea. The effects of the United States exceed those of Japan in the first and second years, but from the third year onward, the relative magnitudes of macro effects are reversed. The larger short-term effects on Korea from US robotization are generated by the relatively high propensity to import in the US, which tends to increase Korean exports to the US.

7. Concluding Remarks

The purpose of this chapter is to evaluate the probable global impact of robotization on the macro and sectoral economies, using a world model of industry and trade. We find that robotization in Japan and Korea has a positive impact on their economic growth, whereas robotization in the US has a negative effect on her own economic growth. We also find that the international impacts of robotization in Japan are negative in the United States, but positive with regard to the Korean economy.

Of course, these findings from the simulation experiments depend on the structure of the global model we used, as well as on the assumptions made for the simulation. We focus our attention on robotization in the machinery industry, in which Japan has a comparative advantage over the United States and the NIEs. We are not concerned with robotization in industries such as textile products, where the NIEs have a comparative advantage over developed countries. Because exchange rate variables are exogenous in the current version of the model, the impacts through exchange rate changes are neglected.

In conclusion, continued efforts should be made to improve the whole model system and to examine alternative cases in simulation studies.

References

Japan Industrial robot Association (1985). *The Report (Manufacturing) on the Long-term Forecast of the Demand for Industrial Robots*, Tokyo. (in Japanese)

Kinoshita, S *et al.* (1982). *The Development and Application of the World Industry-Trade Model for the Analysis of the International Industry-Trade Structure around Japan*, Tokyo: Economic Planning Agency. (in Japanese)

Kinoshita, S (1983). "Structure and Application of a World Industry and Trade Model," Paper presented at the Project Link Project meeting at Tsukuba.

Kinoshita, S *et al.* (1987). "The Economic Impacts of Robotization: Domestic and International," Paper presented at the IIASA CIM Workshop.

Leontief, W and F Duchin (1986). *The Future Impact of Automation on Workers*, New York: Oxford University Press.

Mitsuo, S (1988). "Economics of Robotization," Kokumin Keizai Zasshi, 158(6), December. (in Japanese)

Moriguchi, C (1983). Forecasting and simulation analysis of the world economy, *American Economic Review*, 63(2).

Chapter 4

Japanese Overseas Production within the Asia International Input-Output Model: Japan, the US, and Asia*

Mitsuo Yamada

1. Introduction

It is widely known that foreign direct investment (FDI) played an important role in the economic development of the countries of East Asia. After the Plaza Accord was signed in 1985, the rapid appreciation of the Japanese yen forced Japanese manufacturers to extend overseas production. Although the long recession following the collapse of the bubble economy in the 1990s somewhat dampened the enthusiasm of Japanese firms vis-à-vis FDI, the globalization of the Japanese economy seemed a long-term trend. Furthermore, the 1997 Asian financial crisis threw Asian economies into confusion and many firms came to a standstill. However, the following year, Asia's economy recovered gradually and the volume of FDI conducted by Japanese firms also recovered to pre-crisis levels.

The overseas activities of Japanese firms are examined in surveys published by the Ministry of Economy, Trade, and Industry (METI): the *Basic Survey of Overseas Business Activities* every three years and the *Trend Survey of Overseas Business Activities* in other years. According

*This paper was published in The Journal of Econometric Study of Northeast Asia, October, 2004 (Vol. 5, No. 1). The original version was presented at the 8th international convention of the EAEA held in Kuala Lumpur in 2002. The author wishes to thank to Dr. Keiko Ito of ICSEAD for her valuable comments, and Professor Ichiro Tokutsu of Konan University for his helpful comments.

to the reports, there were about 13,000 overseas affiliates of Japanese firms, with sales by these firms reaching 126 trillion yen in 1998 (50 trillion yen in the manufacturing sector and 76 trillion yen in non-manufacturing sectors). The total value of sales accounted for 13.1% of total Japanese output in 1998.

It is well known that input-output analysis is one of the most useful tools for carrying out impact analysis of hollowing-out in the manufacturing sector. According to Inaba (1999), much Japanese research carried out in this field from 1979 to 1995 involved estimating the effects of FDI on international trade and then evaluating the direct and indirect impacts of this change in international trade on internal production and labor demand. Input-output analysis was applied to this latter phase. There were many disparities in the methods used to link FDI to international trade and in the usage of input-output tables, which led to differences in their results. However, analysis using internal input-output tables cannot completely capture the interdependence between firms based in the home country and their overseas affiliates.

Yamada (2002) modified the 1995 US-Japan international input-output table and analyzed the relationship between the US and Japanese economy by looking at Japanese overseas activities. This analysis explicitly demonstrated the activities of the Japanese overseas firms in the US market in the input-output table, and evaluated the impact of Japanese overseas production in the US economy on both the US and Japanese economies.

In this chapter, we will reconstruct the Asian international input-output table for 1995 to extract from it information about Japanese overseas activities in the US and Asian economies, and to integrate those activities into one table. Using this modified table, we are able to analyze the effects of Japanese overseas production in the US and Asian economies on Japan, the US, and Asian economies. We are also able to discuss the differences between Japanese overseas activities in the US and Asian economies.

In the next section, we discuss the theoretical framework of the input-output model in brief. We then state the database for our recompiled input-output table. Finally, we examine some analytical results showing the relationship between those economies and the impact of Japanese overseas activities on each economy.

2. Theoretical Framework

As is well known, an international input-output table shows the internal and international transactions among sectors in each country, and is compiled from each country's input-output table and international trade statistics. Here, we consider the international input-output tables of two countries: Japan and the relevant foreign country. Furthermore, we extract the Japanese overseas activity from the foreign country, using the Figure 1 to denote Japan, 2 to denote the foreign country excluding Japanese overseas activity, and 3 to denote Japanese overseas activity. Our model is expressed as follows:

$$\begin{bmatrix} \mathbf{A}_{11} & \mathbf{A}_{12} & \mathbf{A}_{13} \\ \mathbf{A}_{21} & \mathbf{A}_{22} & \mathbf{A}_{23} \\ \mathbf{A}_{31} & \mathbf{A}_{32} & \mathbf{A}_{33} \end{bmatrix} \begin{bmatrix} \mathbf{x}_1 \\ \mathbf{x}_2 \\ \mathbf{x}_3 \end{bmatrix} + \begin{bmatrix} \mathbf{F}_{11} \\ \mathbf{F}_{21} \\ \mathbf{F}_{31} \end{bmatrix} + \begin{bmatrix} \mathbf{F}_{12} \\ \mathbf{F}_{22} \\ \mathbf{F}_{32} \end{bmatrix} + \begin{bmatrix} \mathbf{E}_1 \\ \mathbf{E}_2 \\ \mathbf{E}_3 \end{bmatrix} = \begin{bmatrix} \mathbf{x}_1 \\ \mathbf{x}_2 \\ \mathbf{x}_3 \end{bmatrix}.$$

Here, $\mathbf{A}_{13}, \mathbf{A}_{23}$, and $\mathbf{A}_{33}$ signify the input coefficient matrices of Japanese overseas activity. Sales of the intermediate products of Japanese overseas activity to each region are expressed as $\mathbf{A}_{31}\mathbf{x}_1, \mathbf{A}_{32}\mathbf{x}_2$, and $\mathbf{A}_{33}\mathbf{x}_3$ respectively. Exports of finished goods to the Japanese market are expressed as $\mathbf{F}_{31}$ for Japanese overseas activity. On the other hand, the sales value of finished goods in the domestic market is expressed as $\mathbf{F}_{32}$, while exports to a third county are expressed as $\mathbf{E}_3$.

Solving this equation for the output, we obtain

$$\begin{bmatrix} \mathbf{x}_1 \\ \mathbf{x}_2 \\ \mathbf{x}_3 \end{bmatrix} = \begin{bmatrix} \mathbf{I}-\mathbf{A}_{11} & -\mathbf{A}_{12} & -\mathbf{A}_{13} \\ -\mathbf{A}_{21} & \mathbf{I}-\mathbf{A}_{22} & -\mathbf{A}_{23} \\ -\mathbf{A}_{31} & -\mathbf{A}_{32} & \mathbf{I}-\mathbf{A}_{33} \end{bmatrix}^{-1} \left\{ \begin{bmatrix} \mathbf{F}_{11} \\ \mathbf{F}_{21} \\ \mathbf{F}_{31} \end{bmatrix} + \begin{bmatrix} \mathbf{F}_{12} \\ \mathbf{F}_{22} \\ \mathbf{F}_{32} \end{bmatrix} + \begin{bmatrix} \mathbf{E}_1 \\ \mathbf{E}_2 \\ \mathbf{E}_3 \end{bmatrix} \right\}$$

$$\begin{bmatrix} \mathbf{x}_1 \\ \mathbf{x}_2 \\ \mathbf{x}_3 \end{bmatrix} = \begin{bmatrix} \mathbf{B}_{11} & \mathbf{B}_{12} & \mathbf{B}_{13} \\ \mathbf{B}_{21} & \mathbf{B}_{22} & \mathbf{B}_{23} \\ \mathbf{B}_{31} & \mathbf{B}_{32} & \mathbf{B}_{33} \end{bmatrix} \left\{ \begin{bmatrix} \mathbf{F}_{11} \\ \mathbf{F}_{21} \\ \mathbf{F}_{31} \end{bmatrix} + \begin{bmatrix} \mathbf{F}_{12} \\ \mathbf{F}_{22} \\ \mathbf{F}_{32} \end{bmatrix} + \begin{bmatrix} \mathbf{E}_1 \\ \mathbf{E}_2 \\ \mathbf{E}_3 \end{bmatrix} \right\}.$$

Assuming $\Delta\mathbf{F}_{11} = \Delta\mathbf{F}_{12} = \Delta\mathbf{E}_1 = \mathbf{0}$ and $\Delta\mathbf{F}_{21} = \Delta\mathbf{F}_{22} = \Delta\mathbf{E}_2 = \mathbf{0}$ in this equation, we can derive the output induced by finished goods resulting from Japanese overseas activity as follows:

$$\begin{bmatrix} \Delta\mathbf{x}_1 \\ \Delta\mathbf{x}_2 \\ \Delta\mathbf{x}_3 \end{bmatrix} = \begin{bmatrix} \mathbf{B}_{13}(\Delta\mathbf{F}_{31} + \Delta\mathbf{F}_{32} + \Delta\mathbf{E}_3) \\ \mathbf{B}_{23}(\Delta\mathbf{F}_{31} + \Delta\mathbf{F}_{32} + \Delta\mathbf{E}_3) \\ \mathbf{B}_{33}(\Delta\mathbf{F}_{31} + \Delta\mathbf{F}_{32} + \Delta\mathbf{E}_3) \end{bmatrix}.$$

This shows the degree to which the induced production in each economy stems from the Japanese overseas production of finished goods.

On the other hand, Japanese overseas production will substitute for domestic final demand and exports from Japan to some extent. If we assume that $100\alpha_i\%$ of Japanese overseas production of finished goods i substitutes for these, that is

$$\mathbf{\Delta F}_{11} + \mathbf{\Delta F}_{12} + \mathbf{\Delta E}_1 = -[\alpha_i](\mathbf{\Delta F}_{31} + \mathbf{\Delta F}_{32} + \mathbf{\Delta E}_3),$$

where $[\alpha_i]$ means a diagonal matrix whose diagonal elements are α_i, then the induced effect on production is derived from the following equation:

$$\begin{bmatrix} \mathbf{\Delta x}_1 \\ \mathbf{\Delta x}_2 \\ \mathbf{\Delta x}_3 \end{bmatrix} = -\begin{bmatrix} \mathbf{B}_{11}[\alpha_i](\mathbf{\Delta F}_{31} + \mathbf{\Delta F}_{32} + \mathbf{\Delta E}_3) \\ \mathbf{B}_{21}[\alpha_i](\mathbf{\Delta F}_{31} + \mathbf{\Delta F}_{32} + \mathbf{\Delta E}_3) \\ \mathbf{B}_{31}[\alpha_i](\mathbf{\Delta F}_{31} + \mathbf{\Delta F}_{32} + \mathbf{\Delta E}_3) \end{bmatrix}.$$

3. Database for the Input-Output Model

The Asian international input-output table for 1995 was compiled and published by the Institute of Developing Economies (IDE) in 2000. This table includes ten countries or regions: Japan, the US, Indonesia, Malaysia, the Philippines, Singapore, Thailand, China, Taiwan, and South Korea. Hong Kong is also included but treated as exogenous. In European countries, the UK, France, and Germany appear as exogenous. IDE Asian international input-output tables were published for 1985, 1990 and 1995. However, we concentrate our attention on the most recent year for which input-output tables exist, because the overseas expansion of Japanese firms has continued to accelerate since 1985.

Firstly we integrate ten countries or regions from this table into three: Japan, the US, and Asia.[1] Then, we recompile the table so that Japanese overseas production activities in the US and Asia are become explicit. Here we use statistics obtained from a survey carried out the

[1] There may be some differences between Southeast Asian countries and China in considering Japanese overseas production activities. However, we treat them as one region, mainly because of the limited availability of data.

same year by METI regarding the overseas activity of Japanese firms. We make use of data on the regional sales volumes of Japanese overseas affiliates by industry, sales for each market, domestic and foreign, and the purchase of intermediate goods and services from each region.[2]

78 sectors are originally defined for each country or region in the IDE table, and it would seem desirable to use the 78-sector table for the analysis. However, the METI data on Japanese overseas activities gives us information for only 18 sectors: agriculture, fisheries and forestry, mining, construction, 12 manufacturing sectors, wholesale and retail trade, services, finance and real estate. Therefore, we have had to integrate the input-output table to create 20 sectors, adding two sectors: the public sector, and others (public utilities and network sector), in which Japanese firms are assumed not to have expanded overseas. The definition of each sector appears in Table 1.

The basic idea and detailed procedure for estimating the recompiled input-output table can be found in Yamada (2002). In this paper, we discuss the outline of the procedure. (See Fig. 1.)

First of all, we compile the original input-output table to obtain a 20-sector 3-region table as stated above. Then we estimate the activities of Japanese overseas affiliates in 20 sectors of the US and Asia economies: production, intermediate demand, final demand and export demand. Subtracting these overseas activities from the original values in the table, we obtain the activities of firms that have no relationship with Japanese firms in terms of ownership.

To estimate activities of Japanese firms overseas, we make use of METI statistics regarding the overseas activities of Japanese firms. Assuming that the value of sales is equal to the value of production, we can estimate the value of goods produced by Japanese firms overseas by sector and by region.[3] Dividing the value of purchases from each region

[2]These figures are recognized to vary considerably year by year, because they are dependent on sampling data as opposed to estimated values for the population. Fukao *et al.* (1999) tried to estimate population values for these statistics. However, we use the values reported in these statistics with no correction, because we have no appropriate information for correcting it.

[3]The sales value is not equal to the production value in terms of inventory changes. However, we treat them the same, assuming there are no changes in the inventory.

Table 1 Definition of sectors.

	Sectors
1	Agriculture, forestry and fishery
2	Mining
3	Construction
4	Food
5	Textiles
6	Timber, wood, and pulp
7	Chemicals
8	Iron and Steel
9	Nonferrous metals
10	General machinery
11	Electrical machinery
12	Transport equipment
13	Precision instruments
14	Petroleum and coal
15	Miscellaneous manufacturing
16	Commerce
17	Public service
18	Other service
19	Finance and real estate
20	Other

by the estimated value of production, we can derive intermediate input ratios, which are used to assign an input value for each region to each sector. In addition, the sales ratio for each region is used to assign the demand by region to each sector. In this way we can roughly assign the inputs and demands by region and by sector for the overseas activities of Japanese firms. The detailed input coefficients are estimated by applying the relative values of the input coefficients of the original input-output table.[4] Final demand is estimated to fill the identity so that total supply equals total demand in each sector.

Secondly, we integrate the extracted activities of Japanese overseas production to create a single input-output table. In this stage, the domestic input of Japanese overseas activities in the US includes both

[4]Though we use the input coefficients of the original input-output table to estimate the detailed input coefficients of Japanese overseas production, the input structure of Japanese overseas production is not the same as that of the rest of the region. This is simply because of the difference in trade patterns for both activities.

(1) Asian international input output table, original

Asian international input output table		Intermediate demand Japan	Intermediate demand United States	Intermediate demand Asia	Final demand Japan	Final demand United States	Final demand Asia	Export ROW	Production
Intermediate Input	Japan	Axjj	Axju	Axja	Fdjj	Fdju	Fdja	Ejr	Xj
	USA	Axuj	Axuu	Axua	Fduj	Fduu	Fdua	Eur	Xu
	Asia	Axaj	Axau	Axaa	Fdaj	Fdau	Fdaa	Ear	Xa
Import	ROW	Axrj	Axru	Axra	Fdrj	Fdru	Fdra		
Value added		Vj	Vu	Va					
Production		Xj	Xu	Xa					

(2) Separation of activities of Japanese overseas subsidiaries

Asian international input output table(non-overseas subsidiaries)		Intermediate demand Japan	Intermediate demand United States	Intermediate demand Asia	Final demand Japan	Final demand United States	Final demand Asia	Export ROW	Production
Intermediate Input	Japan	Axjj~	Axju~	Axja~	Fdjj~	Fdju~	Fdja~	Ejr~	Xj~
	USA	Axuj~	Axuu~	Axua~	Fduj~	Fduu~	Fdua~	Eur~	Xu~
	Asia	Axaj~	Axau~	Axaa~	Fdaj~	Fdau~	Fdaa~	Ear~	Xa~
Import	ROW	Axrj~	Axru~	Axra~	Fdrj~	Fdru~	Fdra~		
Value added		Vj~	Vu~	Va~					
Production		Xj~	Xu~	Xa~					

Asian international input output table(overseas subsidiaries)		Intermediate demand Japan	Intermediate demand United States	Intermediate demand Asia	Final demand Japan	Final demand United States	Final demand Asia	Export ROW	Production
Intermediate Input	Japan	-	Axju*	Axja*	-	-	-	-	-
	USA	Axuj*	Axuu*	Axua*	Fduj*	Fduu*	Fdua*	Eur*	Xu*
	Asia	Axaj*	Axau*	Axaa*	Fdaj*	Fdau*	Fdaa*	Ear*	Xa*
Import	ROW	-	Axru*	Axra*	-	-	-		
Value added		-	Vu*	Va*					
Production		-	Xu*	Xa*					

(3) Integration of each activity into one input output table

Asian international input output table			Intermediate demand: non-overseas subsidiaries Japan	United States	Asia	Intermediate demand: overseas subsidiaries United States	Asia	Final demand Japan	United States	Asia	Export ROW	Production
Inter-mediate input	non-overseas subsidiaries	Japan	Axjj~	Axju~	Axja~	Axju*	Axja*	Fdjj~	Fdju~	Fdja~	Ejr~	Xj~
		USA	Axuj~	Axuu~	Axua~			Fduj~	Fduu~	Fdua~	Eur~	Xu~
		Asia	Axaj~	Axau~	Axaa~			Fdaj~	Fdau~	Fdaa~	Ear~	Xa~
	overseas subsidiaries	USA	Axuj*			Axuu*	Axua*	Fduj*	Fduu*	Fdua*	Eur*	Xu*
		Asia	Axaj*			Axau*	Axaa*	Fdaj*	Fdau*	Fdaa*	Ear*	Xa*
Import		ROW	Axrj~	Axru~	Axra~	Axru*	Axra*	Fdrj~	Fdru~	Fdra~		
Value added			Vj~	Vu~	Va~	Vu*	Va*					
Production			Xj~	Xu~	Xa~	Xu*	Xa*					

(4) Input output table, recompiled

Asian international input output table			Intermediate demand: non-overseas subsidiaries Japan	United States	Asia	Intermediate demand: overseas subsidiaries United States	Asia	Final demand Japan	United States	Asia	Export ROW	Production
Inter-mediate input	non-overseas subsidiaries	Japan	Axjj~	Axju~	Axja~	Axju*	Axja*	Fdjj~	Fdju~	Fdja~	Ejr~	Xj~
		USA	Axuj~	Axuu~1	Axua~1	Axuu*1	Axua*1	Fduj~	Fduu~	Fdua~	Eur~	Xu~
		Asia	Axaj~	Axau~1	Axaa~1	Axau*1	Axaa*1	Fdaj~	Fdau~	Fdaa~	Ear~	Xa~
	overseas subsidiaries	USA	Axuj*	Axuu~2	Axua~2	Axuu*2	Axua*2	Fduj*	Fduu*	Fdua*	Eur*	Xu*
		Asia	Axaj*	Axau~2	Axaa~2	Axau*2	Axaa*2	Fdaj*	Fdau*	Fdaa*	Ear*	Xa*
Import		ROW	Axrj~	Axru~	Axra~	Axru*	Axra*	Fdrj~	Fdru~	Fdra~		
Value added			Vj~	Vu~	Va~	Vu*	Va*					
Production			Xj~	Xu~	Xa~	Xu*	Xa*					

Import of intermediate goods from Japan is contained. (Export induced effect)
Export of Intermediate goods from Japan (Export induced effect)
Export of final goods to Japan (Reimport effect)
Purchaging of intermediate goods in the local markets
Export of intermediate goods to Japan (Reimport effect)
These substitute partly the export of Japan (Export substitution effect)

Fig. 1 Recompilation of an international input-output table.

that of Japanese overseas firms and that of non-Japanese firms in the US. The situation is the same for the structure of non-Japanese firms in the US. Consequently, we have to separate these inputs not only for the US but also for Asia. To do this, we need information about the degree to which Japanese firms overseas purchase intermediate goods and services from Japanese firms in the local market and the degree to which they sell intermediate goods and services to non-Japanese firms in the same market. Unfortunately, such information cannot be obtained systematically. In this paper, we divide them up according to their production shares, assuming that purchases depend on the production ability of suppliers.[5]

The recompiled input-output table shows many aspects relating to the activities of Japanese firms overseas. Their intermediate inputs and final demand from Japan are considered in terms of the induced export demand effect for Japan. The table includes exports of intermediate and finished goods and services to Japan, which is described as the re-import effect of Japan. However, in order to measure the export substitution effect, we need additional information regarding the degree to which the final demand of Japan is affected by production at overseas affiliates.

Table 2 is the estimated input-output table, which is aggregated to one sector for each region. From this table, we can find that production by Japanese firms in the US is worth $211.34 billion, which is larger than the $158.62 billion produced by Japanese firms in Asia. Japanese firms sell a great deal of intermediate and finished goods to the local market in both the US and Asia. However, there are some differences between the two markets. In the US market, Japanese firms sell more finished goods than intermediate goods, while the opposite is true in the Asian market. Japan imports more goods and services from Japanese affiliates in Asia than it does from those in the US. The local content ratio of firms in the US seems larger than that of firms in Asia as a whole.

4. Some Simulation Results

In this section, we discuss some results of simulations. The first one is intended to evaluate international links using induced production stemming from one unit increase in final demand by sector and region. Secondly, we outline the regional contribution of Japanese overseas

[5] Because this division of intermediate demand violates the demand-supply relationship, we have modified final demand to compensate for this.

Table 2 Recompiled input-output table. (Unit: $1 billion)

	Intermediate demand					Final demand				
	Japan	United States	Asia	JOS in United States	JOS in Asia	Japan	United States	Asia	Other	Production
Japan	4283.03	31.06	77.07	24.12	26.40	4967.46	65.30	55.01	216.48	9745.93
United States	38.90	5722.33	61.24	71.96	0.94	24.74	6711.06	33.48	580.48	13245.14
Asia	48.45	63.32	2192.48	2.89	47.91	29.00	63.70	1859.97	400.46	4708.18
JOS in United States	4.02	95.12	1.65	2.67	0.03	2.37	103.05	0.87	1.57	211.34
JOS in Asia	13.66	2.40	65.96	0.13	3.00	11.72	2.33	54.55	4.87	158.62
Other	192.80	360.07	273.57	2.09	6.75	87.39	272.74	147.88	0.00	0.00
Value added	5165.07	6970.85	2036.21	107.48	73.59	0.00	0.00	0.00	0.00	0.00
Production	9745.93	13245.14	4708.18	211.34	158.62	5122.68	7218.19	2151.75	1203.86	28069.21

	Intermediate demand					Final demand				
%	Japan	United States	Asia	The United States, Japanese	Asia, Japanese	Japan	United States	Asia	Other	Production
Japan	43.95	0.23	1.64	11.41	16.65	96.97	0.90	2.56	17.98	34.72
United States	0.40	43.20	1.30	34.05	0.59	0.48	92.97	1.56	48.22	47.19
Asia	0.50	0.48	46.57	1.37	30.20	0.57	0.88	86.44	33.26	16.77
The United States, Japanese	0.04	0.72	0.04	1.26	0.02	0.05	1.43	0.04	0.13	0.75
Asia, Japanese	0.14	0.02	1.40	0.06	1.89	0.23	0.03	2.54	0.40	0.57
Other	1.98	2.72	5.81	0.99	4.26	1.71	3.78	6.87	0.00	0.00
Value added	53.00	52.63	43.25	50.86	46.39	0.00	0.00	0.00	0.00	0.00
Production	100.00	100.00	100.00	100.00	100.00	100.00	100.00	100.00	100.00	100.00

production through the induced value added in each region. Finally, we discuss the overall effect of Japanese overseas production on Japan, comparing its induced demand and substitution effects.

4.1. *The induced production of one unit increase in final demand*

Figure 2 shows the degree to which production is induced by one unit increase in final demand by sector and region. The effect on production is the largest in the home market for each sector. Here we mainly examine international interdependence. A unit increase in most manufacturing sectors in Japan has a significant effect on both the US and Asian economies. However, some differences are observed. Final demand increases in food, timber, wood and pulp, and electrical machinery in Japan have a great effect on the US economy. For the Asian economy, the effects of petroleum and coal are the largest, followed by those of textiles, timber, wood and pulp, iron and steel, non-metal products, and electrical machinery.

In the US case, the increase in final demand for electrical machinery in the US has the greatest effect on the Asian economy, followed by transport equipment, precision instruments and textiles. In addition, increases in the final demand for general machinery, electrical machinery, transport equipment, and precision instruments have a significant effect on Japan. This situation arises due to the fact that exports from Japan to the US are concentrated in the machinery sectors, because induced demand is transferred through international trade. The textile sector also has an influence over the Asian economy.

The relationship between the US and Japanese firms in the US economy is very similar to that between the US and the Japanese economy, in both size and direction, which is very interesting. The leading export sectors in Japan, such as electrical machinery and transport equipment, have expanded into the US market through FDI. However, the relationship with Japanese overseas firms in Asia seems very weak.

In the case of Asia, the increase of final demand in the electrical machinery sector has the highest effect on Japan, while the effects of general machinery, transport equipment are also considerable. The

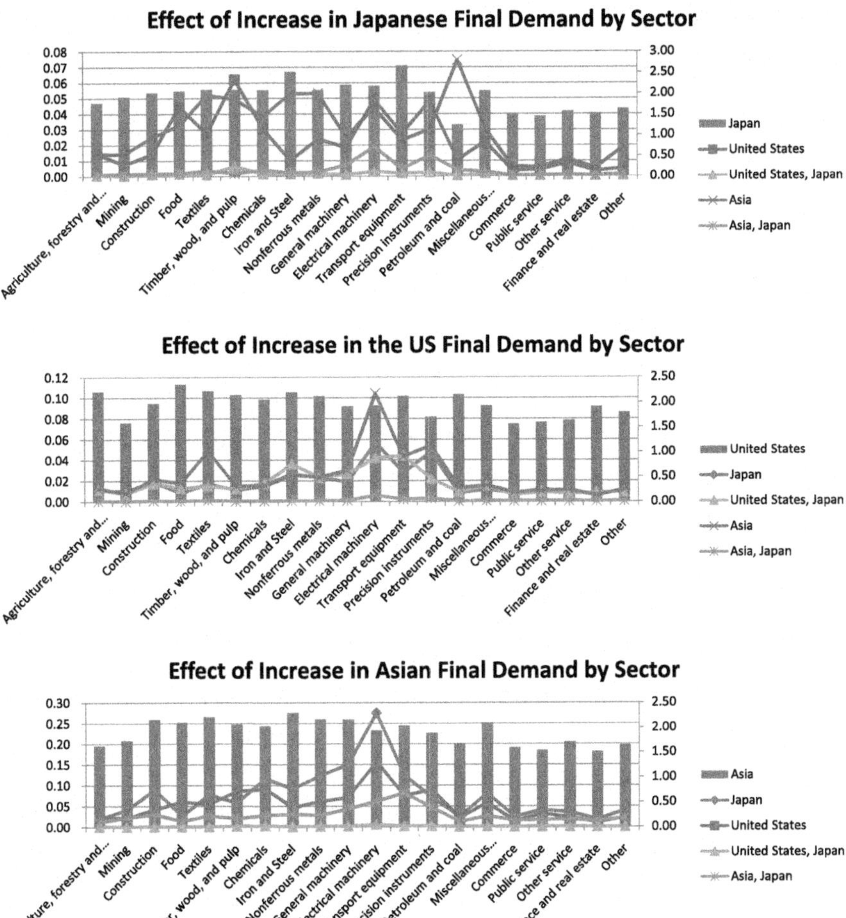

Fig. 2 Induced production stemming from a unit increase of final demand for each sector and country.

Note: The own effect, shown as a bar, is measured on the right-hand axis, while the others, shown as lines, are measured on the left-hand axis.

increase of final demand in Asia's machinery sectors has a relatively large impact on the US economy, but this is not so great as the effect on Japan. Asian production is connected to Japan more than to the US, especially in the machinery sectors. An increase in Asian demand has an impact on Japan overseas affiliates in Asia to some extent, though the effect on Japanese overseas affiliates in the US is almost negligible.

4.2. *Contribution in terms of the induced value added*

The sum of the increases in import demand and value added, which are induced by a unit increase in final demand, is known to be same as the value of the initial increase in final demand (see Matsumura & Fujikawa (1998)). From this relationship, we can evaluate regional contributions to unit production of final demand in terms of value added and imports. Here we are able to determine who benefits from this. Figure 3 shows regional contributions to the production of finished goods by Japanese overseas affiliates in the US and Asia, respectively.

With regard to production by Japanese overseas firms in the US, the contribution of own value added is obviously the highest in almost all sectors. In this case, "own" denotes Japanese overseas firms. Accordingly, we will focus on the contributions of the others in Fig. 3. We find that the US contributions are dominant. Japan makes a relatively significant contribution in the following sectors: general machinery, electrical machinery, precision instruments, petroleum and coal, and miscellaneous manufacturing. Most of these sectors are export-intensive sectors in Japan. The Asian contribution is almost negligible, but slightly more significant in the case of electrical machinery and miscellaneous manufacturing. The contribution of Japanese overseas firms in Asia is also negligible.

In the case of Japanese overseas production in Asia, the contribution of the local economy in Asia is also the largest except in terms of the own contribution. Japan's contribution is almost as much as that of the local economy in the case of the machinery, textile, chemical industry, iron and steel, and non-metal industry sectors. The contribution of the US is not so high, and that of Japanese overseas firms in the US is negligible.

Japan has different patterns in terms of its contributions to overseas firms by sector in the US and Asia. A relatively high contribution is observed in the case of the machinery sectors in the US, though its contribution to overseas firms in Asia is not insignificant in such sectors as textiles, chemical industry, iron and steel, non-ferrous metals and machinery. The relationship between Japanese overseas activities in the US and in Asia seems to be negligible.

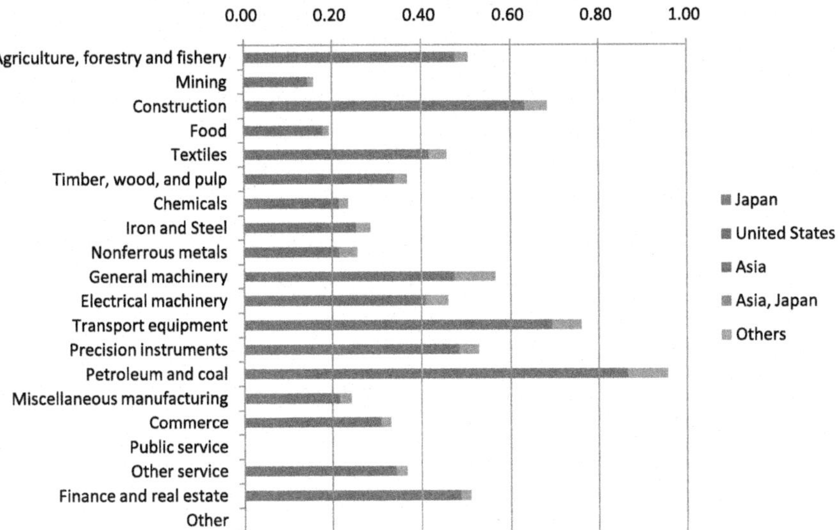

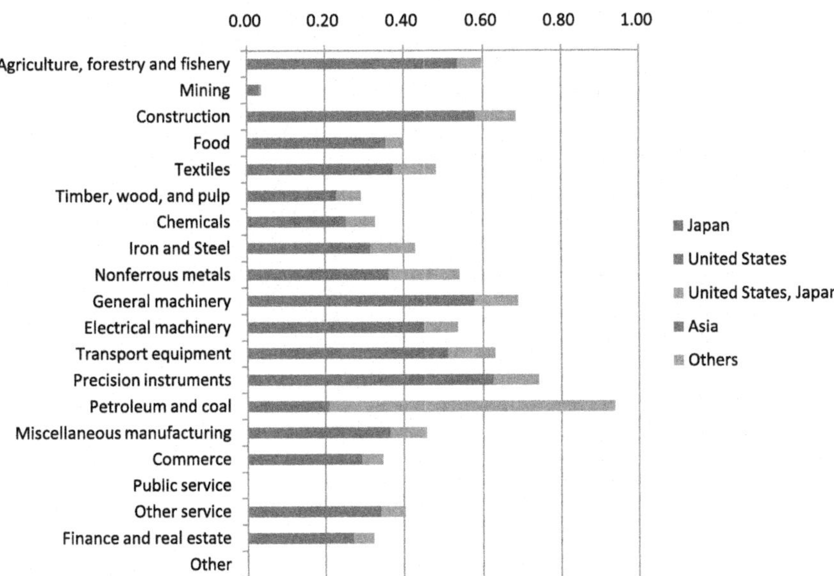

Fig. 3 Value added by region.

4.3. *The induced production effect versus the substitution effect of overseas production*

Finally, we discuss the induced production and substitution effects that Japan incurs due to Japanese overseas production. How much production in Japan is induced by the overseas production of Japanese firms? How much production is substituted by this overseas production?[6]

Table 3 shows the results of a simulation. In Case 1, the induced production of Japanese overseas production is calculated. The production of finished goods by Japanese overseas firms in the US totals $108.99 billion, which increases Japanese production by $30.07 billion and US production by $78.75 billion. Total induced production is $224.53 billion. On the other hand, production by overseas firms in Asia is $73.18 billion, which increases Japanese production by $31.20 billion and US production by $46.51 billion, to give total induced production of $156.12 billion. Although production by overseas firms in Asia is about 70% of the US level, the induced production effects in Japan are almost the same in both cases.

Production by Japanese overseas firms substitutes for Japanese final domestic demand and exports to some extent. What value can be placed on this substitution? If we assume that overseas production substitutes for Japanese final demand completely, the reduction would be $76.74 billion in the US case and $61.29 billion in the Asian case, as shown in Case 2.[7]

In Case 2, we find that Japanese final demand is substituted by $76.74 billion, while Japanese production is reduced by $183.60 billion with regard to overseas production in the US and by $140.04 billion in the case of overseas production in Asia. The reductions in production are dominant only in Japan.

It may, however, be unrealistic to assume full substitution, so our alternative assumption is that final demand is substituted by the same

---

[6]R. E. Lipsey and E. D. Ramstetter (2001) and E. D. Ramstetter (2002) investigated the relationship between affiliate activity in Japan, US multinationals and Japanese exports, concluding that there were no significant negative relationships.

[7]These values are smaller than those of Case 1, because the substitution would be limited to tradable goods.

Table 3 The effect of the Japanese overseas production. Unit: $1 billion

	Case-1		Case-2		Case-3		Case-4		Case-5	
	Induced production effect		Substitution effect		Substitution effect		Induced production and substitution effect		Induced production and substitution effect	
Changes in final demand	Japanese Subsidiary in US	Japanese Subsidiary in Asia	Japanese Subsidiary in US $\alpha = 1$	Japanese Subsidiary in Asia $\alpha = 1$	Japanese Subsidiary in US $\alpha = 0.13$	Japanese Subsidiary in Asia $\alpha = 0.13$	Japanese Subsidiary in US $\alpha = 1$	Japanese Subsidiary in Asia $\alpha = 1$	Japanese Subsidiary in US $\alpha = 0.13$	Japanese Subsidiary in Asia $\alpha = 0.13$
Japan	0.00	0.00	−76.74	−61.29	−10.11	−7.81	−76.74	−61.29	−10.11	−7.81
United States	0.00	0.00	0.00	0.00	0.00	0.00	0.00	0.00	0.00	0.00
Asia	0.00	0.00	0.00	0.00	0.00	0.00	0.00	0.00	0.00	0.00
JOS in United States	108.99	0.00	0.00	0.00	0.00	0.00	108.99	0.00	108.99	0.00
JOS in Asia	0.00	73.18	0.00	0.00	0.00	0.00	0.00	73.18	0.00	73.18
Total	108.99	73.18	−76.74	−61.29	−10.11	−7.81	32.25	11.89	98.88	65.36
Induced Production										
Japan	30.07	31.20	−183.60	−140.04	−24.77	−18.27	−153.53	−108.85	5.29	12.92
United States	78.75	2.69	−2.54	−2.23	−0.34	−0.30	76.22	0.45	78.41	2.38
Asia	3.99	46.51	−2.34	−2.13	−0.30	−0.27	1.65	44.38	3.69	46.24
JOS in United States	111.40	0.09	−0.15	−0.13	−0.02	−0.02	111.25	−0.04	111.38	0.07
JOS in Asia	0.32	75.63	−0.61	−0.64	−0.09	−0.10	−0.30	75.00	0.22	75.54
Total	224.53	156.12	−189.24	−145.18	−25.53	−18.96	35.29	10.94	199.00	137.16
Induced Production(%)										
Japan	27.59	42.63	−168.46	−191.38	−22.73	−24.97	−140.87	−148.74	4.86	17.66
The United States	72.26	3.67	−2.33	−3.05	−0.31	−0.41	69.93	0.62	71.95	3.26
Asia	3.66	63.56	−2.15	−2.92	−0.28	−0.37	1.51	60.65	3.38	63.19
JOS in United States	102.22	0.12	−0.14	−0.18	−0.02	−0.02	102.08	−0.06	102.20	0.10
JOS in Asia	0.29	103.36	−0.56	−0.87	−0.08	−0.13	−0.27	102.49	0.21	103.22
Total	206.01	213.34	−173.64	−198.39	−23.42	−25.91	32.38	14.95	182.59	187.43

*The value of final demand in Case-1 is not equal the sum of the corresponding final demand in the Table 2, because the statistical discrepancy, which is included in the Table 2, is excluded here.

proportion as the share of Japanese exports among total world exports in each sector; this constitutes Case 3. The export shares are shown in the first column of Table 4. The average shares are 13.18% in the US case, and 12.75% in the Asian case. We therefore express these cases as $\alpha = 0.13$ in Tables 3 and 4. As a result, Japanese domestic production is reduced by \$24.77 billion and \$18.27 billion respectively.

Comparing these values, we can gain a picture of the overall effects for the different degrees of substitution. Case 4 shows the overall effect, assuming that overseas production completely substitutes for Japanese final demand. However, if the substitution is more moderate, this might be an overestimate. Then we assume that the substitution is about 13% of average[8] overseas production, as shown in Case 5. In this case, the induced production effect overcomes the substitution effect in Japan as a whole. Japanese domestic production increases by \$5.29 billion due to overseas production in the US, causing own production to reach \$111.38 billion. Of course, the US economy gains mainly in terms of production, while the Asian economy experiences only small gains. On the other hand, overseas production in Asia worth \$75.31 billion causes an increase in Japanese production of \$12.92 billion. The increase in Japanese production in the Asian case is more than twice that seen in the US case, although the value of Japanese overseas production in the US case is actually larger than in the Asian case.

Table 4 shows the effect on Japanese production by sector in Cases 4 and 5. As has already been demonstrated, the overall effects on Japanese production are positive in Case 5. However, we find that production of transport equipment brings about a reduction of \$4.16 billion in the US case, but electrical machinery production gives rise to an increase of \$4.13 billion. Japanese automobile companies began investing in the US market in 1990s, leading to a reduction in automobile exports from Japan. We also find negative effects on the production of precision instruments. We can therefore conclude that the induced production effect overcomes the substitution effect in Japan as a whole. However,

[8]We express these cases as $\alpha = 0.13$ in Tables 3 and 4, because the average export ratio is about 13% in both cases. However, export substitution depends on the different export ratios by sector as stated in Table 4.

Table 4 The effect of Japanese overseas production on Japan. (Unit: $1 billion)

		Case-4		Case-5	
		Induced production and substitution effect on Japan		Induced production and substitution effect on Japan	
	Japanese export ratio to the World Total	Japanese subsidiary in US	Japanese subsidiary in Asia	Japanese subsidiary in US	Japanese subsidiary in Asia
Sectors	(%)	$\alpha = 1$	$\alpha = 1$	$\alpha = 0.13$	$\alpha = 0.13$
1 Agriculture, forestry and fishery	0.52	−1.36	−1.07	0.02	0.03
2 Mining	0.27	−0.45	−0.17	0.01	0.02
3 Construction	0.00	−2.28	−3.65	0.05	0.10
4 Food	0.57	−5.56	−3.72	0.01	0.05
5 Textiles	2.22	−1.08	−3.49	0.07	0.33
6 Timber, wood, and pulp	0.50	−2.40	−1.49	0.13	0.20
7 Chemicals	6.05	−6.69	−3.00	0.29	1.17
8 Iron and Steel	11.26	−5.95	−2.09	0.65	2.42
9 Nonferrous metals	5.23	−3.59	−3.08	0.73	0.89
10 General machinery	14.65	−6.87	−3.61	0.41	0.79
11 Electrical machinery	15.87	−21.04	−28.25	4.13	1.94
12 Transport equipment	15.34	−58.77	−26.18	−4.16	0.34
13 Precision instruments	17.11	−0.91	−2.30	−0.02	−0.06
14 Petroleum and coal	1.94	−0.92	−0.75	0.06	0.17
15 Miscellaneous manufacturing	4.73	−9.81	−7.07	0.49	0.74
16 Commerce	0.00	−6.63	−4.73	1.17	1.57
17 Public service	0.00	−0.37	−0.27	0.02	0.03
18 Other service	0.00	−8.48	−6.54	0.50	0.83
19 Finance and real estate	0.00	−3.02	−2.21	0.18	0.34
20 Other	0.00	−7.34	−5.19	0.57	1.00
Average for US	13.18	—	—	—	—
Average for Asia	12.75	—	—	—	—
Total	—	−153.53	−108.85	5.29	12.92

the hollowing-out of production may be apparent in such sectors as transport equipment and precision instruments.[9]

5. Concluding Remarks

In this paper, we recompile the IDE Asian international input-output table for 1995 to deal explicitly with Japanese overseas production activities and to analyze the relationship between Japanese overseas activities and the economies of the home and invested countries. For this purpose, we make use of METI survey statistics on the overseas activities of Japanese firms in the same year. The recompiled input-output table shows the interdependence among them, allowing us to clarify the role of Japanese overseas firms.

Japanese overseas production in the US is about 2.17% of production of Japan, while that in Asia is 1.63%. Japanese purchases of intermediate and finished goods from subsidiaries in Asia amount to 16.00% of Japanese subsidiaries' production in Asia, whereas purchases from subsidiaries in the US total just 3.02%. On the other hand, the purchase of intermediate goods from Japan is 11.41% of overseas production in the US and 16.64% in Asia. These show that Japanese subsidiaries in Asia have a stronger link to the Japanese economy than do those in the US.

Moreover, looking at the effect on production of increased final demand, the relationship between Japan and Japanese subsidiaries in Asia demonstrates a close interdependence in the case of machinery sectors. In addition, Japanese subsidiaries in the US are affected strongly in the case of US machinery sectors, which is similar to the effect on Japanese production. This reflects the fact that overseas production in the US is concentrated in the machinery sectors, where Japan has export competitiveness.

The simulation of the contribution in terms of value added shows that overseas production is connected, to a considerable extent, to each local economy, i.e. that of the US and Asia. Overseas production affects

[9]This conclusion is heavily dependent on the assumption of substitution. If the substitution ratio is higher than our assumption, the overall effect on Japanese production might be negative, as shown in Case 4, which is an extreme case.

the home country in two different ways: the induced production effect and the substitution effect. The overall effect on home production depends on the degree of substitution. If the degree of substitution is the same as the share of Japanese exports in total world exports for each sector, then the two different effects on home production would cancel each other out. However, hollowing-out in production might occur in such sectors as transport equipment and precision instruments. Of course, these are tentative results. We need more evidence, especially with regard to the degree of the substitution of overseas production.

Issues to be settled when we apply the METI survey to the input-output table include the definition of terms, whether the fiscal or calendar year is used, the definition of sectors, data coverage problems attributable to survey statistics and the definition of Japanese affiliates. In spite of these outstanding issues, our analytical framework provides a new way of investigating the relationship between the home and invested economies arising from overseas production. Furthermore, China is such an important economy as to warrant its being dealt with separately from Asia. The relationship between Japan and Europe is also significant. These issues should be considered in our future research.

References

Inaba, K (1999). *Kaigai Chokusetsu Toushi no Keizaigaku* (The Economics of Foreign Direct Investment), Sobun-sha, Japan.

Institute of Developing Economies (2000). *Asian International Input-Output Table 1995.*

Ito, T and OK Anne (2000). *The Role of Foreign Direct Investment in East Asian Economic Development*, University of Chicago Press.

Fujikawa, K (1999). *Global Keizai no Sangyou Renkan Bunseki* (Input-Output Analysis of the Global Economy), Sobun-sha, Japan.

Fukao, K, Y Tangjun and S Makoto (1999). "Kohyo no Paneruka to Nai-Gaisou ni yoru Kaigai Jigyou Katsudo Kihon Chousa, Doukou Chousa no Boshudan Suikei". (Estimating Total Overseas Business Activities of Japanese Companies from Extrapolations of Panel Data Underlying the Basic and Annual Surveys), in Institute for International Trade and Investment, ed., pp. 3–34 (in Japanese).

Lipsey, RE and DR Eric (2001). Affiliate activity in Japanese and US multinationals and Japanese exports, 1986–1995. ICSEAD Working Paper Series Vol. 2001–29, Kitakyushu, Japan.

Ramstetter, ED (2002). Is Japanese manufacturing really hollowing out? ICSEAD Working Paper Series Vol. 2002–24, Kitakyushu, Japan.

Sano, T and T Chiharu (1994). Asia taiheiyou chiiki no kokusai sangyou renkanhyou (international industrial linkages in the Asia pacific region). *Innovation & I-O Technique*, 5(1), pp. 19–31 (in Japanese).

Yamada, M (2002). Overseas production of Japanese firms and Japan–US interdependence: An input-output analysis. *Journal of Applied Input-Output Analysis*, 8, pp. 15–36.

Chapter 5

Econometric Evaluation of the Fiscal Expansion and Stimulus Packages in Three Asian Countries and the United States*

Taiyo Ozaki*

1. Introduction

During the last few years, the world economy has been hit by global financial shocks. A large amount of government spending on infrastructure and subsidies, called stimulus packages, has been put rapidly into place to rescue the sharply declining economy. Can stimulus packages, however, boost the economy in reality? If they are effective in the short term, then what is the size of the multiplier for GDP from the stimulus packages? There are several conflicting views in relation to this question. As for the multiplier, it ranges from "negative" to two or three. Our research focuses mainly on this topic. There is also another question, in that fiscal expansion will necessarily bring an increase in debt and cause crowding-out effects in the long term. The model employs a fixed-exchange-rate assumption, however, so we

*This chapter was published in *The Journal of Econometric Study of Northeast Asia*, January 2011 (Vol. 7, No. 2). The author would like to express his gratitude to professors Soshichi Kinoshita, Mitsuo Yamada and Jiro Nemoto for their helpful comments.

only evaluate the effects under the crowding-out through domestic absorption.

Regarding the model structure itself, the research is aimed at analyzing the properties of the Asian Link Model developed from 2005–2006, (see Ozaki, 2006), which consists of models for China, Japan, the United States and the ROK and a bilateral trade linkage model. The model is also designed to evaluate the recent fiscal stimulus packages.

This model has expanded conventional econometric models in several directions. One is to carry out further investigation of the changing bilateral trade patterns which include the four countries. Trade relations have been transformed so dramatically that it is inevitable that many countries assign a vertical structure to production across boundaries, and we must develop a new method which is more flexible and is able to evaluate properly the indirect role of third-country effects. Changes in trading patterns require the expressing of the explicit relationships in substitution or complementation effects between nations. We tried applying the translog function to the import share functions. Another direction is that the model uses forward-looking variables to evaluate the anticipated expectations in new economic policy. Recent neo-Keynesian econometric models usually adopt these formulations in the specification of consumption, and investment functions, *et al.* As we have no exact information about the future, however, the historical data in the forerunning period are assumed to be the future expected values and we estimate the parameters which give the minimum prediction errors; in this sense, the expectation is called "model-consistent" rather than "rational" when the model is simulated for a future period.

The model is annual and data are mainly obtained from OEF (Oxford Economic Forecasting, at present Oxford Economics) and the COMTRADE database, which covers the period from 1980–2005/2006. As the economic structure and the trade relationships have changed so greatly since the collapse of the bubble economy, however, the sample period used here is in reality somewhat reduced to 1990–2005 in many cases.

2. Model and Specifications

1) GDP definition

Each country model has a simple demand-side structure, generally as follows:

GDP = C + IF + GC + X − M
GDPV = CV + IFV + GCV + XV − MV

An affixed "V" denotes a nominal value. This is also the case for the following:

CV = PC*C/100
IFV = PIF*IF/100
GCV = PGC*GC/100
XV = PX*X/100
MV = PM*M/100

2) Consumption

The consumption function is formulated applying the Permanent Income Hypothesis, in which technically "model-consistent" expectations (sometimes confused with rational expectations) are assumed. This type of specification originally appeared in MULTIMOD, IMF (1998), in which forward-looking formulations were adopted.

The income constraint for a household is as follows;

$$W_{t+1} = (1 - t_w)YL_t - C_t + (1 + r)W_t$$

where W = wealth, t_w = tax rate, YL = household income, C = consumption, and r = interest rate.

We made the assumption of determining the consumption at the present time under the conditions maximizing the discounted total utility/income in the future:

$$\max_{C_t} E\left(\sum_{i=0}^{\infty}\left(\frac{1}{1+\delta}\right)^i u(C_{t+i})|\Omega\right)$$

where u = utility function, δ = discount rate, and Ω = the available information set.

The expectation of future gain is approximately substituted for the expectation of the series for future income. There are many types of expectation such as a typical distributed lag model, but the most natural way to express future income is to induce forward-looking variables.

$$E\left(\sum_{i=0}^{\infty}\left(\frac{1}{1+\delta}\right)^{i} u(C_{t+i})|\Omega\right) = E\left(\sum_{i=0}^{\infty}\left(\frac{1}{1+\delta}\right)^{i} YL_{t+i}|\Omega + W_t\right)$$

$$C_t = \left(\frac{\delta}{1+\delta}\right) E\left(\sum_{i=0}^{\infty}\left(\frac{1}{1+\delta}\right)^{i}(1-t_w)YL_{t+i} + W_t\right)$$

The final specification of the consumption function is given by:

$$C_t = c_0 + c_1\left(\sum_{i=0}^{\infty}\left(\frac{1}{1+\delta}\right)^{i}(1-t_w)YL_{t+i}\right) + c_2 W_t$$

The brief notation using EViews is as follows:

C = F(PEDYV/PC*100ΣPENW(+i)/PC(+i)/(1 + RLG(+i)))

where PEDY = disposabl eincome, PENW = wealth, and RLG = interest rate.

The table below shows the propensity to consume of each country; it should be noted that Japan has a low propensity and the United States has a high propensity, exceeding 1.0 in the long term.

PEDYV = PEWFP + PEOY − TY

Table 1 Propensity to consume.

	Income	Lag	Wealth
China	0.85 (*)	with lag	0.005
Japan	0.68 (*)	with lag	0.01
ROK	0.81 (*)	without lag	0.06
US	1.04 (*)	with lag	0.001

(*) propensity to consume in the long term

where PEWFP = wage income, PEOY = property income, and TY = income tax.

SV = PEDYV − CV
PENW = PENW(−1) + SV

where SV = savings.

PEWFP = F(ER*ET)

where ER = earnings per capita, and ET = employment.

PEOY = F(RLB*PENW)
TY = F(PEDYV)

3) Investment

The ratio of the shadow value of capital to the unit of investment is known as the marginal Q, and this derives from the linear relationship between marginal Q and investment.

The marginal Q here is defined by the following formulation originally developed in Behr and Bellgardt (2002).

In the basic Q-model, firms are assumed to maximize the expected value of the sum of discounted profits:

$$\max_{\pi_t} E\left(\sum_{i=0}^{\infty}\left(\frac{1}{1+\delta}\right)^i \pi_{t+i}\,|\Omega\right)$$

where π = corporate profit.

We assume a Cobb-Douglas production function, $Y_t = AK_t^{\alpha}L_t^{\beta}$, and a profit function as follows:

$$\pi_t = pAK_t^{\alpha}L_t^{\beta} - w_t - q_t I_t$$

where p = output price, K = capital stock, L = labor, w = wage rate, q = unit cost of investment, and I = investment.

The marginal productivity of capital, MPK, is given by:

$$\frac{\partial\pi}{\partial K} = \frac{\partial Y}{\partial K}p + \frac{\partial p}{\partial Y}\frac{\partial Y}{\partial K}Y = \theta\frac{Yp}{K}$$

Here we presume $Yp \approx V$ (value added), therefore the estimate of θ is:

$$\hat{\theta} = \frac{\sum (r_i + d_i)}{\sum \frac{V_i}{K_i}}$$

The ratio of the shadow value of capital to the unit of investment is known as the marginal Q, and this derives from the linear relationship between the marginal Q and investment.

The marginal Q is defined by the next formulation:

$$Q_t = \sum_{i=1}^{\infty} E(MPK_i)\frac{(1+d_t)^i}{(1+r_t)^i} \approx \hat{\theta}\sum_{i=1}^{\infty} \frac{1}{(1+r_t)^i}\frac{V_i}{K_i}$$

As $d_t = \bar{d}$ is assumed, the effect of the depreciation is absorbed in $\hat{\theta}$. Lastly, we get the specification of the investment function:

$$\frac{I_t}{K_{t-1}} = \alpha_0 + \alpha_1\left(\sum_{i=1}^{\infty} \frac{1}{(1+r_t)^i}\frac{GDP_i}{K_i}\right) + \alpha_2\frac{Z_t}{K_{t-1}}$$

$$K_t = I_t + (1 - d_t)K_{t-1}$$

where Z = additional explanatory variables such as the corporate operating surplus.

IF = IBUD + IFOR + ILON + IFF

where IBUD = investment from government funds, IFOR = investment via foreign capital, ILON = investment via private loans, and IFF = private corporate investment.

IFF/K(−1) = F(ΣGDP(i)/K(i)/(1 + RLG(i)) Z(k)/K(−1))

where ΣGDP(i)/K(i)/(1 + RLG(i)) = a proxy for marginal Q, and Z(k) = additional elements such as:

Z1 = COGTP
Z2 = RLB*PENW
Z3 = money supply, etc.

Table 2 Investment functions.

	ΣGDP(i)/K(i)	*t*-value	Z(k)/K(−1)	*t*-value
China	0.22	3.29	43.1 (**)	4.05
Japan	0.20	2.18	21.5 (*)	2.48
ROK	0.13	0.94	50.1 (**)	3.46
US	0.43	3.71	27.0 (**)	1.27

(*) Z = money supply
(**) Z = corporate profit
K = IFF + K(−1)

The estimated parameters are as follows:
China's foreign investment

$$IFOR = F(GDP(i)W(i)/W(j)GDP(j))$$

Foreign investment (FDI inflow) in China is substantially affected by Japan's GDP.

A typical example is as follows:

$$\log(IFOR) = -49.5 - 0.08^{*}\log(ER\$/WWC\$) + 0.86^{*}\log(CN\_GDP) + 3.63^{*}\log(JP\_GDP)$$

In this estimation, CN_GDP is not significant, and its elasticity is rather low.

4) Exports and Imports

Drastic changes in trading patterns have taken place since 1995. The role of China especially is rapidly becoming greater in exports to and imports from the rest of the world. Alongside this, the ROK has reinforced its dependency on China and the United States. In contrast, Japan increases its exports in the area of industrial supplies, in particular, and this causes the increase in imports of equipment and components from developing countries through FDI.

By way of an example, US imports have been growing, and if exports from Japan have diminished, the reduction must have been filled by third-country exports; therefore US imports are not determined solely by bilateral relationships. The role of trade substitution and complementation with third countries is becoming greater notwithstanding the conventional bilateral trade relationships.

Table 3 Trading partners: Exports and imports.

	China	Japan	US	Korea	RW	World	
China	—	$T(c,j)$					
Japan	$T(j,c)$	—	$T(j,u)$	$T(j,k)$	$T(j,r)$	$T(j,w)$	XV$ Total Export
US		$T(u,j)$	—				
Korea		$T(k,j)$		—			
RW		$T(r,j)$			$T(r,r)$		
World		$T(w,j)$					
		MV$ Toatal Import					

Trade functions are specified by each of the combinations of trading partners (see Table 3). The row sum for Japan, for example, equals the total exports of Japan, with X$V denoting nominal exports in US dollars, and the column sum M$V consequently equals Japan's total imports.

The functions, as we present later, contain indirect relative price combinations to reflect the substitution effects with respect to third-party countries.

Consider a specific bilateral trade relationship between countries i and j. Of course country i has several options regarding trading partners importing and/or exporting goods. In the conventional model, the formulation of export T_{ij}, or import T_{ji} is typically a function of the demand of country j and the relative price, $\frac{p_i}{p_j}$. This model implicitly implies that the domestic demand of country j can be substituted by foreign goods from country i, but it does not describe explicitly how the change in the $i-j$ relationship affects the $i-k$ relationship.

To avoid this problem, we adopt the translog function formation to denote the $j-i$ and $i-k$ relationships.

We assume a linear homogeneous function:

$$M = f(M_1, M_2, \dots)$$

where M = total real imports, and M_j = imports from country j, with $j = 1, 2, 3, 4$ here.

To minimize the cost function of M, we use the translog function with a second-order approximation, and this is denoted by:

$$\ln MV = \ln \alpha_0 + \sum_{i=1}^{n} \alpha_i \ln P_i + \frac{1}{2}\sum_{i=1}^{n}\sum_{j=1}^{n} \gamma_{ij} \ln P_i P_j$$

$$+ \alpha_M \ln M + \frac{1}{2}\gamma_{MM}(\ln M)^2 + \sum_{i=1}^{n} \gamma_{iM} \ln P_i \ln M$$

where MV = total cost, namely total imports in nominal terms.

Using Shephard's lemma:

$$\frac{\partial \ln MV}{\partial \ln P_i} = \frac{\partial MV}{\partial P_i}\frac{P_i}{MV} = \frac{P_i M_i}{MV} = S_i$$

$$= \alpha_i + \sum_{j=1}^{n} \gamma_{ij} \ln P_i + \gamma_{iM} \ln M$$

$$= \alpha_i + \sum_{j=1}^{n} \gamma_{ij} \ln P_i + \gamma'_{iM} \ln GDP$$

and here we simply assume that $M = f(GDP)$.

The parameter constraints are as follows:

$$\sum_{i=1}^{n} \alpha_i = 1$$

$$\sum_{j=1}^{n} \gamma_{ij} = 0$$

$$\sum_{i=1}^{n} \gamma_{iM} = 0$$

The sum of column j of $T(i, j)$ equals the total imports of country j. Each element reflects the export prices of the respective countries, which differ from each other, and form the composite import prices.

In reality, parameter constraints are so crucial that we only adopt $\sum \gamma_{ij} = 0$, and some calibration techniques to estimate parameters are applied: for example, we assume the demand elasticity of the importing country and the elasticity of the export price to be 0.1 and −0.01, respectively, if the estimation is not successfully carried out and it is needed.

Crude oil and natural gas are imported from the rest of the world and treated separately to be able to evaluate the effect of oil price changes: they are treated as exogenous, however.

5) Deriving Import Prices and Imports in Real Terms

In this model the export price is fixed and treated as an exogenous variable, while the import price is determined as the combination of the export prices of partner countries. For the purposes of illustration, we refer to the case for China:

$$
\begin{aligned}
&\mathrm{CN\_M\$V} = \mathrm{T(jpcn)\$} + \mathrm{T(krch)\$} + \mathrm{T(usch)\$} + \mathrm{T(rsch)\$}\\
&\mathrm{CN\_M\$} = \mathrm{T(jpch)\$/JP\_PX\$}{*}100 + \mathrm{T(krch)\$/KR\_PX\$}{*}100\\
&\qquad\qquad + \mathrm{T(usch)\$/US\_PX\$(us)}{*}100 + \mathrm{XVrsch\$}\\
&\mathrm{MVrsch\$} = \mathrm{MOIL\$} + \mathrm{MGAS\$} + \mathrm{MCOAL\$} + \mathrm{MrsCN\_others\$}\\
&\mathrm{CN\_PM\$} = \mathrm{CN\_MV\$/CN\_M\$}{*}100\\
&\mathrm{PM} = \mathrm{F(CN\_PM\$}{*}\mathrm{CN\_RXD)}\\
&\mathrm{MV} = \mathrm{F(CN\_M\$V}{*}\mathrm{CN\_RXD)}\\
&\mathrm{M} = \mathrm{MV/PM}{*}100
\end{aligned}
$$

6) Tax and Financial Sector

Example: China

$$\mathrm{TAXES} = \mathrm{TXAV} + \mathrm{TXIV} + \mathrm{TXTV} + \mathrm{TY} + \mathrm{TXOTH} + \mathrm{TINT}$$

where TXAV = tax on the agricultural sector, TXIV = tax on industry and commerce, TXTV = tariff on trade, TY = income tax, TXOTH = tax, miscellaneous, and TINT = tax on interest.

$$
\begin{aligned}
&\mathrm{GREV} = \mathrm{TAXES} + \mathrm{GREVO}\\
&\mathrm{GEXP} = \mathrm{GCV} + \mathrm{GIV} + \mathrm{GEOTH}\\
&\mathrm{GB} = \mathrm{GBPRIM}\\
&\quad = \mathrm{GREV} - \mathrm{GEXP} = -(\mathrm{GGDBTX}) = \mathrm{GGDBT} - \mathrm{GGDBT}(-1)
\end{aligned}
$$

7) Money Demand and Interest Rates

We chose the model with the monetary policy rule formulated originally by Clarida, Gali and Gertler (2000) and re-quoted in Cho and Moreno

(2006). The theoretical model is as follows:

$$R_t = \alpha + \rho R_{t-1} + (1 - \rho)[\beta E_t \hat{p}_{t+1} + \beta YGAP] + \varepsilon_{MP}$$

R_t is the combination of the past interest rate and the expected inflation rate and the deviation of output from the trend or the potential output. ε_{MP} is the monetary policy rules or the monetary shocks. The parameter α denotes the long-term reaction of the central bank to the expected inflation, and in addition β denotes the measure to evaluate the effects of the deviation of the output from the potential output, and here we adopt the money supply as a proxy instead of the difference in GDP.

The short-term interest rate

$$\mathrm{RSH} = \mathrm{F}(\alpha \mathrm{RSH}(-1)\ (1-\alpha)\mathrm{PGDP}(+1)/\mathrm{PGDP}\beta \mathrm{MON}/\mathrm{PGDP})$$

The long-term interest rate

$$\mathrm{RLG} = \mathrm{F}(\alpha \mathrm{RLG}(+1)\ (1-\alpha)\mathrm{RLG}(-1)\beta \mathrm{RSH})$$

8) Balance of Payments

RES\$ = RES\$(−1) + BCU\$ + BCAP\$
BCU\$ = X\$V − M\$V

X\$V = nominal exports in dollars
M\$V = nominal imports in dollars

BCAP\$ = FDI\$ + NFDI\$

9) Deflators and Price Indexes

Most deflator equations involve wage variables (earnings: ER) as a main explanatory variable. Wage growth is conventionally linked to the

Table 4 Interest rate functions.

	α	t-value	β	t-value
China	0.63	3.28	−0.99	−1.66
Japan	0.68	6.43	−1.50	−1.59
Korea	0.59	9.70	−3.51	−7.11
US	0.59	6.01	−2.16	−1.00

Phillips curve in which the difference in GDP is usually applied instead of the unemployment rate. This kind of specification seems to make the model unstable during simulation from 1990, however. Therefore, we adopt the formulation that labor productivity affects earnings in the long term.

$$\log ER_i = \alpha + \beta \log\left(\frac{GDP_t}{L_t}\right) + \gamma \log PC_{t-1}$$

This type of specification is rather conventional. We tried several types of specification in the context of the aggregate supply equation for new Keynesian macro models (Calvo, 1983; and Cho and Moreno, 2006); simulation results were not satisfactory, however.

PGDP = GDPV/GDP*100
PC = F(PC(−1) ER)
PIF = F(PM ER)
PGC = F(PC)
PX = exogenous
PM = determined by the trade sector, a combination of the prices of exporting countries

10) Labor

ET = F(GDP GDP(−1)/ET(−1))
U = LS − ET
URATE = U/LS*100
ET = employment
U = unemployment
LS = labor supply

3. Testing the Model

To test and simulate the model, we need a slightly complicated procedure to deal with forward-looking variables, which was originally developed in Fair (1984) and sometimes called the "extended path method". This method calculates future expected values to determine the present value of endogenous variables; therefore, for example,

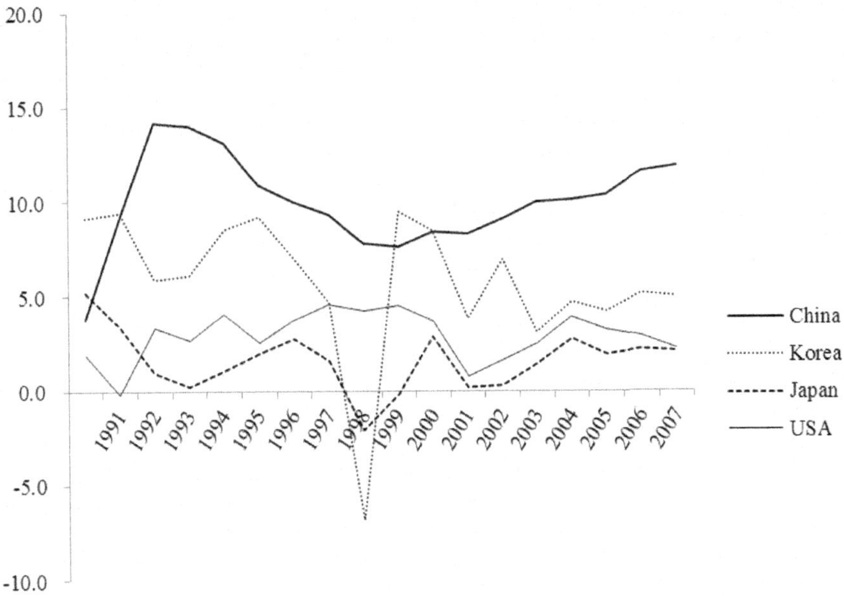

Fig. 1 The growth rates of the four countries.

Table 5 MAPEs.

	GDP	GDPV	C	IF	X	M	PGDP	ET	U
China	1.5	4.4	2.0	4.5	1.3	8.1	3.0	2 3	47.8
Japan	1.9	3.3	0.5	5.2	5.0	1.1	1.4	0.7	13.7
USA	2.4	3.5	2.8	2.4	3.0	5.2	1.2	0.8	15.5
Korea	5.5	6.4	5.7	7.0	6.7	7.8	2.0	2.1	54.1

MAPE(%) 2000–2005

future GDP affects present consumption because we usually anticipate policy changes in the future.

We carried out the final test from 1990 to 2005, and the results with GDP as the baseline for each country are presented below.

In the Asian models, it seems rather difficult to follow up on the deep trough during the 1997–1999 crisis.

The MAPEs (the Mean Absolute Percent Errors) regarding the principal endogenous variables for the period 2000–2005 are shown in the table below. The Korea model has somewhat larger errors for some key variables and needs to be improved, and the same is true for the results for unemployment.

4. Simulation and Results

1) Simulation Scenarios

Case 1: *Fiscal expansion of China* = government investment +1% of real GDP, sustained shock

Case 2: *Fiscal expansion of Japan* = as above

Case 3: *Fiscal expansion of the US* = as above

Case 4: *Fiscal expansion of Korea* = as above

Case 5: *China's expansion of government investment*
= +3.2% of nominal GDP for the 1st year, +5.2% for the second year, as a part of the recent big stimulus package (Mizuho study, the maximum among similar estimates)

It was announced that fiscal expenditure will almost exceed 4,000 billion yuan in total, which amounts for almost 16.0% of nominal GDP as of 2007. However, several organizations such as the IMF (2009a), the Financial Times (15 November 2008) and the Mizuho Research Institute (Japan, 2009) have estimated that expenditure in reality may be restricted to a smaller amount than that announced. Some example estimates follow:

IMF:= 1,100 billion yuan over 3 years, 4.4% of nominal GDP (as of 2007)
Financial Times:= 1,180 billion yuan in 2 years (4.7%)
Mizuho Bank:= 2,100 billion yuan in 2 years (8.4%), 1st year = 800, 2nd year = 1,300 (3.2% and 5.2%, respectively) billion yuan

Case 6: *The US increase in government investment*
As a part of the recent big stimulus package, we assume an increase in investment by 0.742% of nominal GDP for the first year, 0.895% (second year), and 0.548% (third year) according to the proportions quoted by the IMF (2009a).

Table 6 IMF estimates for stimulus packages US Stimulus Package (in billions of dollars, CY basis).

	2009	2010	2011	Total
Total	283	259	121	663
(in percent of GDP)	2.0	1.8	0.8	4.6
Revenue measures	99	116	37	252
Individual income	37	80	32	149
Corporate income	57	32	−2	87
Other	5	4	7	16
Expenditure measures	184	143	84	411
Infrastructure and other	32	47	47	126
Safety nets	77	14	5	96
State aid and education	75	82	32	189

Source: US CBO; Fund staff estimates
Note: This table is quoted from the IMF (2

Table 7 Tax cuts as percentage of nominal GDP.

	1st year	2nd year	3rd year
Income tax cut	0.26	0.56	0.22
Corporate tax cut	0.40	0.22	0.0
Safety net	0.53	0.10	0.0

(*) Calculated from the IMF table above

Here, we assume that the expenditure on infrastructure, state aid and education can be regarded as government investment, which amounts to US$314 billion in total, and is 2.18% of nominal GDP as of 2007. Therefore the figure used in the simulation is rather less than the total for the stimulus packages.

Case 7: *US fiscal expansion* = a package of tax cuts and subsidies

Case 8: *Appreciation of the yuan (China)* = +10%, sustained shock is assumed

Case 9: *Appreciation of the yen (Japan)* = +10%, sustained shock is assumed

Table 8 Summary of stimulus packages Stimulus packages in Large countries (in percent of GDP).

	2008	2009	2010	Total
Canada	0.0	1.5	1.3	2.7
China	0.4	2.0	2.0	4.4
France	0.0	0.7	0.7	1.3
Germany	0.0	1.5	2.0	3.4
India	0.0	0.5	...	0.5
Italy	0.0	0.2	0.1	0.3
Japan	0.4	1.4	0.4	2.2
U.K.	0.2	1.4	−0.1	1.5
US	1.1	2.0	1.8	4.8
Average 1/	0.5	1.6	1.3	3.4

Source: Fund staff estimate
1/PPP GDP-weighted average

Lastly we quote the IMF summary on Stimulus Packages in Large Countries (IMF, 2009a):

2) The Multipliers of Government Investment

Cases 1 to 4 show the multipliers of fiscal expansion for the four countries. As we know, there is debate on the magnitude of the multipliers which range from "negative" to 2 or 3. On average, many studies report that a 1% increase in government investment has been found to increase GDP by close to 1%. See IMF (2009b), Taylor (2009), ESRI (Japan, Cabinet Office, 2008), Christiansen (2008), Botman and Laxton (2006), Perotti (2005), and Ban (2000, 2002). Our results are shown in the following table, in which multipliers affecting the countries themselves range from 1.04 to 1.49. Fiscal expansion in both Japan and the United States does not appear to have such a great effect on their own economies, but does on those of China and Korea.

Comparing the United States and Japan, the United States is more dominant over the developing countries, whereas the role of Japan has recently diminished, but still has a large influence both on China and Korea. It is notable that China's expansion causes a 0.19%

Table 9 Fiscal expansion multipliers (peak values).

		Peak Effect on GDP of.			
Multiplier Summury		China	Japan	US	Korea
Expansion in Government Investment in.	China	1.49	0.04	0.00	0.19
	Japan	0.08	1.16	0.01	0.16
	US	0.19	0.02	1.21	0.21
	Korea	0.01	0.01	0.00	1.04

increase in Korea's GDP and Korea has accelerated its dependency on China.

Dong He, Zhiwei Zhang and Wenlang Zhang (2009) estimate the Chinese multiplier to be around 1.1 in the medium term, as fiscal spending leads to higher household consumption and corporate investment over time. However, this seems rather low compared to other research considering the structural models of input-output frameworks.

Our results are shown in the graphs below:

Regarding multipliers for Japan, Fumikazu Hida *et al.* (2009, ESRI) report the effect of government investment (1% of real GDP) to be 1.0 for the first year, which is a little lower than our result. In their paper

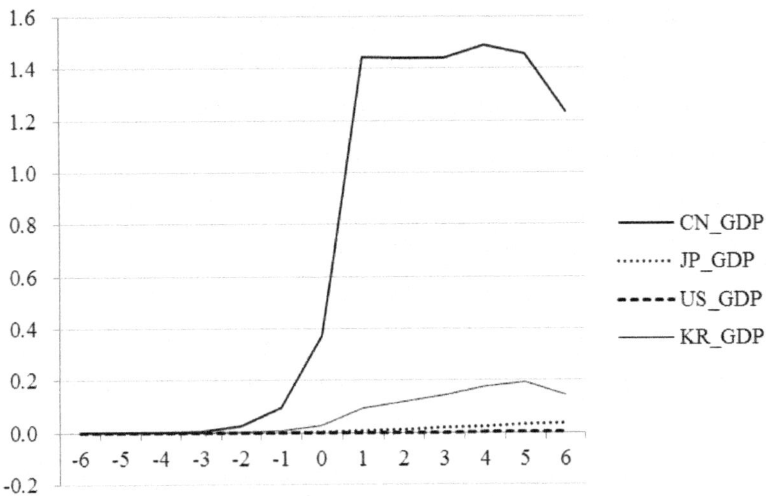

Fig. 2 Fiscal expansion multiplier.

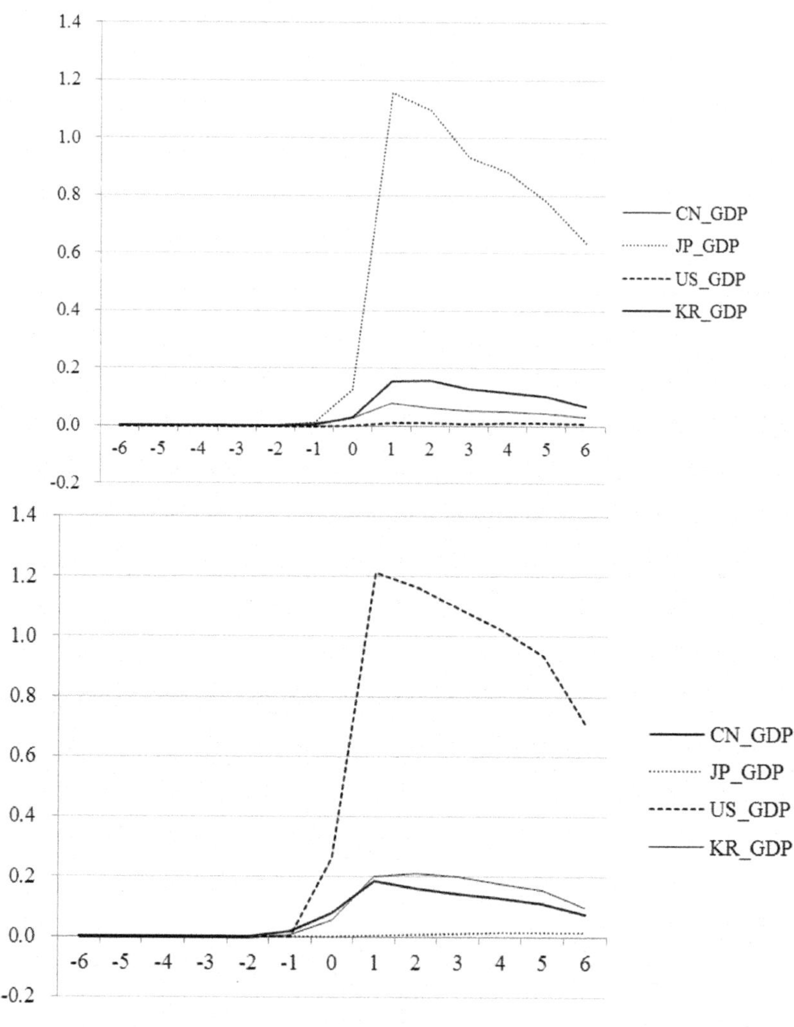

Fig. 2 (*Continued*)

they also argue that the effects of tax cuts will remain less than 60% of those in the case of increased investment, and the interest rate will decline in the short term.

John F Cogan, Tobias J Cwik and John B Taylor (2009) report on the multiplier for the US economy. It is in the range 1.4–1.5 at its peak, and declines rapidly to zero.

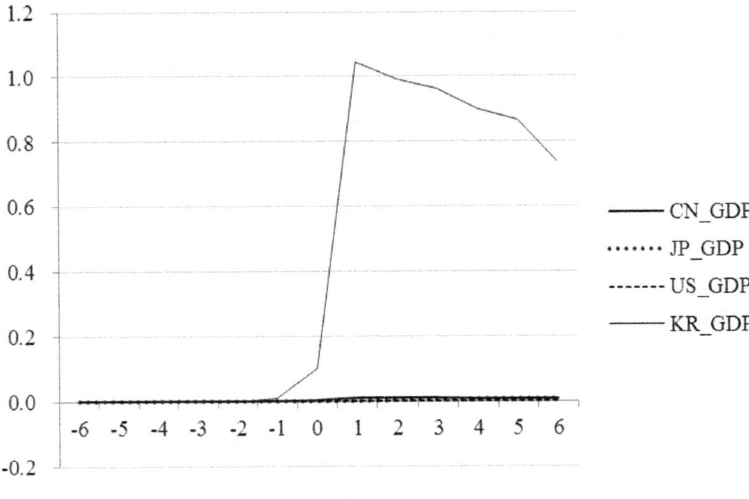

Fig. 2 (*Continued*)

In general the multipliers become smaller for every nation, which reflects the lack of private-sector response and the shift to lower multiplier spending. As we have shown, the fiscal expansion multipliers range from 1.04 to 1.49, which depends on the ratio of investment to total demand, the structure of consumption and the import elasticity relative to GDP and how it raises interest rates in the long term. As for Korea, the increase in GDP augments imports which tend to function to reduce the multiplier.

In the case of Korea the multiplier is the lowest, which is due to the openness of the Korean economy, expanding leakages via trade channels.

China has a strong dependency on the United States, followed by Japan. At the same time, Korea is increasing its dependency on China.

3) The Domestic Effects of Fiscal Expansion

Using the same simulation as above, we examined the domestic effects of fiscal expansion. As the scenario is designed to increase government investment, IF (investment) is necessarily the leading category for demand, whose multipliers range from 3 to 5. However, in the case of Korea, government investment has some tendency to come round to support households and boost consumption.

Table 10 1–3 year average effects of fiscal expansion (%).

	GDP	GDPV	C	IF	X	M	ET (Labor)	PGDP
China	1.44	1.70	0.38	3.87	0.00	0.87	0.46	0.25
Japan	1.06	1.28	0.42	3.40	0.01	0.83	0.16	0.22
US	1.16	1.38	0.25	5.24	0.00	0.40	0.49	0.22
Korea	1.00	1.40	0.51	3.37	0.00	0.71	0.36	0.40

In every country, the fiscal expansion will bring an increase in price deflators by 0.2–0.4%. Among the four nations, Japan has the lowest increase in employment, and the New Deal in Japan will not do much toward increasing new employment.

The distinctive low effect on employment in Japan is shown in the figure below:

4) The Effects of Stimulus Packages

China's stimulus package

China's stimulus package has a great effect on its economy. It raises GDP by 5.88% and also boosts the ROK economy, which greatly depends on China's economy, by 0.63%. In the long term, however, the effects will slow to less than 1%.

This fiscal expansion will increase employment up to 2.47%. Excess employment, however, should be adjusted in the long term: it will fall

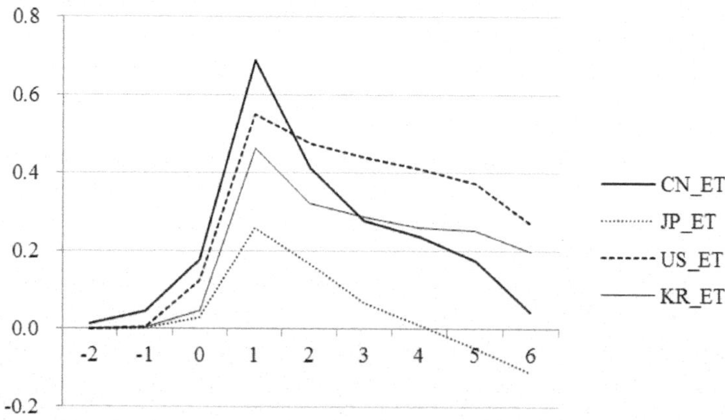

Fig. 3 Effects on employment.

Table 11 The effects of China's stimulus package.

	CN_GDP	JP_GDP	US_GDP	KR_GDP
−2	0.09	0.00	0.00	0.01
−1	0.34	0.00	0.00	0.04
0	1.33	0.00	0.00	0.14
1	5.24	0.01	0.01	0.51
2	5.88	0.01	0.01	0.63
3	−0.02	0.01	0.00	−0.02
4	0.38	0.01	0.00	0.04
5	0.42	0.01	0.00	0.07
6	0.30	0.01	0.00	0.04

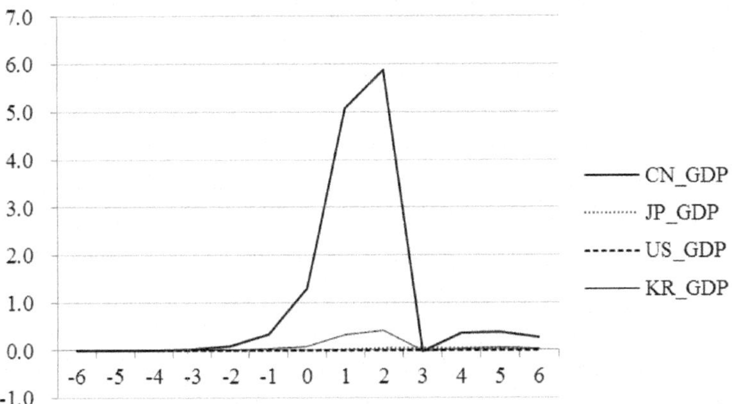

Fig. 4 China's stimulus package.

to −2% within a few years. On the other hand, it is notable that the rise in the GDP deflator will remain less than 1%.

The US stimulus package: government investment

The results for the US stimulus package, which is limited only to the area of construction and related spending, appear somewhat similar to those from the test for fiscal expansion above. The effect on GDP is estimated to be around 0.94%, and expected to increase employment by up to 0.42%.

As for the effects on the world economy, a 0.94% expansion of the US economy brings on a rather small increase in the world economy,

Table 12 The domestic effects for China.

	CN_GDP	CN_GDPV	CN_ET	CN_PGDP
−2	0.09	0.10	0.04	0.01
−1	0.34	0.38	0.16	0.04
0	1.33	1.47	0.64	0.14
1	5.24	5.90	2.47	0.63
2	5.88	6.97	1.82	1.03
3	−0.02	0.68	−1.92	0.71
4	0.38	1.04	−0.74	0.65
5	0.42	1.00	−0.32	0.57
6	0.30	0.77	−0.20	0.47

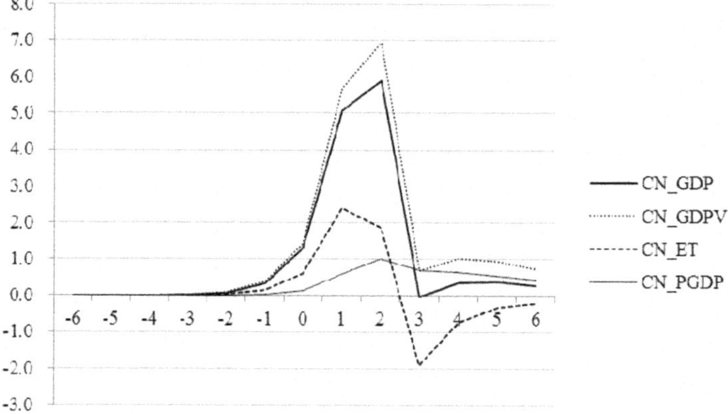

Fig. 5 The domestic effects for China.

remaining negligible for the Japanese economy especially, despite the US expansion.

The US stimulus package: tax cuts and subsidies

This simulation is for the evaluation of the effects relating to the tax cuts and subsidies which are included in the stimulus package and are assumed to increase household disposable income. This stimulus expands US GDP by up to 0.68%, and therefore the combined effect on GDP together with government investment amounts to around 1.61%.

A predominant part of the increase comes from private consumption, which shows a 0.9% increase at its peak. In addition, this

Table 13 The effects of the US stimulus package.

	CN_GDP	JP_GDP	US_GDP	KR_GDP
−2	0.00	0.00	0.01	0.00
−1	0.01	0.00	0.06	0.01
0	0.02	0.00	0.25	0.02
1	0.05	0.00	0.94	0.07
2	0.04	0.00	0.94	0.07
3	0.02	0.00	0.40	0.02
4	0.00	0.00	−0.14	−0.01
5	0.00	0.00	−0.12	−0.01
6	0.00	0.00	−0.09	−0.01

Table 14 The domestic effects for the United States.

	US_GDP	US_GDPV	US_ET	US_PGDP
−2	0.01	0.00	0.00	−0.01
−1	0.06	0.06	0.03	0.00
0	0.25	0.27	0.11	0.01
1	0.94	1.00	0.42	0.06
2	0.94	1.14	0.38	0.20
3	0.40	0.73	0.13	0.32
4	−0.14	0.19	−0.09	0.32
5	−0.12	0.09	−0.05	0.21
6	−0.09	0.03	−0.03	0.11

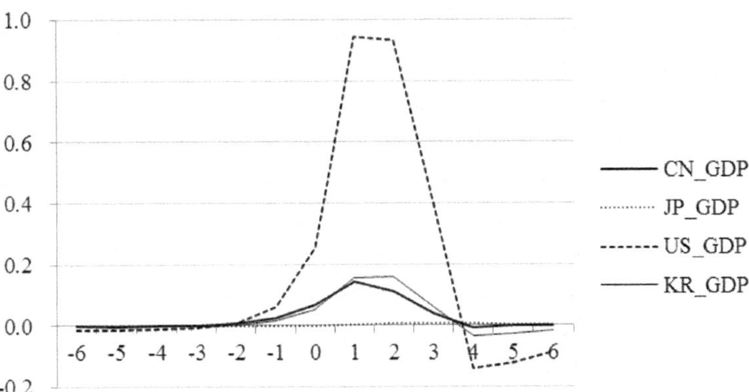

Fig. 6 The US stimulus package.

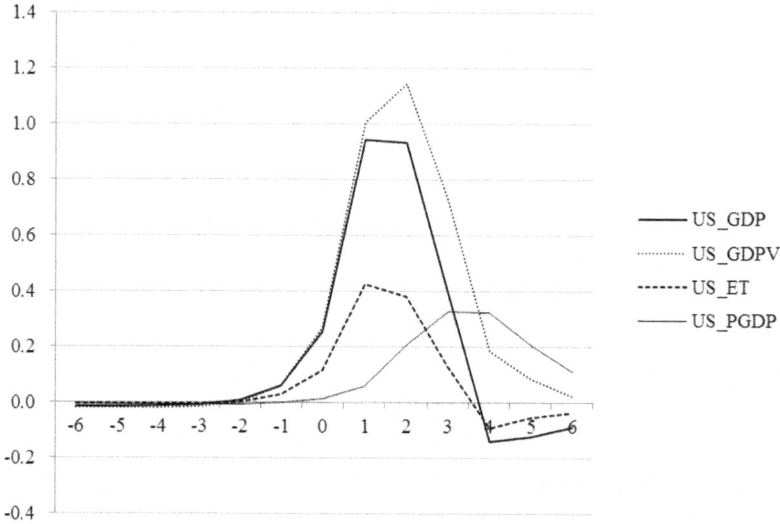

Fig. 7 The domestic effects for the United States.

Table 15 The effects of tax cuts and subsidies.

	CN_GDP	JP_GDP	US_GDP	KR_GDP
−2	0.00	0.00	0.00	0.00
−1	0.00	0.00	−0.12	−0.01
0	0.01	0.00	0.05	0.01
1	0.04	0.00	0.65	0.05
2	0.03	0.00	0.68	0.05
3	0.02	0.00	0.41	0.03
4	0.01	0.00	0.22	0.01
5	0.01	0.00	0.13	0.01
6	0.00	0.00	0.07	0.00

type of fiscal spending has more labor-augmenting characteristics than government investment, and therefore appears to be more efficient in securing employment.

5) Changes in Exchange Rates

Appreciation of the yuan (RMB)

The appreciation of the yuan leads to a drastic slowdown in China's economy by around 3–4%. In addition to this, it is very distinctive that China's slowdown makes other nations' economies shrink at the same

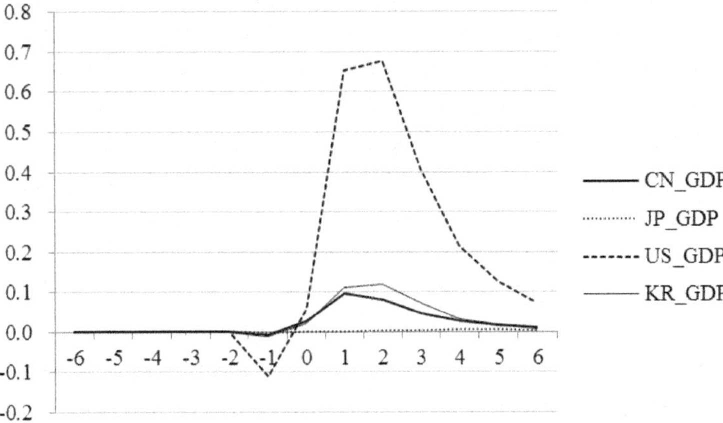

Fig. 8 The effect of tax cuts and subsidies.

Table 16 Domestic effects.

	US_GDP	US_GDPV	US_ET	US_PGDP	US_C
−2	0.00	0.00	0.00	0.00	0.02
−1	−0.12	−0.22	−0.04	−0.10	0.04
0	0.05	−0.04	0.03	−0.09	0.07
1	0.65	0.59	0.30	−0.05	0.69
2	0.68	0.75	0.28	0.07	0.90
3	0.41	0.59	0.15	0.19	0.65
4	0.22	0.44	0.08	0.22	0.35
5	0.13	0.32	0.04	0.20	0.19
6	0.07	0.23	0.03	0.16	0.10

time by up to 1% and its slowdown in exports leads to a simultaneous reduction in Korea's exports.

In Ban (2000), the reduction of GDP is estimated at around 3% in 2001. Our estimate is rather drastic, and this reflects the fact that the Chinese economy has enhanced its export-dependent characteristics compared to previously; the export to GDP ratio was 23% in 2001, and exceeded 34% in 2005.

Appreciation of the yen

The appreciation of the yen also largely affects the Japanese economy: it slows down the GDP of Japan by around −1.3%. There may be a large drop in the GDP of the neighboring country, Korea, of −0.2%.

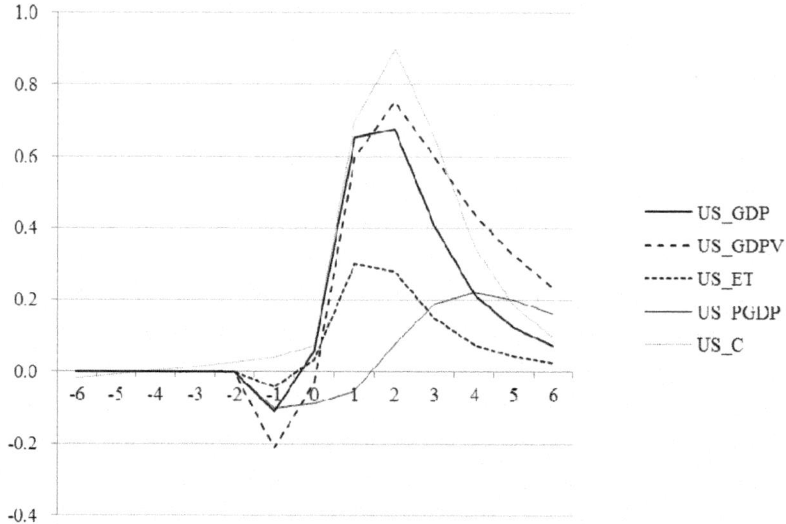

Fig. 9 Domestic effects.

Table 17 Total effect of US stimulus package.

	CN_GDP	JP_GDP	US_GDP	KR_GDP
−2	0.00	0.00	0.00	0.00
−1	0.02	0.00	−0.05	0.00
0	0.09	0.00	0.31	0.07
1	0.24	0.00	1.60	0.26
2	0.19	0.01	1.61	0.28
3	0.09	0.01	0.80	0.13
4	0.02	0.01	0.08	0.00
5	0.02	0.01	0.00	−0.01
6	0.01	0.01	−0.02	−0.01

The reduction in the GDP of Japan will greatly induce simultaneous Chinese and ROK reductions in exports, because of the growing mutual dependency compared with one or two decades before.

For reference, we quote the results of the simulation carried out by Ban (2000), and the reaction of China is quite different compared to the case above. According to their work, the reduction in Japanese exports was simultaneously filled by the exports of third countries, which boosted the other nations' economies. This means that substitution

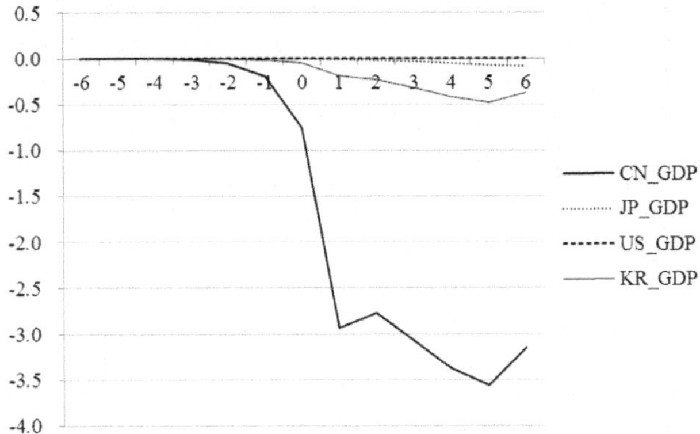

Fig. 10 Effects of the appreciation of the Yuan.

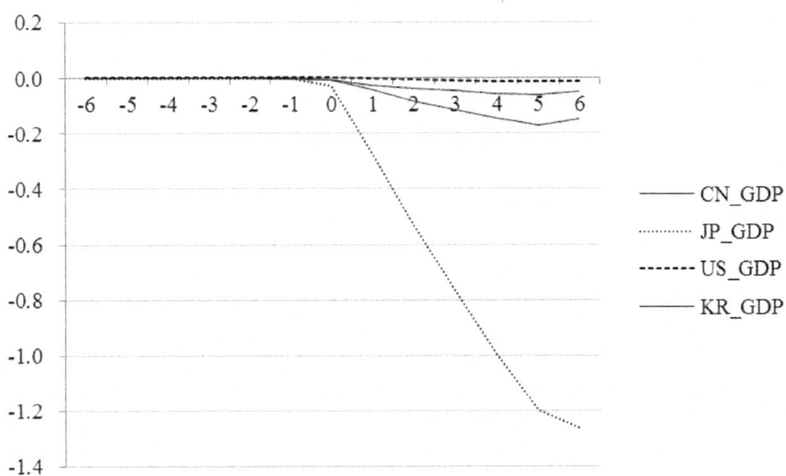

Fig. 11 Effects of the appreciation of the Yen.

among exporting countries has diminished with the rising trend of cooperative and complementary relations.

The effects of stimulus packages estimated by the IMF

IMF (2009b) estimates of the multipliers of fiscal expansion use the GIMF model (Kumhof and Laxton, 2009). Japanese multipliers are estimated as much smaller than in our case. The effects on other countries regarding US and Japanese expansion are ot estimated to be high, which is similar to our results.

Tables 18 and 19 IMF estimates.

Growth Effects of Fiscal Stimulus in 2009 and 2010 (Deviation from baseline in percentage point)

	Stimulus in					
	All	US	Euro Area	Japan	Em.Asia	RoW
Effects on Growth in 2009						
World	1.4	0.5	0.2	0.1	0.4	0.2
United States	1.5	1.3	0.0	0.0	0.1	0.1
Euro Area	0.9	0.2	0.5	0.0	0.1	0.1
Japan	1.1	0.2	0.0	0.7	0.1	0.0
Emerging Asia	2.1	0.6	0.1	0.1	1.3	0.1
Remaining Countries	1.0	0.3	0.1	0.0	0.2	0.4
Effects on Growth in 2010						
World	0.7	0.9	0.0	0.0	−0.2	0.0
United States	1.5	1.4	0.0	0.0	0.0	0.0
Euro Area	0.3	0.5	-0.2	0.0	0.0	0.0
Japan	0.4	0.5	0.0	-0.2	0.0	0.0
Emerging Asia	0.2	1.1	0.0	0.0	−0.9	0.0
Remaining Countries	0.6	0.7	0.0	0.0	0.0	−0.1

Level Effects of Fiscal Stimulus in 2009 and 2010 (Percent Deviation from baseline in percent)

	Stimulus in					
	All	US	Euro Area	Japan	Em.Asia	RoW
Effects on GDP in 2009						
World	1.4	0.5	0.2	0.1	0.4	0.2
United States	1.5	1.3	0.0	0.0	0.1	0.1
Euro Area	0.9	0.2	0.5	0.0	0.1	0.1
Japan	1.1	0.2	0.0	0.7	0.1	0.0
Emerging Asia	2.1	0.6	0.1	0.1	1.3	0.1
Remaining Countries	1.0	0.3	0.1	0.0	0.2	0.4
Effects on GDP in 2010						
World	2.0	1.4	0.1	0.1	0.2	0.2
United States	3.1	2.7	0.1	0.1	0.1	0.1
Euro Area	1.2	0.6	0.3	0.1	0.1	0.1
Japan	1.5	0.7	0.1	0.5	0.1	0.1
Emerging Asia	2.3	1.6	0.1	0.1	0.4	0.1
Remaining Countries	1.7	1.0	0.1	0.1	0.2	0.3

According to our measurement, Japan and the United States seem rather "isolated" despite the era of integration, because both countries are too large to be able to detect separately the effects of the fiscal stimulus.

References

Ban, K, Kiyomi Watanabe *et al.*, (2000). A Prototype of Macroeconometric Models for Analyzing Asian Crises, *Discussion Paper 92*, Economic Research Institute, EPA.

Ban, K (2002). *Feedback Relationships between Japan and the World Economy: Some Simulation Results based on the Asian LINK Model*, paper presented at the Workshop on Forward-Looking Type Model Building, 21–22 November 2002, NIESR, London.

Behr, Andreas and Egon Bellgardt (2002). Dynamic Q-investment functions for Germany using panel balance sheet data and a new algorithm for the capital stock at replacement values, *Discussion paper 23/02*, Economic Research Centre of the Deutsche Bundesbank.

Botman, Dennis, Douglas Laxton *et al.*, (2006). A New-Open-Economy-Macro Model for Fiscal Policy Evaluation, *IMF Working Paper WP/06/45*, February.

Cho, Seonghoon and Antonio Moreno, (2006). "A Small-Sample Study of the New-Keynesian Macro Model", *Journal of Money, Credit, and Banking* Vol. 38, No. 6.

Christiansen, L (2008). Fiscal Multipliers — A Review of the Literature", Appendix II to *IMF Staff Position Note 08/01, Fiscal Policy for the Crisis.*

Clarida, Richard, J Gali, and Mark Gertler (2000). "Monetary Policy Rules and Macroeconomic Stability: Evidence and Some Theory", *The Quarterly Journal of Economics*, February.

Cogan, John F, Tobias J Cwik, John B Taylor, and Volker Wieland (2009). "New Keynesian versus Old Keynesian Government Spending Multipliers", *Stanford University Working Paper No. 47.*

ESRI (2008, 2009). *The ESRI Short-Run Macroeconometric Model of the Japanese Economy: Basic Structure, Multipliers, and Economic Policy Analyses* (2008 version), Economic and Social Research Institute, Cabinet Office of Japan, November.

Fair, Ray C (1984). *Specification, Estimation, and Analysis of Macroeconometric Models*, Harvard University Press.

He, Dong, Zhiwei Zhang and Wenlang Zhang (2009). "How Large Will Be the Effect of China's Fiscal-Stimulus Package on Output and Employment?", *Pacific Economic Review*, Vol. 14, Issue 5, pp. 730–744, December.

IMF (1998). MULTIMOD Mark III, The Core Dynamic and Steady-State Models, *IMF Occasional Paper No. 164*, http://www.imf.org/external/np/res/mmod/index.htm.

IMF (2009a). *The Size of the Fiscal Expansion: An Analysis for the Largest Countries; February 2009*, IMF Staff Position Note on 1 February.

IMF (2009b). *The Case for Global Fiscal Stimulus*, IMF Staff Position Note.

Kumhof, Michael and Douglas Laxton, (2009). *The Global Integrated Monetary and Fiscal Model (GIMF)*, IMF Macro-Linkage, Oil Prices and Deflation Workshop, 6–9 January.

Mizuho (2009). An Analysis of the Chinese Fiscal Expansion by 4,000 Billion Yuan, *Mizuho Insight for Asia and Oceania*, January. (in Japanese)

Ozaki, Taiyo (2006). An East Asian Link Model and Simulation Analysis, *Journal of the Faculty of Economics Kyoto Gakuen University*, Vol. 15, No. 3.

Perotti, R (2005). "Estimating the Effects of Fiscal Policy in OECD Countries", *CEPR Discussion Paper No. 4842* (London: Centre for Economic Policy Research).

Taylor, John B (2009). "The Financial Crisis and the Policy Responses: An Empirical Analysis of What Went Wrong", *NBER Working Paper No. 14631.*

Appendix A: List of the Principal Equations of the Model

(1) China Model

(Identity)

CN_GDP = CN_C + CN_IF + CN_GC + CN_X − CN_M
CN_GDPV = CN_CV + CN_IFV + CN_GCV + CN_XV − CN_MV
CN_CV = CN_C*CN_PC/100
CN_IFV = CN_IF*CN_PIF/100
CN_GCV = CN_GC*CN_PGC/100
CN_XV = CN_X*CN_PX/100
CN_BAL = CN_XV − CN_MV
CN_PEDYV = CN_PEWFP + CN_PEOY + CN_GEOTH − CN_TY
CN_PEWFP = CN_ER*CN_ET/1000000
CN_IF = CN_IBUDV/CN_PIF*100 + CN_IFOR + CN_ILON + CN_IFF + CN_GISIM

(Consumption)

CN_C = +55.11 + 0.108*CN_PEDYV/CN_PC*100
(2.53) (5.52)
+ 0.0052*(1/(1 + CN_RLG(+1)/100))*CN_PENW(+1)/CN_PC(+1)*100
(2.12)
+ 0.871*CN_C(−1)
(4.96)

D.W. = 1.20 R^2(adj) = 0.997

CN_PENW = 1364.81 + CN_PENW(−1) + 0.329*(CN_PEDYV − CN_CV)
(1.00) (2.76)
+ [AR(1) = 0.916]
(12.7)

D.W. = 1.35 R^2(adj) = 0.999

(Investment)

CN_IFF/CN_K(−1) = −0.0816 + 0.223*(1/(1 + CN_RLG(+1)/100)
(−0.95) (3.29)
*CN_GDP(+1)/CN_K(−1)) + 43.06*CN_COGTP/CN_PIF/CN_K(−1)
(4.05)
+ 8.895e-13*EXP(TREND)
(2.91)

D.W. = 0.83 R^2(adj) = 0.999

CN_COGTP = 221.87 + 0.839*(CN_GDPV − CN_PEDYV) + 0.580*CN_TXIV
(0.64) (5.04) (0.82)
+ [AR(1) = 0.776]
(3.90)

D.W. = 1.23 R^2(adj) = 0.991

(Prices and Wages)
LOG(CN_PC) = 0.113 + 0.718*LOG(CN_PC(−1)) + 0.128*LOG(CN_ER)
(0.72) (7.54) (2.39)
+0.388*LOG(CN_MON2/CN_MON2(−1))
(3.29)
D.W. = 0.69 R^2(adj) = 0.976

LOG(CN_PIF) = 0.107 + 0.374*LOG(CN_PM) + 0.308*LOG(CN_ER)
(0.56) (4.29) (6.93)
+ 0.255*LOG(CN_MON2/CN_MON2(−1))
(0.95)
D.W. = 0.76 R^2(adj) = 0.967

LOG(CN_ER) = 8.669 + 0.849*LOG(CN_GDP/CN_ET) + 0.838*LOG(CN_PC(−1))
(17.0) (14.0) (14.5)
D.W. = 0.89 R^2(adj) = 0.995

(Interest rates)
CN_RLG = 10.67 + 0.375*CN_RLG(−1)
(4.88) (3.24)
+(1 − 0.375)*LOG(CN_PGDP(+1)/CN_PGDP)
−1.533*LOG((CN_MON2 − CN_GGDBT)/CN_PGDP)
(−4.65)
−19.28*LOG(CN_YHAT(−1)/CN_GDP(−1))
(−0.50)
D.W. = 1.52 R^2(adj) = 0.899

CN_RSH is exogenous for the China model
(Labor)
LOG(CN_ET) = 6.309 + 0.5452*LOG(CN_GDP)
(5.76) (7.44)
−0.493*LOG(CN_GDP(−1)/CN_ET(−1))
(−5.09)
D.W. = 1.09 R^2(adj) = 0.921

CN_U = CN_LS − CN_ET
CN_UP = 1*(CN_U/CN_LS*100)
(Trade and Import Prices)
TX_CHWD99 = TM_CHJP99 + TM_CHKR99 + TM_CHUS99 + TX_CHRW99
TX_CHWD99R = TX_CHWD99/CN_PX$*100
TM_WDCH99R = TM_JPCH99/JP_PX$*100 + TM_KRCH99/KR_PX$*100
+TM_USCH99/US_PX$*100 + TX_RWCH99/RW_PX$*100
TM_WDCH99 = TM_JPCH99 + TM_KRCH99 + TM_USCH99 + TX_RWCH99
TM_JPCH99/TM_WDCH$ = −1.578 + 0.296*LOG(CN_GDP) −
0.01*LOG(JP_PX$/WD_WPI)
(−3.39) (4.38)
−0.164*LOG(KR_PX$/WD_WPI) − 0.0277*LOG(US_PX$/WD_WPI)
(−3.55) (−0.71)
−0.0505*TREND
(−5.87)
D.W. = 1.53 R^2(adj) = 0.717

TM_KRCH99/TM_WDCH$ = −0.805 + 0.138*LOG(CN_GDP)
(−1.58) (1.83)
−0.0915*LOG(JP_PX$/WD_WPI) − 0.0364*LOG(KR_PX$/WD_WPI)
(−1.23) (−0.93)
−0.0206*LOG(US_PX$/WD_WPI) − 0.0198*TREND
(−0.43) (−2.01)
D.W. = 0.85 R^2(adj) = 0.917

TM_USCH99/TM_WDCH$ = 0.232 + 0.00245*LOG(CN_GDP)
(0.58) (0.96)
−0.0469*LOG(JP_PX$/WD_WPI
(−0.79) −0.0131*LOG(KR_PX$/WD_WPI) − 0.000233*LOG(US_PX$/WD_WPI)
(−0.42) (0.1)
−0.00854*TREND
(−1.08)
D.W. = 1.46 R^2(adj) = 0.744
CN_PM$ = −0.000895 + 1.00*TM_WDCH99/TM_WDCH99R*100
CN_PM = 7.707 + 0.120*CN_PM$*CN_RXD

(2) Japan Model

(Identity)
JP_GDP = JP_C + JP_IF + JP_GC + JP_X − JP_M
JP_GDPV = JP_CV + JP_IFV + JP_GCV + JP_XV − JP_MV
JP_CV = JP_C*JP_PC/100
JP_IFV = JP_IF*JP_PIF/100
JP_GCV = JP_GC*JP_PGC/100
JP_BAL = JP_XV − JP_MV
JP_PEDYV = JP_PEWFP + JP_PEOY + JP_GEOTH − JP_TY − JP_TYSIM
JP_IF = JP_GIV/JP_PIF*100 + JP_IFF + JP_GISIM
(Consumption)
JP_C = 23545.51 + 0.295*JP_PEDYV/JP_PC*100
(1.05) (2.60)
+0.010*(1/(1 + JP_RLG(1)/100))*JP_PENW(1)/JP_PC(1)*100 + 0.564*JP_C(−1)
(2.07) (5.81)
D.W. = 1.40 R^2(adj) = 0.983
JP_PENW = JP_PENW(−1) + 1.991*(JP_PEDYV − JP_CV)
(Investment)
JP_IFF/JP_K(−1) = −0.024 + 0.2002*(1/(1 + JP_RLG(+1)/100)*JP_GDP(+1)/JP_K)
(−0.31) (2.18)
+21.454*JP_MON(−1)/JP_PIF(−1)/JP_K(−1) + [AR(1) = 1.056]
(2.48) (25.7)
D.W. = 1.36 R^2(adj) = 0.768
(Prices and Wages)
LOG(JP_PC) = 0.633 + 0.294*LOG(JP_ER(−1)) + 0.435*LOG(JP_PC(−1))
(3.59) (2.49) (2.52)
−0.0335*LOG(TREND)
(−7.44) D.W. = 1.38 R^2(adj) = 0.956
LOG(JP_PIF) = 0.318 + 0.00174*LOG(JP_PM(−1)) + 0.699*LOG(JP_ER(−1))
(0.64) (0.96) (11.4)
−0.208*LOG(TREND)
(−23.7) D.W. = 0.91 R^2(adj) = 0.954
LOG(JP_ER) = −0.511 + 1.636*LOG(JP_PC(−1)) − 0.669*LOG(JP_YHAT/JP_GDP)
(−1.15) (16.8) (−5.84)
D.W. = 1.86 R^2(adj) = 0.965
(Interest rates)
JP_RSH = 16.03 + 0.684*JP_RSH(−1) + (1 − 0.684)*LOG(JP_PGDP(+1)/JP_PGDP)
(1.40) (6.43)
−1.50*LOG((JP_MON − JP_GGDBT/100)/JP_PGDP)
(−1.59)

−30.27*LOG(JP_YHAT/JP_GDP)
(−3.31) D.W. = 1.70 R^2(adj) = 0.924

JP_RLG = 1.257 + 0.203*JP_RLG(+1) + 0.595*(JP_RSH)
(4.04) (1.09) (4.34)
D.W. = 1.87 R^2(adj) = 0.940

(Labor)

LOG(JP_ET) = 1.725 + 0.231*LOG(JP_GDP)
(1.87) (2.17)
−0.272*LOG(JP_GDP(−1)/JP_ET(−1)) + 0.620*LOG(JP_ET(−1))
(−2.64) (8.20)
D.W. = 1.31 R^2(adj) = 0.887

LOG(JP_U) = 6.897 − 25.42*LOG(JP_ET/JP_LS) + [AR(1) = 0.927]
(27.6) (−11.9) (9.25)
D.W. = 0.69 R^2(adj) = 0.994

JP_UP = JP_U/JP_LS*100

(Trade and Import Prices)

TX_JPWD99 = TM_JPCH99 + TM_JPKR99 + TM_JPUS99 + TX_JPRW99
TX_JPWD99R = TX_JPWD99/JP_PX$*100
TM_WDJP99R = TM_CHJP99/CN_PX$*100 + TM_KRJP99/KR_PX$*100
+ TM_USJP99/US_PX$*100 + TX_RWJP99/RW_PX$*100
TM_WDJP99 = TM_CHJP99 + TM_KRJP99 + TM_USJP99 + TX_RWJP99

TM_CHJP99/TM_WDJP$ = −2.180 + 0.174*LOG(JP_GDP)
(−1.47) (1.55)
−0.0956*LOG(CN_PX$/WD_WPI) − 0.0952*LOG(KR_PX$/WD_WPI)
(−1.95) (−2.79)
+ 0.137*LOG(US_PX$/WD_WPI)
(3.61) D.W. = 0.56 R^2(adj) = 0.948

TM_KRJP99/TM_WDJP$ = −1.298 + 0.105*LOG(JP_GDP)
(−1.71) (1.80)
−0.0107*LOG(CN_PX$/WD_WPI) − 0.05*LOG(KR_PX$/WD_WPI)
(−0.45) (*)
+ 0.0705*LOG(US_PX$/WD_WPI) − 0.00294*TREND
(3.93) (−2.44)
D.W. = 1.40 R^2(adj) = 0.08

TM_USJP99/TM_WDJP$ = −.022+ 0.119*LOG(JP_GDP)
(−0.92) (1.38)
+ 0.0945*LOG(CN_PX$/WD_WPI) − 0.122*LOG(KR_PX$/WD_WPI)
(3.16) (−5.14)
−0.0620*LOG(US_PX$/WD_WPI) − 0.0196*TREND
(−2.00) (−10.1)
D.W. = 1.72 R^2(adj) = 0.965

JP_PM$ = 0.905*TM_WDJP99/TM_WDJP99R*100
JP_PM = 0.01*JP_PM$*JP_RXD

(3) Korea Model

(Identity)

KR_GDP = KR_C + KR_IF + KR_GC + KR_X − KR_M
KR_GDPV = KR_CV + KR_IFV + KR_GCV + KR_XV − KR_MV
KR_CV = KR_C*KR_PC/100
KR_IFV = KR_IF*KR_PIF/100
KR_GCV = KR_GC*KR_PGC/100
KR_XV = KR_X*KR_PX/100

KR_BAL = KR_XV − KR_MV
KR_PEDYV = KR_PEWFP + KR_PEOY + KR_GEOTH − KR_TY
KR_IF = KR_GIV/KR_PIF*100 + KR_IFF + KR_GISIM
(Consumption)
KR_C = −39773.85 + 0.807*KR_PEDYV/KR_PC*100
(2.21) (10.5)
+ 0.0573*(1/(1 + KR_RLG(1)/100))*KR_PENW(1)/KR_PC(1)*100 − 48812.36*D98
(6.79) (−5.30)
D.W. = 1.20 R^2(adj) = 0.972
KR_PENW = KR_PENW(−1) + 2.750*(KR_PEDYV − KR_CV)
(Investment)
KR_IFF/KR_K(−1) = −0.0761 + 0.127*(1/(1 + KR_RLG(+ 1)/100)*
(−1.14) (0.94)
*KR_GDP(+1)/KR_K) + 50.07*KR_COGTP(−1)/KR_PIF(−1)/KR_K(−1)
(3.46)
D.W. = 1.02 R^2(adj) = 0.785
KR_COGTP = 245346.37 + 0.236*(KR_GDPV − KR_PEDYV)
(1.97) (1.33)
−0.860*KR_TC + [AR(1) = 0.908]
(−0.85) (14.2)
D.W. = 2.00 R^2(adj) = 0.973
(Price and Wages)
LOG(KR_PC) = 0.174 + 0.635*LOG(KR_PC(−1)) + 0.203*LOG(KR_ER)
(5.39) (14.2) (7.46)
D.W. = 1.29 R^2(adj) = 0.998
LOG(KR_PIF) = 0.464 + 0.247*LOG(KR_PM) + 0.401*LOG(KR_ER)
(3.96) (6.22) (33.4)
D.W. = 0.65 R^2(adj) = 0.994
LOG(KR_ER) = −0.0527 + 1.381*LOG(KR_GDP/KR_ET)
(−0.19) (2.75)
+ 0.655*LOG(KR_PC(−1))
(2.07 D.W. = 0.49 R^2(adj) = 0.987
(Interest Rates)
KR_RSH = 17.04 + 0.590*KR_RSH(−1)
(1.72) (9.70)
+ (1 − 0.590)*LOG(KR_PGDP(+1)/KR_PGDP) − 3.513*LOG((KR_MON
(−7.11)
− KR_GGDBT/100)/KR_PGDP) − 7.441*LOG(KR_YHAT/KR_GDP)
(−0.28)
D.W. = 2.33 R^2(adj) = 0.729
KR_RLG = 1.366 + 0.385*KR_RLG(+1) + 0.583*(KR_RSH)
(2.02) (3.49) (5.02)
D.W. = 1.57 R^2(adj) = 0.931
(Labor)
LOG(KR_ET) = 4.636 + 0.457*LOG(KR_GDP)
(7.88) (6.92)
−0.224*LOG(KR_GDP(−1)/KR_ET(−1))
(−2.51)
D.W. = 1.19 R^2(adj) = 0.983
KR_U = KR_LS − KR_ET
KR_UP = KR_U/KR_LS*100
(Trade and Import Prices)
TX_KRWD99 = TM_KRCH99 + TM_KRJP99 + TM_KRUS99 + TX_KRRW99
TX_KRWD99R = −21592.23+ 1.00*TX_KRWD99/KR_PX$*100

TM_WDKR99 = TM_CHKR99 + TM_JPKR99 + TM_USKR99 + TX_RWKR99
TM_WDKR99R = TM_CHKR99/CN_PX$*100 + TM_JPKR99/JP_PX$*100 + TM_USKR99/US_PX$*100 + TX_RWKR99/RW_PX$*100
TM_JPKR99/TM_WDKR$ = −2.485 + 0.223*LOG(KR_GDP)
(−2.04) (2.28)
−0.01*LOG(JP_PX$/WD_WPI) − 0.128*LOG(CN_PX$/WD_WPI)
(−1.99)
+0.162*LOG(US_PX$/WD_WPI) − 0.0150*TREND(−1)
(3.33) (−2.94)
D.W. = 1.22 R^2(adj) = 0.819
TM_CHKR99/TM_WDKR$ = −1.021 + 0.0679*LOG(KR_GDP)
(−1.34) (1.10)
+ 0.0622*LOG(JP_PX$/WD_WPI) + 0.00393*LOG(CN_PX$/WD_WPI)
(1.19 (0.09)
+ 0.0353*LOG(US_PX$/WD_WPI) + 0.0116*TREND
(1.01) (3.31)
D.W. = 1.28 R^2(adj) = 0.960
TM_USKR99/TM_WDKR$ = 0.467 + 0.00181*LOG(KR_GDP)
(0.48) (0.02)
−0.123*LOG(JP_PX$/WD_WPI) + 0.0171*LOG(CN_PX$/WD_WPI)
(−2.76) (0.32)
−0.01*LOG(US_PX$/WD_WPI) − 0.0172*TREND
(*) (−4.31)
D.W. = 1.19 R^2(adj) = 0.920
KR_PM$ = 65.41 + 0.260*TM_WDKR99/TM_WDKR99R*100
KR_PM = KR_PM$*KR_RXD/1000

(4) US Model

(Identity)
US_GDP = US_C + US_IF + US_GC + US_X − US_M
US_GDPV = US_CV + US_IFV + US_GCV + US_XV − US_MV
US_CV = US_C*US_PC/100
US_IFV = US_IF*US_PIF/100
US_GCV = US_GC*US_PGC/100
US_BAL = US_XV − US_MV
US_PEDYV = US_PEWFP + US_PEOY + US_GEOTH − US_TY + US_TYSIM + US_GESIM
US_IF = US_GIV/US_PIF*100 + US_IFF + US_GISIM
TX_USWD99 = TM_USCH99 + TM_USJP99 + TM_USKR99 + TX_USRW99
TX_USWD99R = TX_USWD99/US_PX$*100
US_M = US_MV/US_PM*100
US_TAXES = US_TY + US_TX + US_TP + US_TSS + US_TC
US_GREV = US_TAXES + US_GREVO
US_GEXP = US_GCV + US_GIV + US_GEXPO
(Consumption)
US_C = −371.55 + 0.502*US_PEDYV/US_PC*100
(3.91) (4.65)
+ 0.000904*((1/(1 + US_RLG(1)/100))*US_PENW(1)/US_PC(1)
(2.53)
*100 + (1/(1 + US_RLG/100)) *US_PENW/US_PC*100) + 0.515*US_C(− 1)
(5.2)
D.W. = 1.12 R^2(adj) = 0.999
US_PENW = US_PENW(−1) + 8.512*(US_PEDYV − US_CV) + 3.912*US_PENAF

(Investment)
US_IFF/US_K(−1) = −0.282 + 0.434*(1/(1 + US_RLG(+1)/100)
(−3.08) (3.71)
*US_GDP(+1)/US_K) + 26.979*US_COGTP/US_PIF/US_K(−1) + 0.0321*D2000
(1.27) (9.71)
D.W. = 2.08 R^2(adj) = 0.923

(Prices and Wages)
LOG(US_PC) = −3.252 + 0.642*LOG(US_ER) + 0.430*LOG(US_PM(−1))
(−5.40) (29.1) (4.01)
D.W. = 0.95 R^2(adj) = 0.975

LOG(US_PIF) = 0.901 + 0.217*LOG(US_ER) + 0.376*LOG(US_PM(−1))
(2.25) (10.9) (5.57)
D.W. = 0.95 R^2(adj) = 0.975

LOG(US_ER) = 4.728 + 0.571*LOG(US_GDP(−1)/US_ET(−1))
(2.80) (2.41)
+ 0.651*LOG(US_ER(−1))
(5.57)
D.W. = 1.36 R^2(adj) = 0.985

(Interest Rates)
US_RSH = 13.47 + 0.592*US_RSH(−1)
(4.20) (6.01)
+ (1 − 0.592)*LOG(US_PGDP(+1)/US_PGDP) − 2.16*LOG((US_MON
(−1.00)
− US_GGDBT/100)/US_PGDP) − 74.563*LOG(US_YHAT/US_GDP)
(−8.46)
D.W. = 1.83 R^2(adj) = 0.873

US_RLG = 0.0388 + (1 − 0.398)*US_RLG(+1) + 0.398*US_RLG(−1)
(0.05) (4.45)
+ 0.0607*(US_RSH) − 0.0104*TREND
(0.75) (−0.40)
D.W. = 2.89 R^2(adj) = 0.867

(Labor)
LOG(US_ET) = 7.253 + 0.466*LOG(US_GDP)
(7.31) (6.51)
−0.101*LOG(US_GDP(−1)/US_ET(−1)) + 0.0161*D2000
(−0.80) (4.77)
D.W. = 1.21 R^2(adj) = 0.993

US_U = −0.505 + 1.00*(US_LS − US_ET)
US_UP = −0.0222 + 1.00*(US_U/US_LS*100)

(Trade and Import Prices)
TM_WDUS99 = TM_CHUS99 + TM_JPUS99 + TM_KRUS99 + TX_RWUS99
TM_WDUS99R = TM_CHUS99/CN_PX$*100 −TM_JPUS99/JP_PX$*100
+ TM_KRUS99/KR_PX$*100
+ TX_RWUS99/RW_PX$*100

TM_JPUS99/TM_WDUS$ = 0.0663 + 0.0388*LOG(US_GDP)
(0.03) (0.14)
−0.0453*LOG(JP_PX$/WD_WPI) + 0.150*LOG(KR_PX$/WD_WPI)
(−0.53) (1.05)
−0.278*LOG(CN_PX$/WD_WPI) − 0.0148*TREND
(−1.41) (−1.24)
D.W. = 1.49 R^2(adj) = 0.910

TM_KRUS99/TM_WDUS$ = −0.666 + 0.0800*LOG(US_GDP)
(−2.12) (2.16)

+ 0.0288*LOG(JP_PX$/WD_WPI) – 0.01*LOG(KR_PX$/WD_WPI)
(3.76) (*)
+ 0.000722*LOG(CN_PX$/WD_WPI) – 0.00173*TREND
(0.06) (–1.25)
D.W. = 0.755 R^2(adj) = 0.744

TM_CHUS99/TM_WDUS$ = –1.0222 + 0.120*LOG(US_GDP)
(–0.45) (0.45)
– 0.101*LOG(JP_PX$/WD_WPI) + 0.281*LOG(KR_PX$/WD_WPI)
(–1.28) (4.59)
– 0.35*LOG(CN_PX$/WD_WPI) + 0.00225*TREND
(*) (0.24)
D.W. = 1.54 R^2(adj) = 0.826

US_PM$ = 0.01*TM_WDUS99/TM_WDUS99R*100
US_PM = 1.00*US_PM$

Note: (*) denotes calibrated parameters

Appendix B: List of Variables

Unless otherwise stated, the unit for all local currencies is one billion.

The list below is quoted from Oxford Economic Forecasting, now Oxford Economics. With respect to the Japan Model, however, the variable names are the same as in all the other countries' models.

BAL	Balance of payment	Identity
BASET	Bank total assets (yen trillion)	IFS Banking
BBIS	Bank BIS ratio (BT1 + BT2 as % BRWA)	BOJ/other estimate
BBIST1	Bank tier 1 ratio (BT1 as % BRWA)	BOJ/other estimate
BBOND	Bank bond finance (yen trillion)	IFS Banking
BBP	Benchmark bond prices	Datastream
BCAP	Capital/financial account in BOP (yen billion) NSA	Datastream
BCU	Current account of the balance of payments (yen billion) SA	Datastream
BCURRATE	Current account as % nominal GDP	OEF calculated
BFORA	Bank foreign assets (yen trillion)	IFS Banking
BFORL	Bank foreign liabilities (yen trillion)	IFS Banking
BGOV	Bank claims on central government (yen trillion)	IFS Banking

BINEX	Bank interest expenses (yen trillion)	BOJ/other estimate
BININ	Bank interest income (yen trillion)	BOJ/other estimate
BLIAB	Bank total liabilities (yen trillion)	IFS Banking
BNPERF	Bank non-performing loans within BPRIV (yen trillion)	OEF estimate
BPERF	Bank performing loans within BPRIV total (yen trillion)	BPRIV– BNPERF
BPRIV	Bank domestic claims on non-cent. govt. (yen trillion)	IFS Banking
BPROF	Bank total operating profits (yen trillion)	BOJ/other estimate
BRES	Bank total reserves (yen trillion)	IFS Banking
BRWA	Bank risk-weighted assets (yen trillion)	BOJ/other estimate
BSER	Invisibles/services balance in BCU (yen billion) SA	Datastream
BSURP	Bank cumulative surplus after write-offs (yen trillion)	BPRIV – BNPERF
BT1	Bank tier 1 capital (yen trillion)	BOJ/other estimate
BT2	Bank tier 2 capital (yen trillion)	BOJ/other estimate
BTOTH	Bank other capital (yen trillion)	BOJ/other estimate
BTUSD	Bank subordinated debt (yen trillion)	BOJ/other estimate
BTUSP	Bank unrealized stock profits, net (yen trillion)	BOJ/other estimate
BVI	Visible trade balance, BOP basis (yen billion) SA	Datastream
BWAGE	Bank wage bill (yen trillion)	BOJ/other estimate
BWCUM	Bank cumulative write-offs of bad loans (yen trillion)	OEF estimate

BWRITE	Bank write-offs of bad debt out of profits (yen trillion)	OEF estimate
C	Consumer expenditure (yen billion, 1995 prices) SA	Datastream
CARB	Carbon emissions, million metric tons	OEF calculated
CARS	Car sales, registrations (thou., av. quarterly, SA)	Datastream
CBANK	Bank credit from monetary auth. (yen trillion)	IFS Banking
CD	Consumer exp. — durables (yen billion, 1995 prices)	Datastream, SA
CND	Consumer exp. — non-durables (1995 prices)	Identity C–CD
CODIV	Company sector dividend payments (yen billion)	Identity = PEDIV
COGTP	Company profits (yen billion)	OEF calculated
CONAF	Assets, net acquisition fin. assets — companies (yen billion)	Identity
CONIR	Company sector net interest receipts (yen billion)	OEF calculated
CONSTR	Construction activity (1995 = 100) SA	METI
CONW	Company sector net wealth (yen billion)	Identity
CPI	Prices, CPI – total (1995 = 100) NSA	Datastream
CPIFU	Prices, CPI – fuel (1995 = 100) NSA	Datastream
CPIX	Prices, CPI – non-fuel goods and services	OEF calculated
CU	Capacity utilization (%)	ESM key statistics
CUMOD	Capacity utilization — model consistent version	OEF calculated

CV	Consumer Expenditure (yen billion) SA	Datastream
DCOAL	Coal, total demand (mtoe)	OECD IEA Energy
DELTA	Depreciation rate for capital stock	OEF calculated
DGAS	Gas, total demand (mtoe)	OECD IEA Energy
DIV	Dividends index	Datastream
DIVT	Target dividend yield ratio	OEF estimate
DOIL	Oil, total demand (mtoe)	OECD IEA Energy
DOMD	Domestic demand SA	C + IF + GC + IS
DOTH	Banks' other liabilities (yen trillion)	IFS Banking
DPRIV	Bank demand/time/savings deposits (yen trillion)	IFS Banking
DSMP	Stockmarket prices based on DY ratio model	OEF calculated
EE	Employees in employment (thou.)	QLFS Item 40
EQMON	Money supply, equilibrium	OEF calculated
ER	Earnings, economy-wide average (yen thou.)	OEF calculated
ES	Employment, self employed (thou.)	OEF calculated
ESTAR	Employment at NAIRU (thou.)	OEF calculated
ET	Employment, total (thou.) SA	Datastream
FASSET$	Foreign assets (US$ billion)	IFS
FDI$	Incoming foreign direct investment, net total (US$m)	Datastream
FLIAB$	Foreign liabilities (US$ billion)	IFS
GB	Government (general) balance (yen billion)	ARNA
GBCEN	Government balance, alternative (yen billion) NSA	Datastream
GBPUB	Government balance, public sector (yen billion) NSA	Datastream

GC	Public consumption (yen billion, 1995 prices) SA	Datastream
GCGPE	Transfers, personal sector from central govt. (yen billion)	ARNA Part 3 II
GCV	Public consumption (yen billion) SA	Datastream
GDIP	Government interest payments, gross (yen billion)	ARNA Part 3 SA
GDIR	Government debt interest receipts (yen billion)	Identity GDIP – GNIP
GDP	GDP (yen billion, 1995 prices) SA	Datastream
GDP$	GDP, US$ million, 1995 prices SA	World Bank, WDI
GDP$V	GDP nominal in US$ millions (SA)	Identity
GDPV	GDP (yen billion) SA	Datastream
GEOTH	Government expenditure, others	
GEXP	Government expenditure, total (yen billion)	ARNA Part 3, II
GGDBT	Government (central) debt — stock gross (fin. liab.)	Datastream
GI	Investment by government (yen billion, 1995 prices) SA	Datastream
GIV	Public investment spending (yen billion) SA	ARNA Part 3, II
GNDBT	Government NET debt — stock, net (yen billion)	OEF calculated
GNIP	Government interest payments, net (yen billion)	ARNA Part 3 SA
GREV	Government revenue, total (yen billion)	ARNA Part 3, II
GREVO	Government revenue, others	
IBUDV	Investment from government budget	

IF	Investment, total (yen billion, 1995 prices) SA	Datastream
IFF	Investment, private sector, real	
IFOR	Investment, net FDI	
IFV	Investment, total (yen billion) SA	Datastream
ILON	Investment funded by loans	
INRS	Investment, private nonresidential — structures	(12.4/26.1) *IPNR
IP	Industrial production index (1995 = 100) SA	Datastream
IPDE	Investment, private nonresidential — equipment	IPNR-INRS
IPEO	Investment, private investment — other equipment	0.7*IPDE
IPETR	Investment, private, equipment, transportation	0.3*IPDE
IPNR	Investment, private-sector business (yen billion, 1995 prices) SA	Datastream
IPRD	Investment in private dwellings (yen billion, 1995 prices) SA	Datastream
IS	Stock-building (yen billion, 1995 prices) SA	GDP−C−IF −GC
ISV	Stock-building (yen billion) SA	GDPV−CV−IFV
K	Capital stock, constant prices	OEF calculated
LS	Labor supply (thou.)	Identity ET+U
M	Imports of goods and services, total, constant prices SA	Datastream
M$V	Imports of goods and services, total in US$	
MCOAL	Imports of coal, mtoe	
MFU	Imports of fuels, constant prices (1995 based)	OECD ITCI
MG	Imports of goods (yen billion, 1995 prices)	100*MGV/ PMG

MGAS	Imports of natural gas, mtoe	
MGNF	Imports of goods, non-fuel, constant prices	MG–MFU
MGV	Imports of goods (yen billion) SA	Datastream
MMWP	Macro-model weighted profits	OEF calculated
MOIL	Imports of crude oil, mtoe	
MON or MON2	M2 Money demand (yen billion)	Datastream
MPK	Marginal physical productivity of capital (%)	OEF calculated
MS	Imports of services (yen billion, 1995 prices) SA	M–MG
MSV	Imports of services, current prices SA	MV–MGV
MV	Imports of goods and services, total (yen billion) SA	Datastream
NAIRU	Non-Accelerating Inflation Rate of Unemployment (%)	OEF calculated
NAIRUR	Parameter used in wage equation = NAIRU/UP	OEF calculated
NETR	Net transfers abroad on BCU, BOP basis (yen billion) SA	Datastream
NFDI$	Inflow of foreign investment excluding FDI	
NIPDV	Net IPD, BOP basis (yen billion) SA	Datastream
NLCOST	Costs of production, non-labor (index 1995 = 100)	OEF calculated
PART	Labor-force participation rate (%)	OEF calculated
PC	Consumer expenditure deflator (1995 = 100) SA	100*CV/C
PCOAL$	Coal, price average incl. carbon tax, US$ per toe	OECD IEA Energy
PCOLBT	Coal, price average in US$ per toe	OECD IEA Energy

PDFU	Fuel price, average 1995 = 100, local currency	Identity
PEDIP	Income, pers. sect. debt interest payments (yen billion)	ARNA Part 3 SA
PEDIR	Income, pers. sect. debt interest receipts (yen billion)	ARNA Part 3 SA
PEDIV	Income, personal sect. dividend receipts (yen billion)	ARNA Part 3 SA
PEDY	Income, real personal disposable, constant price	OEF calculated
PEDYV	Income, personal disposable, current prices	ARNA Part 3, II
PEMPY	Income, compensation from employment (yen billion)	Datastream
PENAF	Assets, acquisitions of financial assets — persons	ARNA Part 1 (2)
PENIR	Interest, pers. sect. net debt int. receipts (yen billion)	Identity
PENW	Wealth, personal sector net wealth (yen billion)	OEF calculated
PEOCR	Pension fund contribution by employers (yen billion)	ARNA Part 3 SA
PEOY	Income, "other" personal income (yen billion)	OEF calculated
PERF	Bank performing loans as proportion of BPRIV	(BPERF/ BPRIV)
PERT	Target PE ratio	OEF estimate
PESR	Savings, personal sector savings rate (%)	OEF calculated
PESV	Savings, personal sector (yen billion)	OEF calculated
PEWFP	Wages and salaries (yen billion)	ARNA Part 3 SA
PGAS$	Gas, price average incl. carbon tax, US$ per toe	OECD IEA Energy

PGASBT	Gas, price average in US$ per toe	OECD IEA Energy
PGC	Public consumption deflator (1995 = 100) SA	100*GCV/GC
PGDP	GDP deflator (1995 = 100) SA	100*GDPV/GDP
PGDPX	Expected price level for exchange rate eq	OEF/user defined
PIF	Investment deflator (1995 = 100) SA	100*IFV/IF
PM	Import deflator — total (1995 = 100) SA	100*MV/M
PM$	Import deflator in $	
PMFU	Import price of fuels (1995 = 100)	OECD ITCI
PMG	Import deflator, goods NSA (1995 = 100)	Datastream
PMGNF	Imports deflator — goods, non fuel	OEF calculated
PMS	Import price of services (1995 = 100) SA	100*(MSV/MS)
POIL$	Oil, price average incl. carbon tax, US$ per toe	OECD IEA Energy
POILBT	Oil, price average in US$ per toe	OECD IEA Energy
POP	Population, total (thou.)	OECD/World Bank
POPW	Population of working age (thou.)	World Bank
PPI	Prices, producer (1995 = 100) NSA	Datastream
PROD	Productivity, trend	OEF calculated
PSH	Stock exchange index, Tokyo (4 January 1968 = 100)	Datastream
PSMP	Stockmarket prices based on PE ratio model	OEF calculated
PSTAR	Price level target for interest rate rule	OEF/user fixed
PX	Export deflator — total (1995 = 100) SA	100*XV/X

PX$	Export deflator in US$	
PXFU	Export price of fuels (1995 = 100)	OECD ITCI
PXG	Export deflator, goods NSA (1995 = 100)	Datastream
PXGNF	Export deflator — goods, non fuel	OEF calculated
PXS	Export price of services (1995 = 100) SA	100*XSV/XS
QCOAL	Coal, total production (mtoe)	OECD IEA Energy
QGAS	Gas, total production (mtoe)	OECD IEA Energy
QOIL	Oil, total production (mtoe)	OECD IEA Energy
QR	Relative return on investment — companies	OEF calculated
RDEP	Bank deposit rate (%)	Datastream
RES$	Reserves, Central Bank forex (US$ billion)	IFS
RES$M	Reserves, months of import cover	Identity
RISK	Exchange rate risk premium	OEF calculated
RLEND	Bank lending rate (%)	IFS via Datastream
RLG	Interest rate, benchmark long-bond (%)	Datastream
RRH	Interest rate, personal sector real (%)	OEF calculated
RRX	Real effective exchange rate (1990 = 100)	OEF
RS	Retail sales, constant prices index (1995 = 100)	(JPRETAILA* 100)
RSH	Interest rate, 3-month rate on CDS (%)	Datastream
RX	Effective exchange rate (1990 = 100)	Datastream
RX1	Effective exchange rate (1990 = 100) OEF definition	OEF

RXD	Exchange rate, dollar rate	Datastream
RXDM	Exchange rate, Deutschmark rate	Datastream
RXDX	Expected exchange rate for exchange rate eq	OEF/user defined
RXEURO	Exchange rate, yen/euro	OEF estimate
RXPPP	Exchange rate, indicator for yen/US$ rate	OEF calculated
RXPPT	Exchange rate, indicator for yen/US$ rate	OEF calculated
SME	Stockmarket earnings	Datastream
SMP	Stockmarket index, Datastream total market	Datastream
ST	Stocks, total (yen billion, 1995 prices) SA	ST(−1) + IS
TAXEX	Tax, total receipts	
TAXRY		
TBALRATE	Trade balance as % nominal GDP	OEF calculated
TC	Tax, corporate taxes (yen billion)	ARNA Part 3, II
TCARB	Carbon tax, US$ per toe flat tax	OEF, zero base
TCOAL	Coal, tax rate, average (%)	OECD IEA Energy
TCOST	Costs, total (index 1995 = 100)	OEF calculated
TCR	Rate of corporate taxation (%)	OEF
TDMD$	Total energy demand	DCOAL* PCOAL + ⋯ +
TFE	Total final expenditure (yen billion, 1995 prices) SA	C + GC + IF + IS + X
TGAS	Gas, tax rate, average (%)	OECD IEA Energy
TINT	Tax on bank deposits	
TM(*i*,*j*) nn	*i*,*j* compromises many combinations of trading partners; *nn* denotes classification item, 99 is all visible trade	COMTRADE

TM_*ij*	Trade from *i* to *j*, current US$ (importing data)	COMTRADE
TOIL	Oil, tax rate average (%)	OECD IEA Energy
TP	Tax, payroll (employer social sec. contrib. yen billion)	ARNA Part 3 SA
TPEN	Energy, total primary energy (mtoe)	OECD IEA Energy
TPR	Rate of payroll taxation (%)	OEF calculated
TRCOL	Time trend used in coal equations	OEF calculated
TREMP	Time trend in employment equation	1980 Q1 = 1
TREND	Trend productivity used in production function	OEF calculated
TRGAS	Time trend used in gas equations	OEF calculated
TRM	Time trend in imports equation	1973 Q1 = 1
TROIL	Time trend used for oil 1973	OEF calculated
TRX	Time trend in exports equation	1973 Q1 = 1
TSS	Social insurance contributions, employees (yen billion)	ARNA Part 3, II
TSSR	Rate of employee social security contributions (%)	OEF calculated
TX	Tax, expenditure tax (yen billion)	ARNA Part 3, II
TX_*ij*	Trade from *i* to *j*, current US$ (exporting data)	COMTRADE
TXAV	Tax, agricultural tax receipts	
TXFU	Tax, expenditure taxes on fuels (yen billion)	OEF calculated
TXIV	Tax, industrial and commercial tax receipts	
TXNFR	VAT rate of expend. taxation (%), excl. fuel taxes	Ministry of Finance
TXOTH	Tax, other receipts	
TXR	Rate of expenditure tax, average effective (%)	OEF (TX/CV)
TXTV	Tax, tariff receipts	

TY	Tax, personal income tax (yen billion)	ARNA Part 3, II
TYR	Rate of income taxation (%)	Min of Finance
U	Unemployment (thou.) SA	Datastream
UP	Unemployment (%) SA	Datastream
WC	Costs — unit wage whole economy (1995 = 100)	OEF calculated
WCMF	Costs — unit wage manufacturing (1995 = 100)	CSO (MRETS)
WCR	Costs, relative unit wage (1995 = 100)	CSO (MRETS)
WEDGE	"Wedge"	OEF calculated
WPI	World average wholesale price index	OEF calculated
WT	World trade index (1995 = 100)	OEF Calculated
WWC$	World wage costs index (1995 = 100)	OEF calculated
X	Exports of goods and services, total constant prices SA	Datastream
X$V	Exports of goods and services, total in US$	
XFU	Exports of fuels, constant prices (1995 base)	OECD ITCI
XG	Exports of goods (yen billion, 1995 prices)	100*XGV/PXG
XGNF	Exports of goods, non fuel, constant prices	XG – XFU
XGV	Exports of goods (yen billion) SA	Datastream
XS	Exports of services (yen billion, 1995 prices) SA	X–XG
XSV	Exports of services, current prices SA	XV-XGV
XV	Exports of goods and services, total (yen billion) SA	Datastream
YHAT	Capacity output (constant prices, yen billion)	OEF calculated

Chapter 6

The Interdependence among Economy, Energy, and Environment in China: An Econometric Analysis 2000–2020*

Mitsuo Yamada

1. Introduction

After introducing market mechanisms into the economy, China has managed to grow as rapidly as it has by actively accepting an inflow of foreign direct investment. In the 1990s the growth rate of China became prominent among East Asian countries (see Fig. 1.1). Generally, rapid development of the economy requires large consumption of energy followed by a great amount of CO_2 emissions. Actually, China's CO_2 emissions are the second largest in the world, after those of the US (see Fig. 1.2). In terms of emissions by GDP, no other country exceeds China. Consequently, China, with its rapid growth, will be required to make more efficient use of energy and reduce CO_2 emissions for the sake of the global environment.

China has abundant coal resources, which have been used mainly as an energy resource. The comparison in Fig. 1.3 of energy resource components among countries shows that China depends heavily on

*This paper was published in The Journal of Econometric Study of Northeast Asia, November 2007 (Vol. 6, No. 1). The original version was presented at the international energy workshop of IIASA, Austria, 2003. The author is grateful to Dr. Mitsuho Uchida of the Central Research Institute of Electric Power Industry, and Dr. Leo Schrattenholzer, the head of the ECS Program, IIASA, for their helpful comments and suggestions.

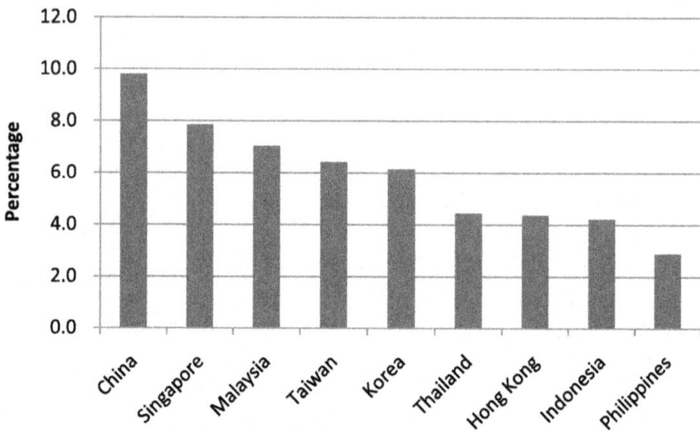

Fig. 1.1
Source: *Key Indicators of Developing Asian and Pacific Countries 2000* Calculated from the database of the Asian Development Bank.

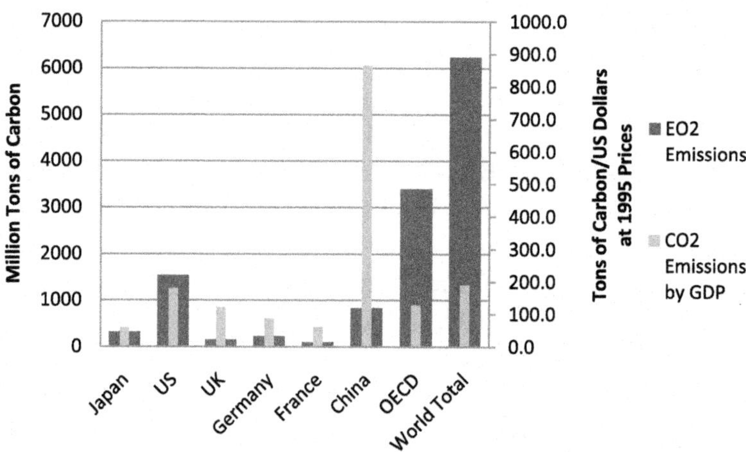

Fig. 1.2 CO_2 Emissions by country in 1999.
Source: IEA Energy Outlook.

domestic coal for energy use. Continued development in China might result in serious environmental problems, thus necessitating improvements in energy efficiency, and a shift in demand from coal to natural gas, which has the lowest CO_2 emissions per calorie of the fossil fuels. Economic cooperation with the developed countries and transfer of

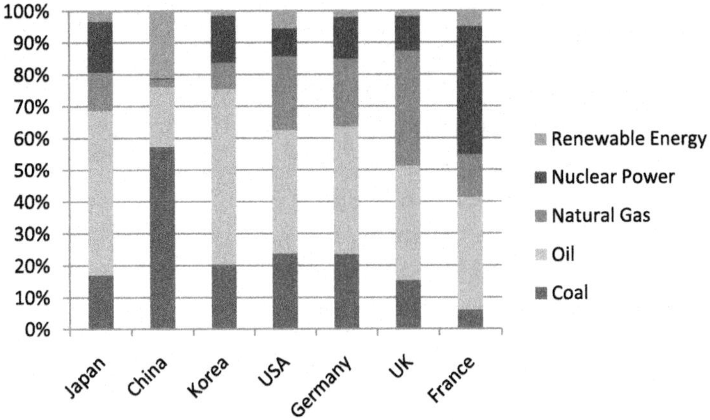

Fig. 1.3 Primary energy composition by country in 1999.
Source: *IEA, Energy Balance of OECD Countries,* Energy Balance of Non-OECD Countries.

advanced technology to China seem important recourses for such a transition.

A large-scale natural gas field was recently discovered in the Tarim Basin, located in western China. Economic development in the eastern coastal area of China has been remarkable, and there appears to be a shortage of energy, and serious air pollution in the region. Therefore, the Chinese government produced a construction plan for a natural gas pipeline to connect both regions in February 2000. This plan was started in 2001 and completion was aimed at for 2004. The project involved the construction of a 4100 km pipeline from the Tarim Basin to Shanghai. The estimated cost was 146 billion yuan. Twelve billion cubic meters of natural gas per year was to be supplied after completion. This amount is to be increased to 19 billion cubic meters after 2010. It is estimated the supply will be stable for 20 years or more, and this plan is expected to contribute to the reduction of CO_2 emissions in China.

The Clean Development Mechanism (CDM) is a system in which a developed country transfers advanced technology to a developing country, for which the developed country receives a certain amount of emission credits, called Certified Emission Reductions (CERs). CERs are authorized amounts of carbon dioxide emissions, which are reduced by a given project. The CDM seems attractive to both developed and developing countries, because the developed country can gain a reduction in CO_2 emissions at a lower cost than that it would be able to at home, and because the developing country achieves environmental improvement by way of introducing advanced technology at a lower cost than it would be able to otherwise. As a rule, the CDM projects, from small- to large-scale, are considered to have a private-sector base. A natural-gas thermal power plant would be a good example of such projects because power generation with natural gas would promote the disuse of coal thermal power stations, which are of small- to medium-scale and superannuated. As a result, this type of project would shift energy usage from coal to natural gas and thus reduce CO_2 emissions.

In this paper, we construct a multi-sectoral econometric model of the Chinese economy, and discuss the economic impacts of the improvement of energy efficiency and the shift of energy demand within this model. In the next section, we explain the outline of our model,

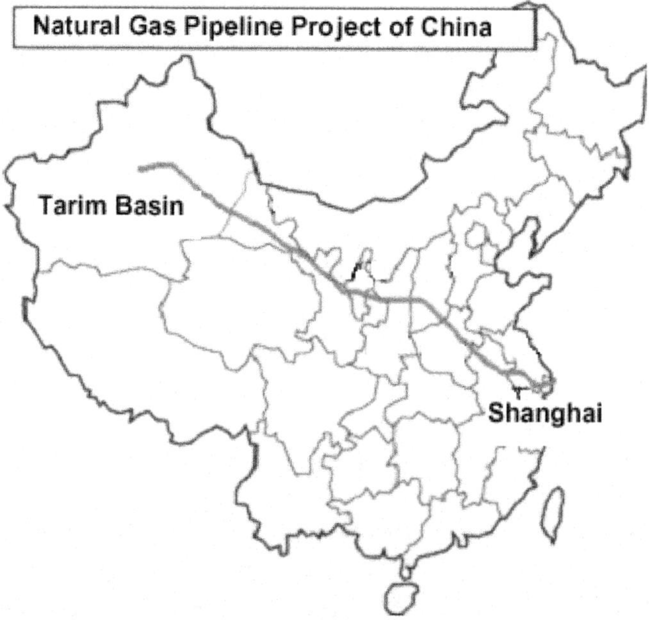

Fig. 1.4

Source: Web site of Search in a Co., Ltd., with some modification (http://news.searchina.ne.jp/2002/0705/general_0705_001.shtml)

and discuss the performance of the estimated model. In Section 3, we present a baseline project from 2000 to 2020, and in Section 4, we analyze scenarios for the pipeline project of the Chinese government, and the natural gas thermal power plant project, which might be a candidate for CDM.

2. Outline and Performance of the Model

The multi-sectoral econometric model of the Chinese economy constructed here is a demand-oriented model of the so-called Keynes-Leontief type. The sectors are categorized into the 15 sectors shown in Table 2.1, which include three energy-related sectors; (1) coal; (2) oil and natural gas; and (3) electric power and heat supply. The data for the model covers the years from 1980 to 2000. However, the period for estimation differs for each equation mainly because of data availability. The sectoral time-series are not officially-published data; therefore, they were estimated by using the Chinese input-output tables.[1]

Table 2.1 Sector classification.

	Sectors
1	Agriculture
2	Mining
3	Food
4	Textile Products
5	Chemical Products
6	Non-Metallic Mineral Products
7	Iron and Steel, and Non-Ferrous Metals
8	Metal Products and Machinery
9	Other Manufacturing
10	Construction
11	Transportation and Communications
12	Services
13	Coal
14	Oil and Natural Gas
15	Electric Power and Heat Supply

[1]The input-output tables are published by the Chinese government National Bureau of Statistics, for the years 1985, 1987, 1990, 1992, 1995, and 1997. The tables were aggregated to the 15 sectors and used, with some interpolations, to estimate the time series data.

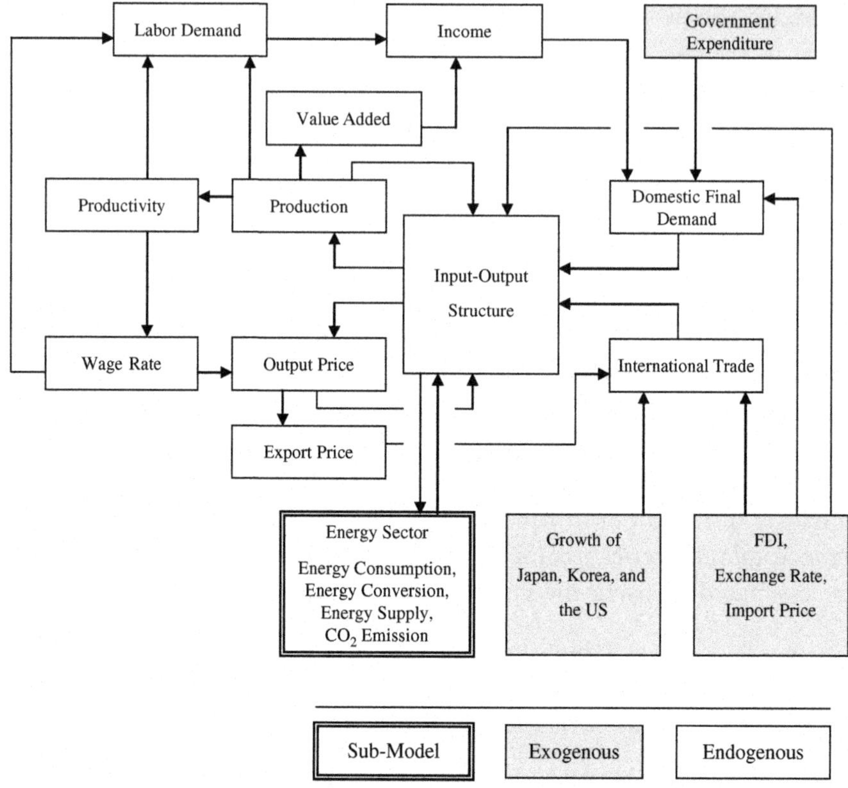

Fig. 2.1 Structure of the model.

2.1. *Structure of the model*

The model structure of the macro and sectoral economy is shown in Fig. 2.1. Expenditures of final demand, production by sector, wage and prices, government expenditure and revenue, current balance and capital balance in international transactions, etc., are shown in this figure. Consumption is explained by income factor and the previous consumption expenditure as a consumption function. Disposable income cannot be obtained from the Chinese official statistics, so we used total value added minus total capital consumption as a proxy variable to represent it.

The investment expenditure contains residential investment, private investment for plant and equipment, and government investment. This is explained by real GDP after subtracting government investment and foreign direct investment. Real GDP is determined as the sum of these expenditures of final demand. In our model, exports are treated as exogenous, and imports by sector are explained endogenously as an import-demand function, in which the explanatory variables are domestic demand by sector and relative price.

The average wage is explained by overall productivity. The wage rate by sector is linked to this average wage. The employment by sector is estimated as the employment-demand function, where the production by sector and real wage are the main explanatory variables. However, employment in the agriculture sector is explained in a different way. The employment in this sector is determined by subtracting the sum of non-agricultural employment from total employment.

Our model contains the fundamental structure of the input-output model. The structure of demand-production determination is expressed as:

$$\mathbf{X} = \mathbf{D} + \mathbf{E} - \mathbf{M}$$

$$\mathbf{X} = \mathbf{AX} + \mathbf{FD} + \mathbf{E} - \mathbf{M}$$

where **X** is a product vector, **D** a domestic demand vector, **E** an export vector, and **M** an import vector. Here, **A** is an input coefficient matrix, and **FD** is a domestic final-demand vector. Meanwhile, the structure of price determination is expressed as:

$$\mathbf{P} = \mathbf{AD}'\mathbf{P} + \mathbf{AM}'\mathbf{PM} + \mathbf{V}$$

$$\mathbf{V} = \hat{\mathbf{X}}^{-1}\hat{\mathbf{L}}\mathbf{W} + \mathbf{O}$$

where **P** is a price vector, **PM** an import price vector, **V** a value added ratio vector, $\mathbf{AD}'$ a transposition of a domestic-input coefficient matrix, and $\mathbf{AM}'$ a transposition of an import-input coefficient matrix. $\hat{\mathbf{X}}^{-1}$ signifies the inverse of the diagonal matrix, whose diagonal elements are from the production vector. $\hat{\mathbf{L}}$ is a diagonal matrix, whose diagonal elements are employed persons by sector. $\mathbf{W}$ is a wage-rate vector, $\hat{\mathbf{X}}^{-1}\hat{\mathbf{L}}\mathbf{W}$ is a unit-wage-cost vector, and $\mathbf{O}$ is a vector that represents other costs.

To simplify the model, however, only one input-output table is used. In the base year, the above relations are strictly maintained, though they do not hold for the other years. We therefore need some adjustment mechanism to explain the discrepancies between the actual domestic demand, $\mathbf{D} = \mathbf{AX}+\mathbf{FD}$, and the calculated domestic demand, $\mathbf{D}^0 = \mathbf{A}^0\mathbf{X} + \mathbf{FD}^0$, which is obtained by assuming that the input coefficient and the distribution ratio of the domestic final-demand in the base year do not change from year to year. These discrepancies are explained by the change in relative prices in our model.

Also, the prices are determined by the sum of the intermediate input cost and unit value-added cost. However, if we apply a fixed input coefficient to this relationship, differences appear between the actual price and the price derived from the costs. In such a case, we apply a regression of the actual price on the calculated price.

In our model, coal, oil, natural gas, and electricity appear in the energy sector[2], though oil and natural gas are treated as one sector in the input-output sector. Figure 2.2 shows the causality among the variables in the energy sector.

Firstly, total power generation is explained by the total demand adjusted for inventory factor and net export. The export and import of electricity are treated as exogenous variables in the model because they are small in scale. The total demand of electricity is calculated as the

[2]Coal, oil and natural gas are measured as tons of coal equivalent. The conversion ratios used were as follows.

Unit	Oil (10,000 tons)	Coal (10,000 tons)	Electricity (100 million kWh)	Natural Gas (100 millon cubic meters)
Calorific Value	10000 kcal/kg	7000 kcal/kg	860 kcal/kWh	9310 kcal/m^3
Standard Coal Conversion	1.429	1.000	0.123	1.330
Conversion Ratio	0.7	1	0.814	0.075

Source: Energy Statistics of China (1997–1999 and 2001).

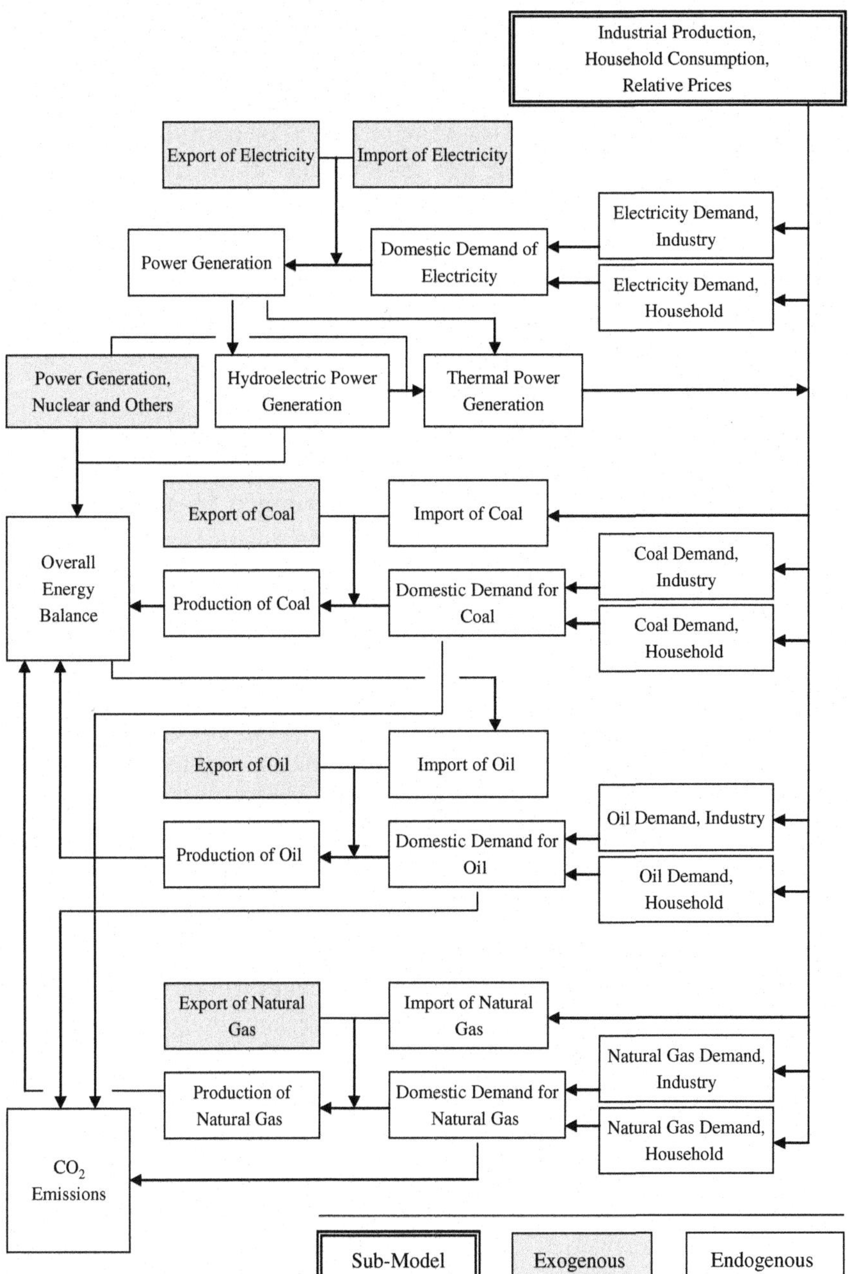

Fig. 2.2 Energy sector flow chart.

sum of industrial demand and household demand. Industrial demand for electricity is a function of the corresponding production or domestic demand and relative price factor. A trend factor is added in some equations. Household demand is also determined by consumption and the relative price factor. Power generation consists of hydroelectric power, thermal power, and other generation methods, mainly nuclear electric-power. Nuclear generation is considered to be exogenous. Hydroelectric generation is explained as a function of total generation and a trend factor, considering that some part of the total generation consists of hydroelectric generation. The remaining part of the total generation is made up by thermal generation.

Assuming exports and imports as exogenous for coal, coal production is explained by the total demand with adjustment for inventory factor and net export. Total demand is determined by the sum of industrial demand and household demand. There is some coal demand for energy conversion. Coal demand for generation is linked to thermal generation via the coal thermal generation ratio and the fuel efficiency of coal generation.

In this equation, the data for the coal thermal ratio and the efficiency ratio of coal thermal generation were obtained from the IEA energy database. According to this data, in 2000 the coal thermal ratio in China was 90.53%, the oil thermal ratio was 8.46%, and the natural gas thermal ratio was 1.02%. The fuel efficiency of generation was 33.26% for coal, 34.14% for oil, and 44.80% for natural gas, respectively, in the same year.

Industrial demand and household demand for coal were determined as a demand function, where the explanatory variables were the production or domestic demand and the relative price. In some equations a trend factor was included.

The oil and natural gas sectors have almost the same structure as the coal sector, with the following differences. Overall energy production is explained by the summation of coal, oil, natural gas, and hydroelectric and nuclear power generation, converted to the same unit. The overall energy demand is explained by summing the sectoral and household demands. Computing the overall energy export in the same way, the overall energy import is determined as the overall demand plus the overall export minus the overall production. In our model, the overall energy import is connected to oil imports, with subtraction of coal imports, which means the shortfall in energy is filled by overseas oil.

Finally, CO_2 emissions are explained from the sum of the demands for coal, oil, and natural gas, after first being multiplied by their respective emission coefficients.[3] The activities of the physical base in the energy sector are connected to the real product in the energy-related sectors.

The main data source we used is the Chiba Statistical Yearbook. However, there were insufficient sectoral data, so we had to estimate sectoral time series for output, intermediate input, value added, employee income, etc. For this estimation, we used the input-output tables for China (see Footnote 1), which we first integrated according to our sectoral classification. Then we interpolated data we lacked between input-output tables, using related time series data. For value added, for example, we used GDP product by sector. We estimated the value-added-to-output ratios by linear interpolation, and obtained output series by sector by dividing the estimated value-added series by the value-added ratios. As a result, we obtained the total intermediate input by sector.

The sum of total intermediate input by sector must be equal to the sum of total intermediate demand by sector. Therefore we could estimate sectoral intermediate demand by multiplying this sum by the relevant ratio of total intermediate demand, which we had linearly interpolated in advance.

We were able to estimate sectoral export and import values from the UN trade database, with some modification for local currency. Total consumption and investment were obtained from the SNA database of China. We estimated the ratios of sectoral values to totals by linear interpolation, and multiplied them by the total value for consumption

[3]The CO_2 emission ratios by type of energy were as follows:

	Coal	Oil	Natural Gas
Emission Coefficient	1.080 (tC/TOE)	0.837 (tC/TOE)	0.641 (tC/TOE)

Source: Revised 1996 IPCC Guidelines for National Greenhouse Gas Inventories.

and investment. Some adjustments were necessary to stay in keeping with the definition that the sum of total intermediate demand and final demand, consumption and investment, and export minus import equals the output for each sector.

After estimating deflators for output, export, and import by sector, we got the corresponding real value by dividing the estimated nominal value by the appropriate deflator.

We ran the model using the following time series data; the period from 1981 to 2000 for the macro equation, and 1985 to 2000 for the energy sector. The estimation methods are mainly ordinal least squares. Regression with autocorrelation of error terms and estimation with coefficient restrictions were applied in some equations.

In our model, individual demand by sector is explained by the computed demand based on the base-year input-output coefficients with appropriate adjustment. This equation is important in our model. We explained it using two factors; the computed demand and the relative price. We were able to obtain statistically significant estimates for almost all sectors. For three energy sectors, we explained real output by the corresponding physical output in the energy sub-model.

Meanwhile, sectoral price was determined by intermediate input cost, labor cost, and the remaining cost. We estimated sectoral price by intermediate input price, which were computed using the base-year input-output coefficients, and wage rates. The intermediate input deflators were significant for all sectors. However, wage rates were significant only for four sectors; mining, food, construction and services. As one explanatory variable, the dependent variable of the previous period was added for each equation of two sectors; coal, and electric power and heat supply, which are expressed by a partial adjustment mechanism.

Table 2.2 shows the mean absolute percentage error of the main variables for the dynamic simulation for the period 1995–1999. The performance of the model can be evaluated from these values. Some variables in the table are slightly high in MAPE. However, the important variables have very low MAPE values: real GDP is 1.90%, the total for real product is 1.59%, the total for nominal value added is 2.08%, the GDP deflator is 2.15%, and total employment is 0.30%.

Table 2.2 Performance of the model.

Macro Variables	MAPE (%)	Real Product	MAPE (%)
Real GDP	1.90	Agriculture	2.24
Real Consumption	1.73	Mining	17.30
Real Government Consumption	4.95	Food	4.44
Real Investment	1.80	Textile Products	4.06
Real Exports	2.66	Chemical Products	4.69
Real Imports	7.63	Non-Metallic Mineral Products	9.95
Nominal GDP	2.74	Iron and Steel, and Non-Ferrous Metals	2.74
Nominal Consumption	0.93	Metal Products and Machinery	2.77
Nominal Government Consumption	5.44	Other Manufacturing	12.48
Nominal Investment	2.52	Construction	1.91
Nominal Exports	2.00	Transportation and Communication	3.04
Nominal Imports	9.13	Services	5.61
GDP Deflator	2.15	Coal	6.49
Producer Price Index	1.89	Oil and Natural Gas	3.26
Consumer Price Index	0.90	Electric Power and Heat Supply	1.85
Employment Total	0.30	Total	1.59
Value Added	**MAPE (%)**	**Product Deflators**	**MAPE (%)**
Agriculture	4.62	Agriculture	6.74
Mining	11.06	Mining	3.23
Food	9.22	Food	1.90
Textile Products	9.09	Textile Products	2.63
Chemical Products	5.23	Chemical Products	4.21
Non-Metallic Mineral Products	9.17	Non-Metallic Mineral Products	1.75
Iron and Steel, and Non-Ferrous Metals	14.13	Iron and Steel, and Non-Ferrous Metals	5.25
Metal Products and Machinery	2.27	Metal Products and Machinery	1.89
Other Manufacturing	18.79	Other Manufacturing	2.34
Construction	1.52	Construction	1.22
Transportation and Communications	7.22	Transportation and Communications	7.71
Services	3.51	Services	3.63

(Continued)

Table 2.2 (*Continued*)

Coal	10.11	Coal	2.43
Oil and Natural Gas	9.41	Oil and Natural Gas	5.16
Electric Power and Heat Supply	6.05	Electric Power and Heat Supply	4.26
Total	2.08	Average	1.49
Employment	**MAPE (%)**	**Energy Variables**	**MAPE (%)**
Agriculture	3.15	Overall Energy Production	2.98
Mining	4.65	Overall Energy Exports	6.65
Food	9.02	Overall Energy Imports	8.78
Textile Products	11.04	Overall Energy Demand	2.70
Chemical Products	11.33	Coal Production	3.23
Non-Metallic Mineral Products	14.10	Coal Demand	3.12
Iron and Steel, and Non-Ferrous Metals	14.15	Coal Demand, Industry	3.61
Metal Products and Machinery	16.17	Coal Demand, Household	5.65
Other Manufacturing	15.66	Coal Demand, Power Generation	2.36
Construction	2.81	Oil Production	5.51
Transportation and Communications	2.27	Oil Demand	2.61
Services	3.34	Oil Demand, Industry	2.54
Coal	4.27	Oil Demand, Household	4.62
Oil and Natural Gas	6.02	Natural Gas Production	3.26
Electric Power and Heat Supply	3.35	CO_2 Emissions	2.66
Total	0.30		

We can thus conclude that the model is sufficient for explanation of the sample period.

3. Baseline Prediction

3.1. *The assumptions made for the prediction*

In this section we discuss the baseline prediction from 2000 to 2020 which was to be used in the scenario analysis. The assumed values, adopted here for the exogenous variables, are shown in Table 3.1. Basically these values were extracted with some adjustments from the

Table 3.1 Assumed values of the exogenous variables, (%).

Variables	2000–2010	2010–2020
Real Export		
Agriculture	10.00	5.00
Mining	0.50	2.00
Food	5.00	3.00
Textile Products	6.49	3.00
Chemical Products	8.00	5.00
Non-Metallic Mineral Products	1.50	1.00
Iron and Steel, and Non-Ferrous Metals	5.00	3.00
Metal Products and Machinery	11.00	8.00
Other Manufacturing	9.00	4.00
Construction	6.49	5.00
Coal	10.00	5.00
Oil and Natural Gas	0.00	0.00
Electric Power and Heat Supply	2.00	1.00
Total	9.40	6.45
Foreign Direct Investment, Net	9.98	10.00
Import Price (dollar base)	3.00	3.00
International Oil Price (dollar base)	3.00	3.00
Exchange Rate (yuan/dollar)	0.00	0.00
Government Debt from Foreign Countries	−6.01	−3.00
Government Investment	10.00	8.00
Government Income Outside Taxation	17.47	10.00
Average Tax Rate	3.44	2.26
Population	0.79	0.62

recent trends from 1995 to 2000, indicated in past research by the IEA and the Institute of Energy Economics, Japan (IEEJ).

We assumed that the growth rate of real exports was about 9.4% for the first 10 years, and 6.45% for the second 10 years. The net value of foreign direct investment would grow by 9.98% and 10.0% for these periods, respectively. The import price would grow at 3%, the exchange rate was fixed at its value in 2000, and the population growth rates were assumed to be 0.79% and 0.62%.

We assumed that the export and import of energy would grow as fast as in the past or would not change in level. The unit ratio of natural gas to production, which is exogenous in the model, was set as constant, at the 2000 value.

Table 3.2 Assumptions on thermal electricity generation.

		2000	2010	2020
Power generation composition	Coal	90.53	89.44	88.13
	Oil	8.46	7.58	6.76
	Natural Gas	1.02	2.98	5.11
Power generation efficiency	Coal	33.26	35.26	37.34
	Oil	34.14	33.65	34.97
	Natural Gas	44.80	50.00	50.00

Table 3.2 shows the composition of thermal power generation and fuel efficiency from 2000 to 2020, which were the values for China indicated in the Energy Outlook of the IEA. In this table, coal thermal generation will be dominant in the future, though natural gas thermal generation will gradually grow. The share of coal generation was assumed to be 88.13% in 2020. It was assumed that the fuel efficiencies of coal, oil, and natural gas would improve. The efficiency of natural gas was 50.0%, that of coal, 37.34%, and of oil, 34.97%.

3.2. *Characteristics of the baseline*

Table 3.3 shows the results for the main variables in the baseline forecast from 2000 to 2020, as average annual growth rates for two ten-year periods. The growth rates for actual data from 1995 to 2000 are also shown.

The growth rate of real GDP is 6.11% for the first 10 years and 4.40% for the second 10 years, which is slightly low compared with the economic growth in the 1990s. Referring to the standard forecast of the IEA, the growth rate of real GDP is 6.0% for 1997–2010, and 3.7% for 2010–2020. The simulation study of the IEEJ shows 7.1% growth for 2000–2010, and 6.1% for 2010–2020 (see Table 3.4). Though comparison between them is limited because the prediction assumptions and the respective model characteristics are different, the growth rate of our model corresponds to the forecasted values of the IEA and the IEEJ.

Table 3.3 Average growth rates of macro variables, (%).

	1995–2000	2000–2010	2010–2020
Real GDP	7.39	6.11	4.40
Real Consumption	7.95	6.45	3.85
Real Government Consumption	9.61	5.91	4.11
Real Investment	8.88	6.43	4.47
Real Exports	20.65	8.97	6.31
Real Imports	21.25	9.12	5.68
Nominal GDP	9.98	9.92	8.33
Nominal Consumption	10.69	10.09	8.05
Nominal Government Consumption	12.39	9.53	8.32
Nominal Investment	10.67	11.14	9.51
Nominal Exports	20.57	9.63	7.57
Nominal Imports	16.94	11.72	9.06
GDP Deflator	2.41	3.60	3.76
Producer Price Index	1.51	3.45	4.18
Consumer Price Index	2.52	3.42	4.04
Employment, Total	0.91	0.59	0.66

Table 3.4 Comparison of real GDP.

Predictions of Our Model	Average Growth Rate (%)		
	1995–2000	2000–2010	2010–2020
Real GDP	7.39	6.11	4.40
	2005–2010	2000–2010	2010–2020
Population	0.89	0.79	0.62
IEA World Energy Outlook 2000	**Average Growth Rate (%)**		
	2000	1997–2010	2010–2020
Real GDP	7.00	6.00	3.71
	1971–1997	1997–2020	
Population	1.50	0.70	
Institute of Energy Economics, Japan	**Average Growth Rate (%)**		
	1998–2000	2000–2010	2010–2020
Real GDP	7.30	7.10	6.10
	1998–2000	2000–2010	2010–2020
Population	1.00	0.75	0.62

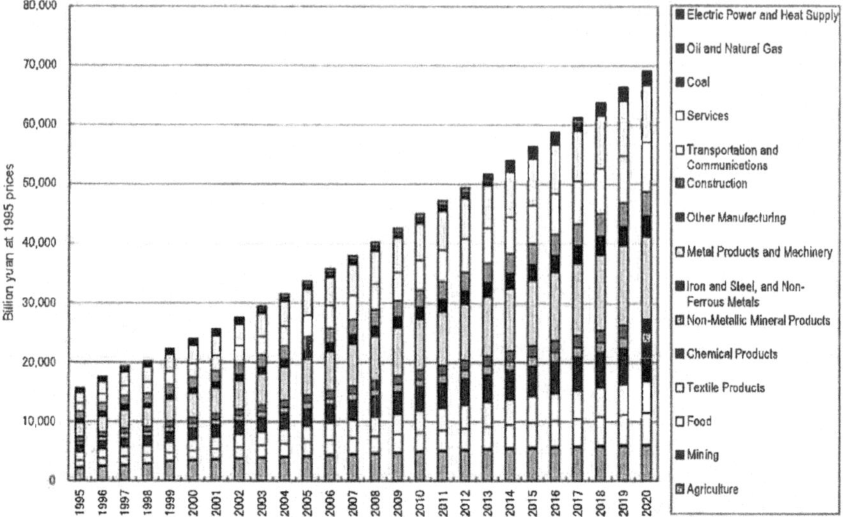

Fig. 3.1 Real production by sector.

Figure 3.1 shows the amount of real production by sector to 2020 and its composition, in which the values from 1995–1999 are actual data. Figure 3.2 shows employed persons by sector. Because we assume the expansion of exports in the metal product and machinery sector, the production in this sector is also growing faster than the other sectors. Moreover, employment in the service sector increases from 40% in 2000 to 48% in 2020, though the employment in the agriculture sector decreases, and the agricultural workers' share of total employment shrinks from 47% to 39% over 20 years. That is, a shift of employment from the agricultural sector to the service sector is expected.

Table 3.5 shows a comparison of primary energy supply. Its growth rate is 5.30% in the first ten-year period and 3.01% in the latter. The energy elasticity to GDP is 0.867 and 0.684 for the same periods, respectively. According to the IEA forecast, the primary energy supply is 3.56% for the period 1997–2010, and 3.11% for the period 2010–2020. The elasticity to GDP is about 0.59 and 0.84 for those same periods, respectively. The IEEJ simulation estimates 3.23% growth for

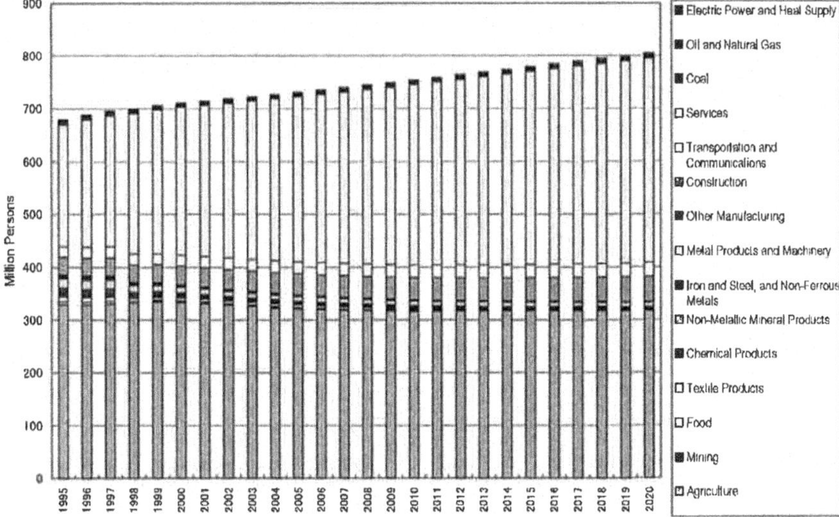

Fig. 3.2 Employment by sector.

2000–2010, and 3.84% for 2010–2020. The elasticity to GDP is 0.45 and 0.63 for those same periods, respectively. The estimates of our model are slightly high in the growth rate for the first period, though almost the same for the latter period.

The primary energy supply is estimated to be 2.480 billion tons of coal equivalent in 2020 in our model, which is slightly lower than the estimates of the IEA and IEEJ, which were 2.767 and 2.747 billion tons of coal equivalent, respectively. The total amount of generation in our model is 3.04 trillion kWh in 2020, which is also lower than the values of the IEA and IEEJ of 3.69 and 4.22 trillion kWh, respectively. The difference may partly stem from the assumption in our prediction that the household demand for electricity decreases by half in its growth according to the data.

We estimate that the supply of natural gas is 0.069 billion tons of coal equivalent, which is much lower than the values of the IEA and IEEJ, which are 0.159 and 0.261 billion tons of coal equivalent, respectively. Our forecasts are basically dependent on past trends in demand and consumption, and we have included policy consideration

Table 3.5 Comparison of primary energy supply.

Predictions of Our Model

	Million Tons of Oil Equivalent			Million Tons of Coal Equivalent			Average Growth Rate (%)	
	2000	2010	2020	2000	2010	2020	2000–2010	2010–2020
Total Primary Energy	770	1,290	1,736	1,100	1,843	2,480	5.30	3.01
Coal	477	810	1,064	682	1,158	1,520	5.43	2.76
Oil	222	355	497	317	507	710	4.81	3.43
Natural Gas	22	35	49	32	49	69	4.41	3.45
Others	48	91	127	69	129	181	6.50	3.44
		(Billion Kwh)						
Electricity	13,158	21,274	30,383	162	261	373	4.92	3.63

IEA World Energy Outlook 2000

	Million Tons of Oil Equivalent			Million Tons of Coal Equivalent			Average Growth Rate (%)	
	1997	2010	2020	1997	2010	2020	1997–2010	2010–2020
Total Primary Energy	905	1,426	1,937	1,293	2,037	2,767	3.56	3.11
Coal	662	940	1,192	946	1,343	1,703	2.73	2.40
Oil	201	371	541	287	530	773	4.83	3.84
Natural Gas	21	56	111	30	80	159	7.84	7.08
Others	21	59	93	30	84	133	8.27	4.66
		(Billion Kwh)						
Electricity	11,630	24,080	36,910	143	296	453	5.76	4.36

(Continued)

Table 3.6 (*Continued*)

Institute of Energy Economics, Japan								
	Million Tons of Oil Equivalent			Million Tons of Coal Equivalent			Average Growth Rate (%)	
	2000	2010	2020	2000	2010	2020	2000–2010	2010–2020
Total Primary Energy	961	1,320	1,923	1,372	1,885	2,747	3.23	3.84
Coal	684	829	1,076	977	1,184	1,537	1.94	2.64
Oil	230	335	513	329	479	733	3.83	4.34
Natural Gas	23	82	183	33	117	261	13.53	8.36
Others	23	73	151	33	105	216	12.11	7.50
		(Billion Kwh)						
Electricity	12,455	22,283	42,200	153	274	518	5.99	6.59

of the future introduction of natural gas, which would make such differences possible.[4]

Table 3.6 shows the amount of CO_2 emissions in relation to energy production. They tally 1.597 billion tons of carbon in 2020, although only 0.835 billion tons of carbon in 2000. In the IEA forecast, the amount of CO_2 emissions in 2020 are 1.753 billion tons of carbon. The IEEJ predicts 1.668 billion tons of carbon in 2020. Our estimate is slightly low compared with the other two results, because energy production and consumption are slightly lower than for the others.

Figure 3.3 shows CO_2 emissions by real GDP in our model. This ratio decreases from 0.1 tons of carbon per thousand yuan in 2000 to 0.0688 tons of carbon per thousand yuan in 2020. The improvement in energy efficiency and the energy shift from coal to natural gas and oil make this ratio lower.

4. Scenario Analyses

In this section, we discuss the following two simulations.

Case 1: The natural gas pipeline project.
Case 2: The construction of natural gas power stations.

In these simulations, we use the baseline prediction, which is explained in the previous section, for the 20 years from 2000 to 2020.

[4]The Energy Research Institute of China estimated the future demands of natural gas, which are shown in the following table. The volume of demand in 2020 is relatively large.

	Actual Data Unit: BCM			Growth Rate (%)	
Sector	1997	2010	2020	2010	2020
Power Generation	2.2	35.0	81.2	23.76	8.78
Chemical Industry	8.4	19.0	32.5	6.45	5.51
Other Industry	6.3	20.0	40.0	9.32	7.18
Household	2.1	22.0	50.0	19.72	8.56
Total	19.6	96.0	203.7	13.02	7.81

Table [illegible] Comparison of CO_2 emissions.

Predictions of Our Model

	Million Tons of CO_2			Million Tons of Carbon			Average Growth Rate (%)	
	2000	2010	2020	2000	2010	2020	1997–2010	2010–2020
CO_2 Emissions	3,061.8	4,393.3	5,855.9	835.0	1,198.2	1,597.1	3.68	2.92
Coal	2,335.2	3,221.5	4,212.9	636.9	878.6	1,149.0	3.271	2.721
Oil	673.8	1,088.9	1,525.5	183.8	297.0	416.0	4.92	3.43
Natural Gas	52.8	82.9	117.5	14.4	22.6	32.1	4.61	3.56

IEA World Energy Outlook 2000

	Million Tons of CO_2			Million Tons of Carbon			Average Growth Rate (%)	
	1997	2010	2020	1997	2010	2020	1997–2010	1997–2020
CO_2 Emissions	3,162.0	4,822.0	6,426.0	862.4	1,315.1	1,752.5	3.30	2.91
Coal	2,548.0	3,638.0	4,624.0	694.9	992.2	1,261.1	2.78	2.43
Oil	567.0	1,060.0	1,555.0	154.6	289.1	424.1	4.93	3.91
Natural Gas	46.0	124.0	247.0	12.5	33.8	67.4	7.93	7.13

Institute of Energy Economics, Japan

	Million Tons of CO_2			Million Tons of Carbon			Average Growth Rate (%)	
	2000	2010	2020	2000	2010	2020	2000–2010	1997–2020
CO_2 Emissions	3,361.5	4,381.3	6,114.6	916.8	1,194.9	1,667.6	2.68	3.39
Coal	2,709.7	3,281.7	4,260.7	739.0	895.0	1,162.0	1.48	2.65
Oil	597.7	905.7	1,426.3	163.0	247.0	389.0	3.25	4.65
Natural Gas	55.0	194.3	429.0	15.0	53.0	117.0	10.20	8.24

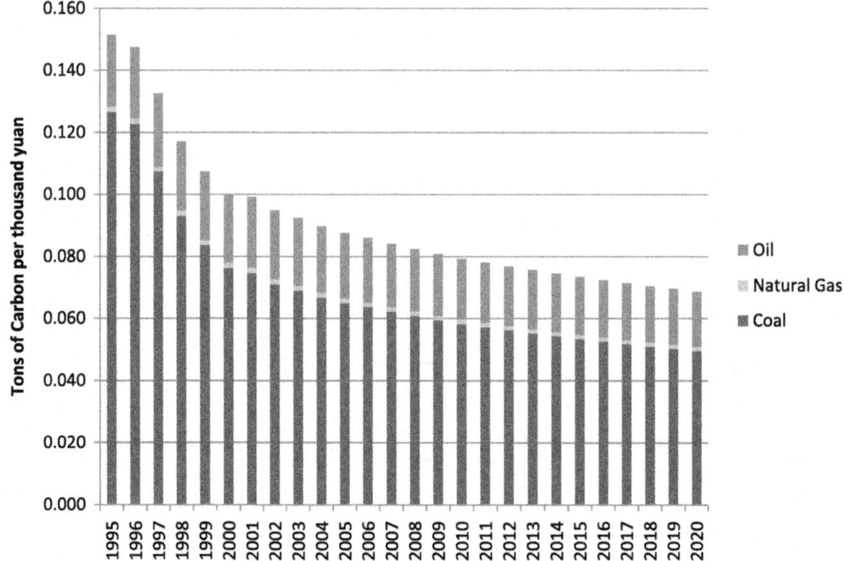

Fig. 3.3 CO_2 Emissions by real GDP.

4.1. *The natural gas pipeline project*

The Chinese government estimated that the cost of the pipeline project from the Tarim Basin to Shanghai of China at about 140 billion yuan, which was 136.25 billion yuan at 1995 market prices. A simulation of this project was performed.

The construction period of this project was to be four years, 2002 to 2005. We therefore divided the total cost by year, assuming that the cost each year was the same, that is, 34 billion yuan. According to the government plan, 90% of the total cost was for the purchase of equipment and materials, 65% of which was to be provided from the domestic market. Considering these circumstances, we assumed the distribution ratios of the investment were as shown in Table 4.1. The scale of this investment, 34 billion yuan, is about 0.3% of GDP in the baseline forecast.

This project was to be completed in 2005, and natural gas supplied from that year. It is assumed that 12 billion cubic meters of natural gas were to be supplied at first, and that the supply will increase to 19 billion cubic meters after 2010. We assume that the natural gas is consumed

Table 4.1 Distribution of investment demand, (%).

Sectors	Share	Domestic	Imports
Agriculture	—	—	—
Mining	—	—	—
Food	—	—	—
Textile Products	—	—	—
Chemical Products	—	—	—
Mon-Metallic Mineral Products	—	—	—
Iron and Steel, and Non-Ferrous Metals	70.0	45.5	24.5
Metal Products and Machinery	20.0	13.0	7.0
Other Manufacturing	—	—	—
Construction	7.0	7.0	—
Transportation and Communications	1.0	1.0	—
Services	2.0	2.0	—
Coal	—	—	—
Oil and Natural Gas	—	—	—
Electric Power and Heat Supply	—	—	—
Total	100.0	68.5	31.5

Table 4.2 Share of natural gas consumption by sector, (%).

Sectors	2005	2010	2020
Electric Power and Heat Supply	60	60	60
Chemical Products	20	20	20
Transportation and Communications	10	10	10
Household	10	10	10
Total	100	100	100

in four sectors; electric power and heat supply, chemical products, transportation and communications, and household, as shown in Table 4.2. It is thought that coal consumption will be replaced by the same amount of natural gas in calorie terms. However, oil consumption will be reduced in the transportation sector. Moreover, the difference of power generation efficiency between natural gas thermal power generation and coal thermal power generation is considered in the electric power sector.[5]

[5]The substitution of natural gas for coal and petroleum will require additional fixed investment in energy-consuming sectors. However, we did not consider such factors in the simulation, because we were not able to obtain sufficient data for their estimation.

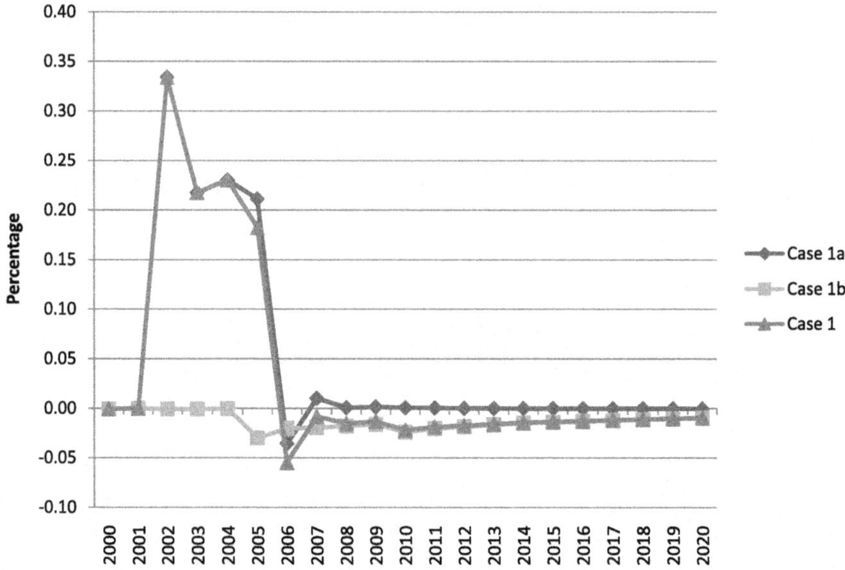

Fig. 4.1 Effect on real GDP.

Figure 4.1 shows the GDP changes from the baseline case. Case 1a shows the effect of increased investment, which expands GDP by 0.20–0.35% of the baseline values for the period of investment. The effect on GDP is concentrated in this period. The investment multiplier is about 1.07–1.28, because the amount of GDP is 25–30 billion yuan and domestic investment is 23.46 billion yuan per year. This effect disappears soon after the completion of the pipeline. Case 1b shows the effect after the completion of the pipeline. A slightly negative influence on GDP is seen. The overall effect is shown by Case 1. The multiplier effect of the investment works and there is a positive effect on GDP until 2005. However, the deflationary effect of the decreased coal demand becomes predominant after 2005.

Figure 4.2 shows the changes in production by sector from the baseline for the years 2005, 2010, and 2020. The primary metal, machinery, construction, transportation and communication, and service sectors receive positive effects in 2005, when investment is increased. Conversely, the natural gas supply starts in 2005, and the demand shift effect of the natural gas begins in 2010 and 2020. Production in the machinery, transportation and communication, and

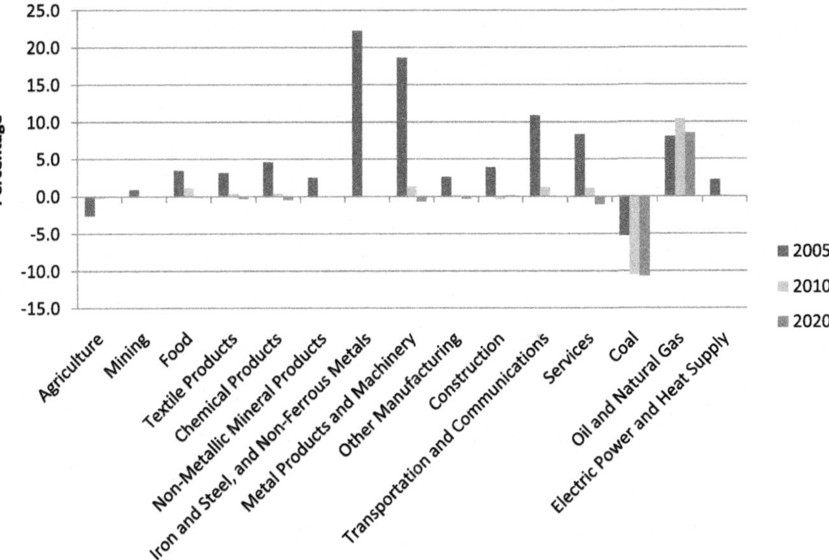

Fig. 4.2 Effect on real production by sector.

service sectors will decrease in line with the production decrease in the coal industry.

Figure 4.3 shows the difference in the amount of the CO_2 emission of each case from the baseline. When the energy demand shift from coal to natural gas occurs, Case 1b shows that the amount of CO_2 emissions decreases, though the CO_2 emissions increase in accordance with the expansion of investment demand, which can also be seen in Case 1a. When natural gas use begins, CO_2 is gradually reduced, though CO_2 increases in the project investment (construction) period, and Case 1 indicates what happens if the two effects are combined

4.2. *Construction of natural gas thermal power plants*

Here we discuss the effect of the construction of natural gas thermal power plants, a project which is widely noted as a candidate for CDM activities. The supply of electricity from the natural gas thermal power plants will reduce that from coal power generation because of the advantage in fuel efficiency. As a result, fuel shifts from coal to natural gas in the power generation process.

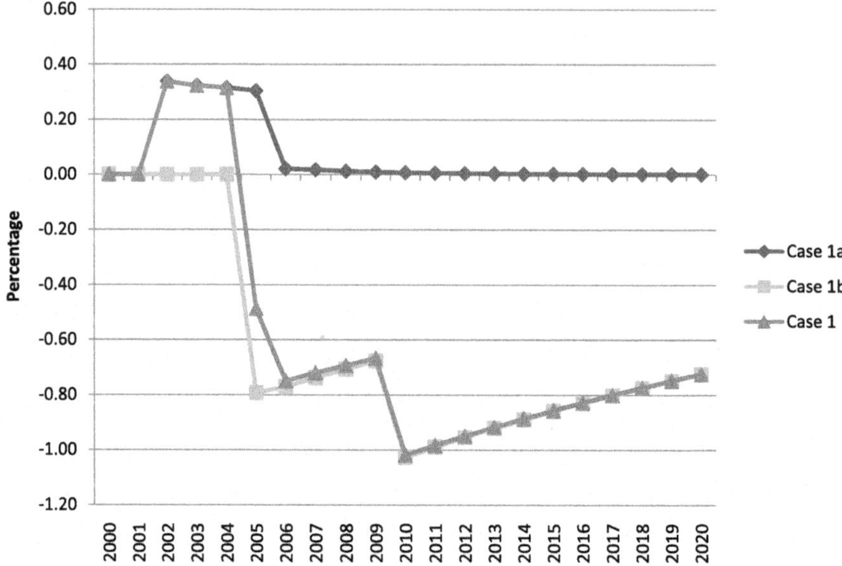

Fig. 4.3 Changes in CO_2 emissions.

From the previous scenario (4.1), we find that the shift from coal to natural gas brings society an immediate reduction in CO_2. However, at the same time, investment demand causes society to experience additional CO_2 emissions. Similar results are expected in this case. The problem then becomes one of whether the effect of the CO_2 reduction is still large even if the investment effect is taken into account.

According to the Energy Research Institute of China, the construction cost of a typical natural gas thermal power plant able to supply electricity of 4.2 billion kWh per year is estimated at 4.2 billion yuan. The present scenario is based on this information.

In order to supply 1% of the amount of power generation in 2010 in our baseline, which is approximately 21 billion kWh, five thermal power plants of the type stated above will be built. The total construction cost is assumed here to be 21 billion yuan, or 20.44 billion yuan at 1995 market prices.

The construction period of the five power plants is assumed to be the five years, 2005–2009. This means that 4.088 billion yuan will be invested each year. Power generation will begin from 2010. Thus the

11 years, up to and including 2020, are evaluated here for the purposes of this analysis.

Natural gas thermal power generation will supply 21 billion kWh of electricity per year. The amount of coal thermal power generation, however, will fall, and coal consumption is reduced as a result. The power generation efficiency of natural gas thermal power is assumed to be 50%, and the efficiency of coal thermal power generation is assumed to be the same as that set in the baseline forecast.

We assume that 80% of the investment expenditure is for machinery products, i.e. machines related to power generation, 15% for construction, 3% for transportation, and 2% for services, as shown in Table 4.3. In addition, 35% of the above-mentioned machinery demand is assumed to be covered by imported goods, and the remainder by domestic ones. It is thought that 72% of the total amount of the investment is domestic.

Figure 4.4 shows the influence on real GDP. The investment has a positive effect on GDP, though the demand shift in energy contributes a negative effect after electricity is supplied by natural gas thermal generation. This pattern is almost the same as that seen in the previous

Table 4.3 Distribution of investment demand, (%).

Sectors	Share	Domestic	Imports
Agriculture	—	—	—
Mining	—	—	—
Food	—	—	—
Textile Products	—	—	—
Chemical Products	—	—	—
Non-Metallic Mineral Products	—	—	—
Iron and Steel, and Non-Ferrous Metals	—	—	—
Metal Products and Machinery	80	52	28
Other Manufacturing	—	—	—
Construction	15	15	—
Transportation and Communications	3	3	—
Services	2	2	—
Coal	—	—	—
Oil and Natural Gas	—	—	—
Electric Power and Heat Supply	—	—	—
Total	100	72	28

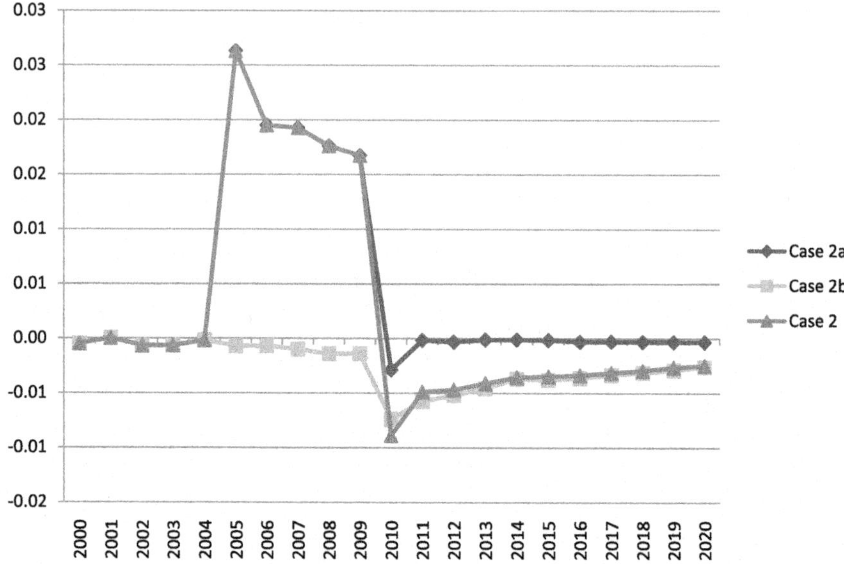

Fig. 4.4 Effect on real GDP.

scenario, though the present scenario shows a difference in the scale of the effects.

Figure 4.5 shows the effect on production by sector. The influence on the machinery sector is the largest, followed by the construction, and transportation and communication sectors. Moreover, coal production is reduced and natural gas production increases after the natural gas generation starts. Many sectors receive a negative influence, though not so large.

Figure 4.6 shows the changes in the amount of CO_2 emissions. An increase of approximately 0.02% in tons of carbon per year is observed in the period of investment (construction), though a decrease of approximately 0.19–0.27% per year is seen after generation starts.

4.3. *Comparison of CO_2 emissions and associated costs*

Figure 4.7 compares the total amount of CO_2 emissions in both scenarios. The pipeline project reduces 170.11 million tons of carbon in the form of CO_2 emissions, though the pipeline investment (construction) increases emissions 12.94 million tons of carbon in the form of

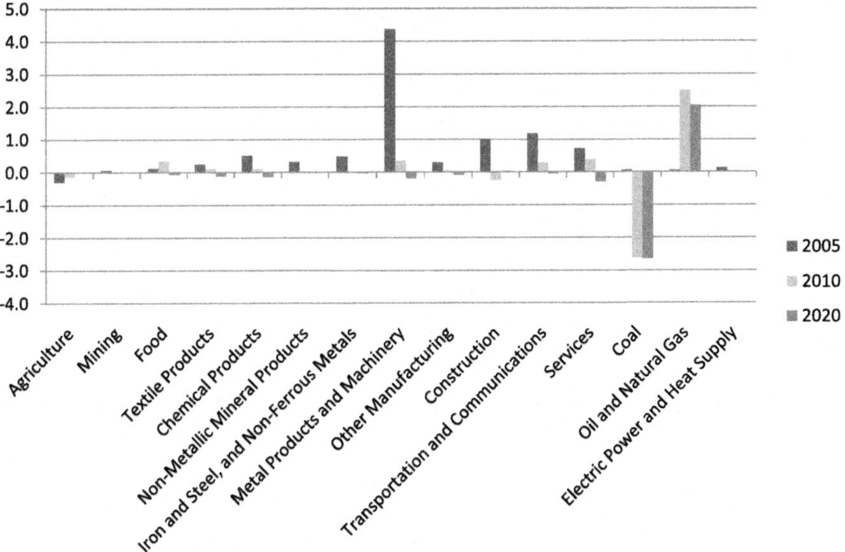

Fig. 4.5 Effect on real production.

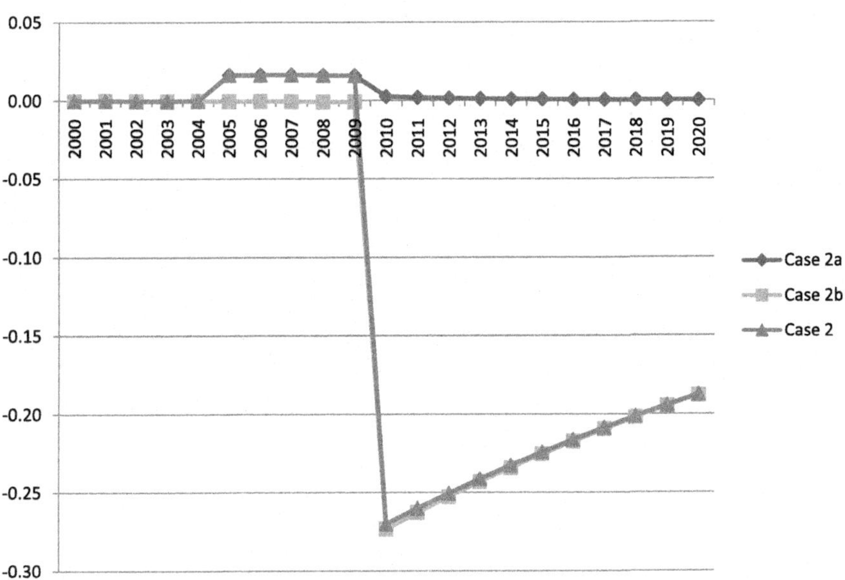

Fig. 4.6 Changes in CO_2 emissions.

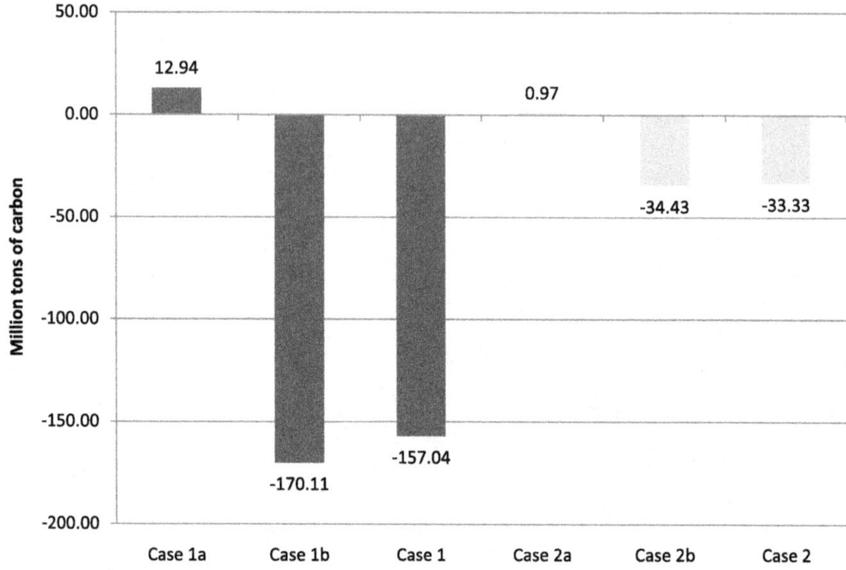

Fig. 4.7 Sum of CO_2 emissions from 2000 to 2020.

CO_2. Overall, the expected reduction is 157.04 million tons of carbon in the form of CO_2. On the other hand, the CO_2 reduction in the natural gas thermal power plant project is expected to be 34.43 million tons of carbon, although an increase of 0.97 million tons of carbon is brought about by the plant investment (construction). In this case, the overall effect is considered to be 33.33 million tons of carbon in the form of CO_2.

Table 4.4 shows a comparison of the effects of the CO_2 reduction. The total amounts of CO_2 reduction in the table are the same values indicated in Fig. 4.7. Values for tons of carbon are converted into tons of CO_2. The reduction cost is the initial investment cost for each project. The unit reduction costs, which are costs by the amount of CO_2 reduced, are evaluated in yuan, yen, and US dollars.[6]

Moreover, "Direct effect" (of the reduction) in the table represents the estimated value for the effect of the CO_2 reduction directly experienced in the sector, which is assumed to shift demand from coal (and

[6]The exchange rates used here are 15 yen to the yuan, and 120 yen to the US dollar.

Table 4.4 Comparison of reduction costs of CO_2 emissions.

			CO_2 Reduction		Reduction Cost	Unit Reduction Cost		
			Million tons of carbon	Million tons of CO_2	Billion yuan	Yuan/ton of CO_2	Yen/ton of CO_2	Dollar/ ton of CO_2
Pipeline Project	Direct Effect		167.39	613.75	140.0	228	3,422	28.51
	Total Effect	Demand Shift Only	170.11	623.74	140.0	224	3,367	28.06
		Demand Shift and Investment	157.04	575.80	140.0	243	3,647	30.39
Natural Gas Electric Power Plant Project	Direct Effect		34.13	125.14	21.0	168	2,517	20.98
	Total Effect	Demand Shift Only	34.43	126.25	21.0	166	2,495	20.79
		Demand Shift and Investment	33.33	122.22	21.0	172	2,577	21.48

in part, oil) to natural gas in both scenarios. These changes, however, affect not only the sector concerned but also other sectors through the interdependence of production among sectors. The amount of the reduction, which occurs in the model simulation, is called "Total effect" (of the reduction) here. This effect is divided between the two cases in the table, Case 1b and Case 2b,to evaluate the effect of demand shift from coal to natural gas, and Case 1 and Case 2 to consider not only the demand shift in energy but also the effect of investment.

"Direct effect" (of the reduction) in the pipeline project is estimated at US$ 28.51 per ton of CO_2, and that of the natural gas thermal power plant project is US$ 20.98 per ton of CO_2. The difference between them is some what large, partly because the sectors in which the demand shift in energy appears directly are not the same. In the former project, not only the electricity sector, but also the chemical, transportation, and household sectors show changes in their energy-demand mix, whereas only the electricity sector is concerned in the latter project. The effect on the electricity sector is expected to be large in terms of CO_2 reduction.

"Total effect" (of the reduction) shows that the unit reduction cost ends up somewhat lower than is the case for "Direct effect" (of the reduction). For the pipeline project, the cost is estimated at US$ 28.06 per ton of CO_2, but rises further to US$ 30.39 per ton of CO_2 when we add the effect of the investment (construction). It becomes US$ 20.79 per ton of CO_2, and US$ 21.48 per ton of CO_2, with the effect of investment (construction) added for the natural gas thermal power plant project.

The demand shift from coal to natural gas increases natural gas production, while decreasing coal production. These changes in production affect other areas of production through changes in the demand of intermediate input and in relative prices. The result of such changes in production is a strengthening of CO_2 reduction in the economy. In addition, investment in (construction of) the project causes additional CO_2 emissions. The CO_2 reduction cost to society as a whole rises when we take the latter into account.

It should be noted that the full lifespan of each project was not considered. The costs obtained are values estimated for our simulation period, 2000 to 2020. Therefore, each reduction cost has the possibility of decreasing further when we consider that the lifetime of the projects is typically longer than those twenty years.[7]

5. Concluding Remarks

Our simulation attempted to predict the growth of the Chinese economy until 2020 and to evaluate the effect of two possible projects on the Chinese economy and environment.

According to our predictions, China will continue to grow at a relatively high rate, although the growth rate will decline gradually to less than 5% per year. The amount of real GDP in 2020 will increase to 2.78 times the amount in 2000. The overall energy demand in 2020 will increase to 1.95 times the amount in 2000. Also, while the efficiency of energy use will increase, the amount of energy demand will continue to rise, which will induce more CO_2 emissions. The emissions will grow to 1.91 times in volume between 2000 and 2020.

The impact analyses of the pipeline project and the thermal power plant project, both of which relate to natural gas usage, raise several points. The pipeline project we evaluated in our model will not have a

[7] If we extend the simulation periods to 2030 under the same conditions, the direct cost of CO_2 reduction decreases to US$ 17.23 per ton of CO_2 for the pipeline project, and US$ 10.93 per ton of CO_2 for the power plant project.

Comparison of the Reduction Costs of CO_2 Emissions.

		CO_2 Reduction		Reduction Cost	Unit Reduction Cost		
		Million tons of carbon	Million tons of CO_2	Billion yuan	Yuan/ton of CO_2	Yen/ton of CO_2	Dollar/ton of CO_2
Pipeline Project	Direct effect through 2020	162.38	595.38	140.0	235	3,527	29.39
	Direct effect through 2030	277.07	1,015.92	140.0	138	2,067	17.23
Natural Gas Electric	Direct effect through 2020	34.31	125.80	21.0	167	2,504	20.87
Power Plant Project	Direct effect through 2030	65.50	240.16	21.0	87	1,312	10.93

large impact on the macro-economy of China on the whole, in the sense that the project will not change the future growth path of the economy. This is simply because investment in the project is only 0.3% of GDP. Investment in the projects will, of course, produce positive impacts on the economy. The effect is limited to the period when the investment occurs, during which time the production in the metal and machinery industries, which produce capital goods, increases greatly. However, the energy shift in both projects will assert a slightly negative impact on production as a whole, mainly because the difference in efficiency induces more reduction in coal use.

CO_2 emissions increase in periods of expansion. On the other hand, the demand shift from coal to natural gas has the effect of reducing CO_2 emissions, because natural gas demonstrates a high level of efficiency in power generation and low CO_2 emissions. Although they offset one another, CO_2 reduction gets the upper-hand throughout the simulation periods. A similar effect is expected for the natural gas thermal power plant project, though the scale of the impact differs. The direct cost of CO_2 reduction is estimated at US$ 28.51 per ton of CO_2 for the pipeline project, and US$ 20.98 per ton of CO_2 for the power plant project. However, the costs increase to US$ 30.39 per ton of CO_2 and US$ 21.48 per ton of CO_2, respectively, for the economy as a whole.

These results are tentative in the sense that our model simulation is limited in the area of demand and in that the effects of changes in the supply situation and improvements in productivity have not sufficiently been taken into consideration. These issues remain to be solved by a future elaboration of our model. At the same time, we should consider the international aspects of interdependency, with the main focus being on interdependency among East Asian countries.

References

Ichimura, Shinichi and Hui-Jiong Wang (2003). *Interregional Input-Output Analysis of the Chinese Economy*, World Scientific, Singapore.

Ito, Kokichi, Yasuhiro Murota, *et al.* (2000). "A Long-Term Econometric Analysis of Macro-Economy and Energy Demand and Supply in China and Korea", *Energy Economics*. The Institute of Energy Economics Japan, pp. 1–15. (in Japanese)

Kim, Yoon Hyung and Mitsuho Uchida (2003). *The New Wave in Northeast Asia: Energy and Electricity Business in the 21st Century*, Keio University Press, Tokyo.

Kinoshita, Soshichi, *et al.* (2002). "An Econometric Analysis on the Growth Patterns and Interdependency of East Asian Economies", The International Centre for the Study of East Asian Development, Kitakyushu (ICSEAD) Working Paper Series Vol. 2002–14. (in Japanese)

Klein, LR and S Ichimura (ed.) (2000). *Econometric Modeling of China*, World Scientific Publishing.

Nakicenovic, N, A Grübler and A McDonald (ed.) (1998). *Global Energy Perspectives*, Cambridge University Press, Cambridge, UK.

Pesaran, MH, RP Smith and T Akiyama (1998). *Energy Demand in Asian Developing Economies*, Oxford University Press.